Combat Leader's Field Guide

12th Edition

Revised and updated by
MSG Brett A. Stoneberger, USA

STACKPOLE
BOOKS

COMBAT LEADER'S FIELD GUIDE
Copyright © 2000 by Stackpole Books

Published by
STACKPOLE BOOKS
5067 Ritter Road
Mechanicsburg, PA 17055
www.stackpolebooks.com

Printed in the United States of America

10 9 8 7 6 5 4 3 2

First edition, 1956, © Military Service Pub. Co.
Second edition, 1960, © The Stackpole Company
Third edition, 1961, © The Stackpole Company
Fourth edition, 1962, © The Stackpole Company
Fifth edition, 1964, © The Stackpole Company
Sixth edition, 1966, © The Stackpole Company
Seventh edition, 1967, © The Stackpole Company
Eighth edition, 1973, © The Stackpole Company
Ninth edition, 1980, © The Stackpole Company
Tenth edition, 1987, © Stackpole Books
Eleventh edition, 1994, © Stackpole Books
Twelfth edition, 2000, © Stackpole Books

Library of Congress Cataloging-in-Publication Data

Combat leader's field guide.—12th ed./rev. and updated by Brett A. Stoneberger.
    p. cm.
  Includes bibliographical references and index.
  ISBN 0-8117-2729-7 (alk. paper)
    1. United States. Army—Field service—Handbooks, manuals, etc.
 I. Stoneberger, Brett A., 1962–

UD443.J8 2000
355.4—dc21
                                 99-056386

Contents

Contents

Preface

This guide is designed to assist leaders or prospective leaders of combat infantry units or other groups that, in an emergency, must fight as infantry. The content is tactical and logistical, administrative matter mostly being omitted. When in the field, especially under stress of combat or simulated combat, the combat leader cannot instantly recall everything he has been taught. Rapid changes in the situation may cause him to assume a position for which he has not yet been trained. He will then appreciate some brief reference material to guide him. He cannot carry a "five-foot shelf" of field manuals, and unlike the staff officer or higher commander, he does not have ready access to organizational files or a library. What he needs he must carry in his pocket, condensed yet in a form approximating at-a-glance capability. This field guide has been compiled from current field manuals and field circulars with those requirements in mind.

You will note that much of the reference material is in fact a comprehensive checklist to ensure that you have not overlooked some important consideration of troop leading.

As with the eleventh edition, the material in this edition is in two parts, unit combat operations and soldier combat skills. The material in Part I focuses on dismounted infantry operations, at the platoon and squad levels, including battle drills—collective actions rapidly executed without applying a deliberate decision-making process. A small unit's ability to accomplish its mission often depends on soldiers and leaders executing key actions quickly. Part II focuses on critical individual soldier skills necessary for battlefield survival. In the post Cold–War era, forces will be called on to deploy almost anywhere in the world on short notice to confront an opponent whose weapons may be as good as our own. This guide includes the considerations applicable to the U.S. Army in its current role of force projection.

PART ONE

Unit Combat Operations

1

The Battlefield

The U.S. Army's current operational doctrine recognizes the end of the Cold War and the change in the nature of the threat. It reflects a shift to stronger joint operations, retains the best of all the doctrine that has gone before, extends the 1986 AirLand Battle doctrine into a wider interservice integration, is more aware of the increasing incidence of combined operations, and recognizes that Army forces operate across the spectrum of war and operations other than war. This doctrine allows for an Army more disposed to force projection (the military's ability to respond quickly and decisively to global requirements) than to forward defense.

ARMY DOCTRINE

It is important for the reader to be aware that the U.S. Army is currently in a phase of doctrinal transition that will carry its forces into the 21st century. It is expected that near the turn of the century each service will have yet another approved version or revision of its warfighting or "operational" doctrine. Army doctrine is alive and therefore able to grow and change based on lessons learned from past and present operations. Additionally, as the U.S. Army looks into the 21st century at its "Army after Next," fighting doctrine will need to adjust accordingly.

Fundamental to operating across the full range of possible operations is an understanding of the Army's doctrinal foundations—the principles of war and the tenets of Army operations. Small-unit leaders must understand the concepts and fundamentals of Army doctrine to effectively lead in combat.

Principles of War

The enduring bedrock of Army doctrine, the principles of war have stood the test of time. Only slightly revised since first published in 1921, today's force-projection Army recognizes the following nine principles of war.

Objective
Direct every military operation toward a clearly defined, decisive, and attainable objective. The ultimate military purpose of war is the destruction of the enemy's armed forces and its will to fight. In operations other than war, the ultimate objective might be more difficult to define, but it must be clear from the beginning.

Offensive
Seize, retain, and exploit the initiative. Offensive action is the most effective and decisive way to attain a clearly defined common objective.

Mass
Mass the effects of overwhelming combat power at the decisive place and time. Synchronizing all the elements of combat power where they will have decisive effect on an enemy force in a short time is to achieve mass.

Economy of Force
Economy of force is the judicious employment and distribution of forces in order to achieve mass elsewhere. Allocate minimum essential combat power to secondary efforts.

Maneuver
Place the enemy in a position of disadvantage through the flexible application of combat power. Maneuver is the movement of forces in relation to the enemy to secure or retain positional advantage.

Unity of Command
For every objective, seek unity of command and unity of effort. At all levels of war, employment of forces in a manner that masses combat power toward a common objective requires unity of command and unity of effort.

Security
Never permit the enemy to acquire unexpected advantage. Security results from the measures taken by a commander to protect his forces.

Surprise
Strike the enemy at a time or place or in a manner for which it is unprepared. The element of surprise can allow forces to achieve success well out of proportion to the effort expended.

Simplicity
Prepare clear, uncomplicated plans and concise orders to ensure thorough understanding. Other factors being equal, the simplest plan is preferable.

Tenets
The fundamental tenets of Army operations describe characteristics of successful operations. The U.S. Army believes that its five basic tenets are the keys to victory. In and of themselves, they do not guarantee victory, but their absence makes it difficult and costly to achieve.

Initiative
Initiative means setting or changing the terms of battle by action. Infantry forces attempt to maintain their freedom of action while limiting the enemy's. This requires an offensive spirit in all operations. Decentralized operations in which small units aggressively fight through enemy resistance with the immediately available resources support the seizure or retention of the initiative. Individuals act independently within the framework of their commander's concept. Leaders and soldiers must understand the intent of commanders two echelons above. Commanders use mission-type orders and clear, concise instructions to ensure that subordinates understand the concept and how they fit within it.

Agility
Infantry forces seize or retain the initiative by acting and/or reacting faster than the enemy. This begins with the commander, who must have the mental agility to rapidly analyze tactical situations, thinking through many possible courses of action and the enemy's likely reaction to them, and determining the most effective and least costly course. Standing operating procedures (SOPs) and drills enable the unit to rapidly execute assigned missions without long, detailed orders.

Depth
Depth is the extension of operations in time, space, and resources. A commander seeks to fight the enemy throughout the depth of the enemy's formations by properly positioning his forces or by skillfully maneuvering his unit. This allows the unit to seek out and concentrate against enemy weaknesses. By swiftly concentrating against first one, then another enemy weakness, a skilled commander can begin to seize the initiative on a local level, allowing a higher commander to then exploit the opportunity.

Synchronization

Synchronization is the arrangement of battlefield activities in time, space, and purpose to produce maximum combat power at the decisive point. A commander synchronizes his subordinates' actions on the battlefield by assigning clear missions, making understood the timing required in the operation, and focusing all actions toward achieving overwhelming combat power at a decisive point. Issuing mission orders, identifying the main effort, and assigning each subordinate element clear tasks and purposes are the best means of maintaining synchronization in a fast-paced, fluid environment.

Versatility

Versatility is the ability of tactical units to adapt to different missions and tasks. In a force-projection army, the demands for versatility increase. Forces must be prepared to move rapidly from one region to another, one type of warfare to another, and one form of combat to another.

Combat Power

Army forces seek to apply overwhelming combat power in order to achieve victory at minimal cost. Four primary elements—maneuver, firepower, protection, and leadership—combine to create combat power.

Maneuver

Maneuver is the movement of forces supported by fire to achieve a position of advantage from which to destroy or threaten destruction of the enemy. Maneuver is the primary means of gaining or retaining the initiative. Forces use stealth, camouflage, dispersion, terrain, and fires to support their movement and close with the enemy. Infantry takes advantage of its ability to move across difficult terrain in any weather to surprise the enemy. The indirect approach guides movement planning: avoiding the enemy's strengths, moving through gaps or weaknesses or around its flanks, and striking at critical locations to rapidly destroy the enemy's will and ability to fight.

Firepower

Firepower is the capacity to deliver effective fire on a target. Firepower and maneuver are complementary. It is the effect of fires on the enemy that matters. A few weapons firing accurately from a location that surprises the enemy are more effective than many weapons with a large volume of fire but without the element of surprise. Before attempting to maneuver, infantry units must establish a base of fire. Leaders must understand the capabilities of organic and supporting weapons, how to position and employ them, and the techniques of integrating and controlling fires.

Protection

Protection is the conservation of the fighting potential of the force. It includes all actions that degrade the enemy's ability to maneuver against or place fires on the friendly force. These include security measures; use of limited visibility, cover, and concealment; air defense; camouflage; and dispersion. Protection also includes maintaining the soldiers' health and morale. Maneuver provides protection for the force by preventing the enemy from fixing it and concentrating firepower against it. Firepower, such as suppressive fire during an assault, can also provide protection. Infantry gains protection by avoiding detection during movement and by digging fighting positions when stationary.

Leadership

The combat power generated by infantry forces is dependent on the concepts and plans developed by the commanders and subordinate leaders. Infantry leaders are expected to lead by personal example and to provide purpose, motivation, and direction for their soldiers. Leaders must know their profession, their soldiers, and the tools of war.

Basic Rules of Combat

These rules appeared in Army doctrine for a short time but are no longer included in recent publications. At the small-unit level, however, they encompass the essence of the above fundamentals.

Secure
- Use cover and concealment.
- Establish local security and conduct reconnaissance.
- Protect the unit.

Move
- Establish a moving element.
- Get in the best position to shoot.
- Gain and maintain the initiative.
- Move fast, strike hard, and finish rapidly.

Shoot
- Establish a base of fire.
- Maintain mutual support.
- Kill or suppress the enemy.

Communicate
- Keep everybody informed.
- Tell soldiers what is expected.

Sustain
- Keep the fight going.
- Take care of soldiers.

2

Command and Control

LEADERSHIP

Military leadership is the process of influencing people—by providing purpose, direction, and motivation—while operating to accomplish the mission and improve the organization. Leaders must motivate their soldiers and give direction to their efforts. They must know their soldiers, their profession, and the tools of war. Only this kind of leader can direct soldiers to do difficult tasks under dangerous and stressful conditions.

Today's Army has a leadership framework that recognizes leaders of character and competence who act to achieve excellence. The model begins with what the leader must BE and spells out the values and attributes that shape the leader's character. It may be helpful to think of these as internal qualities; they define who you are and give you a solid footing. Skills are those things you KNOW how to do, your competence in everything from technical know-how to people skills. But character and knowledge—though absolutely necessary—are not enough. You cannot be an effective leader until you apply what you know, until you act and DO what you must. Be, know, do is a clear, concise statement of the Army's leadership doctrine. Under these headings are all the knowledge and guidance you need.

Infantry Leaders

The infantry leader is closest to the fight and must be a resourceful, tenacious, and decisive warrior as well as a tactician. He must understand and use initiative in accomplishing a mission; he cannot rely on a book to solve tactical problems. He is expected to lead by example, be at the point of decision to maintain control, understand the situation, and issue orders if required. This means that he must know how to quickly analyze a situation and make decisions in light of the commander's intent. He must be prepared to take independent action if necessary. The art of making quick, sound

7

decisions lies in the knowledge of tactics, the military estimate process, and platoon and squad (small-unit) techniques and procedures. The attributes required of infantry leaders include physical toughness, technical knowledge, mental agility, and a firm grasp of how to motivate soldiers to fight in the face of adversity.

Mission Tactics

Mission tactics is a term used to describe the exercise of command authority by a leader; it puts the relationship of command, control, and communications in proper perspective by placing the emphasis on command. This provides for initiative, the acceptance of risk, and the rapid seizure of opportunities on the battlefield. Mission tactics reinforced by knowledge of the higher commander's intent and focused on a main effort establish the basis for small-unit leadership. Leaders must be provided the maximum freedom to command and have imposed on them only that control necessary to synchronize mission accomplishment. The more complex an operation, the more control needed. The challenge to leaders is to provide the minimal amount of control required and still allow for decentralized decision making.

THE COMMAND AND CONTROL PROCESS

The commander accomplishes a mission through the command and control process. He uses this process to find out what is going on, to decide what action to take, to issue orders, and to supervise execution.

Troop-Leading Procedures (TLPs)

Troop leading is the process a leader goes through to prepare his unit to accomplish a tactical mission. It begins when he is alerted for a mission and starts over again when he receives a change or a new mission. Part of TLPs is the commander's estimate of the situation, when he analyzes relevant information to develop the most effective solution to a tactical problem. At company level, the commander's estimate of the situation is a rapid mental process that provides a format for the logical analysis of all relevant factors. TLPs consist of eight steps (see the accompanying chart). Steps 3 through 8 may not follow a rigid sequence. Many steps may be accomplished concurrently. In combat, leaders rarely have enough time to go through each step in detail, but they must use the procedures as outlined—in abbreviated form, if necessary—to ensure that nothing is left out of planning and preparation and that their soldiers understand the unit's mission and are adequately prepared. They continually update their estimates throughout the preparation phase and adjust their plans as appropriate.

Troop-Leading Procedures

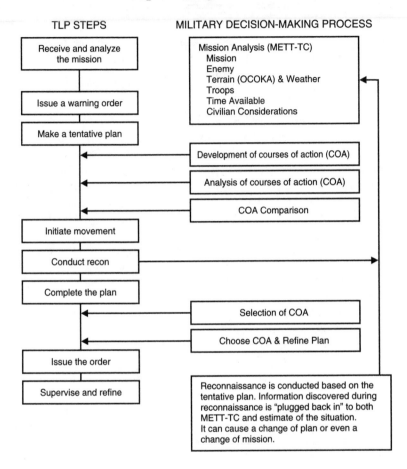

Step 1. Receive the Mission
The leader may receive the mission in a warning order, an operation order (OPORD), or a fragmentary order (FRAGO). He immediately begins to analyze it using the factors of METT-TC:
- What is the MISSION?
- What is known about the ENEMY?
- How will TERRAIN and WEATHER affect the operation?
- What TROOPS are available?
- How much TIME is available?
- Are there CIVILIAN considerations?

The leader should use no more than one-third of the available time for planning and for issuing his OPORD. The remaining two-thirds is for subordinates to plan and prepare for the operation. Leaders should also consider other factors such as available daylight and travel time to and from orders and rehearsals. In scheduling preparation activities, the leader should work backward from the line of departure (LD) or defend time. This is reverse planning. He must allow enough time for the completion of each task.

Step 2. Issue a Warning Order

The leader provides initial instructions in a warning order. The warning order contains enough information to begin preparation as soon as possible. Unit SOPs should prescribe who will receive all warning orders and the actions they must take upon receipt, such as drawing ammunition, rations, and water and checking communications equipment. The warning order has no specific format. One technique is to use the five-paragraph OPORD format. The leader issues the warning order with all the information he has available at the time and provides updates as often as necessary. If available, the following information may be included in a warning order:

- The mission or nature of the operation
- Who is participating in the operation
- Time of the operation
- Time and place for issuance of the OPORD

Step 3. Make a Tentative Plan

The leader develops an estimate of the situation to use as the basis for his tentative plan, using the military decision-making process. This process consists of five steps: detailed mission analysis, situation analysis, and course of action development; analysis of each course of action; comparison of each course of action; selection of a course of action; and refinement of the plan. Selection of a course of action represents the tentative plan. The leader updates the estimate continually and refines his plan accordingly. He uses this plan as the start point for coordination, reconnaissance, task organization (if required), and movement instructions. He works through this problem-solving sequence in as much detail as time allows. As the basis of his estimate, the leader considers the factors of METT-TC:

(M) Mission. The leader considers the mission given to him by his commander and analyzes it in light of the *commander's intent* two command levels higher. He derives the specified task, essential tasks, implied tasks, and limitations and/or constraints of the mission.

(E) Enemy. The leader considers the type, size, organization, tactics, and equipment of the enemy he expects to encounter. He identifies the greatest threat to his mission and the enemy's greatest vulnerability.

(T) Terrain and Weather. The leader considers the effect of terrain and weather on enemy and friendly forces using the guidelines below (OCOKA):

- *(O) Observation and fields of fire.* The leader considers ground that allows him observation of the enemy throughout his area of operation. He considers fields of fire in terms of the characteristics of the weapons available to him; for example, maximum effective range, the requirement for grazing fire, and the arming range and time of flight for antiarmor weapons.
- *(C) Cover and concealment.* The leader looks for terrain that will protect him from direct and indirect fires (cover) and from aerial and ground observation (concealment).
- *(O) Obstacles.* In the attack, the leader considers the effect of restrictive terrain on his ability to maneuver. In the defense, he considers how he will tie in his obstacles to the terrain to disrupt, turn, fix, or block an enemy force and protect his own forces from enemy assault.
- *(K) Key terrain.* Key terrain is any locality or area whose seizure or retention affords a marked advantage to either combatant. The leader considers key terrain in his selection of objectives, support positions, and routes in the offense and in the positioning of his unit in the defense.
- *(A) Avenues of approach.* An avenue of approach is an air or ground route of an attacking force leading to its objective or key terrain in its path. In the offense, the leader identifies the avenue of approach that affords him the greatest protection and places him at the enemy's most vulnerable spot. In the defense, the leader positions his key weapons along the avenue of approach most likely to be used by the enemy.

In considering the effects of weather, the leader is most interested in visibility and trafficability.

(T) Troops Available. The leader considers the strength of subordinate units, the characteristics of his weapon systems, and the capabilities of attached elements as he assigns tasks to subordinate units.

(T) Time Available. The leader refines his allocation of time based on the tentative plan and any changes in the situation.

(C) Civilian Considerations. The leader identifies any civilian considerations that may affect the mission. These factors may include refugees, humanitarian assistance requirements, or specific considerations related to the applicable rules of engagement (ROE) or rules of interaction (ROI).

Step 4. Initiate Movement

The platoon may need to begin movement while the leader is still planning or forward reconnoitering. The platoon sergeant or a squad leader may bring the platoon forward usually under the control of the company executive officer or first sergeant. This step could occur at any time during the TLP.

Step 5. Reconnoiter

If time allows, the leader makes a personal reconnaissance to verify his terrain analysis, adjust his plan, confirm the usability of routes, and time any critical movements. When time does not allow, the leader must make a map reconnaissance. The leader must consider the risk inherent in conducting reconnaissance forward of friendly lines. Sometimes the leader must rely on others (for example, scouts) to conduct the reconnaissance if the risk of contact with the enemy is high.

Step 6. Complete the Plan

The leader completes his plan based on the reconnaissance and any changes in the situation. He should review his mission, as he received it from his commander, to ensure that his plan meets the requirements of the mission and stays within the framework of the commander's intent.

Step 7. Issue the Complete Order

Platoon and squad leaders normally issue oral OPORDs. To aid subordinates in understanding the concept of the mission, leaders should issue the order within sight of the objective or on the defensive terrain. When this is not possible, they should use a terrain model or sketch. Leaders must ensure that subordinates understand the mission, the commander's intent, the concept of the operation, and their assigned tasks. Leaders may require subordinates to repeat all or part of the order or demonstrate on the model or sketch their understanding of the operation. They should also quiz their soldiers to ensure that all soldiers understand the mission. The section on precombat inspections (PCIs) provides a list of questions that leaders can ask to determine whether soldiers understand the mission.

Step 8. Supervise and Refine

The leader supervises the unit's preparation for combat by conducting rehearsals and inspections. The leader uses rehearsals to:
  • Practice essential tasks (improve performance)
  • Reveal weaknesses or problems in the plan
  • Coordinate the actions of subordinate elements

- Improve soldier understanding of the concept of the operation (foster confidence in soldiers)

Rehearsals include having squad leaders brief their planned actions in execution sequence to the platoon leader. The leader should conduct rehearsals on terrain that resembles the actual ground and in similar light conditions. The platoon may begin rehearsals of battle drills and other SOP items before the receipt of the OPORD. Once the order has been issued, the platoon can rehearse mission-specific tasks. Some important tasks to rehearse include:

- Action on the objective
- Assaulting a trench, bunker, or building
- Actions at the assault position
- Breaching obstacles (mine or wire)
- Using specific weapons or demolitions
- Actions on unexpected enemy contact

Squad leaders should conduct initial inspections shortly after receipt of the warning order. The platoon sergeant spot-checks the unit's preparation for combat. The platoon leader and platoon sergeant make a final inspection of the following:

- Weapons and ammunition
- Uniforms and equipment
- Mission-essential equipment
- Soldiers' understanding of the mission and their specific responsibilities
- Communications
- Rations and water
- Camouflage
- Deficiencies noted during earlier inspections

COMBAT ORDERS
Operation Order

An OPORD is a directive issued by the leader to his subordinate leaders to effect the coordinated execution of a specific operation. The leader briefs his OPORD orally from notes that follow the five-paragraph format below.

Task Organization. Explain how the unit is organized for the operation. If there is no change from the previous task organization, indicate "no change."

Paragraph 1. Situation. Provide information essential to the subordinate leader's understanding of the current situation. Subparagraphs include:

a. Enemy Forces. Refer to overlay or sketch. Include pertinent intelligence provided by higher HQ and other facts and assumptions about the enemy. This analysis is stated as conclusions and addresses enemy disposition, composition, strength, capabilities, and most probable course of action.

b. Friendly Forces. Provide information that subordinates need to accomplish their tasks, such as verbatim statements of the missions of the higher unit, left unit, right unit, forward unit, the unit in reserve or following, and units in support or reinforcing the higher unit. Be sure also to include any units attached or detached from the platoon, together with the effective times.

Paragraph 2: Mission. Provide a clear, concise statement of the task to be accomplished and the purpose for doing it (who, what, when, where, and why). The leader derives the mission from the mission analysis.

Paragraph 3: Execution. Intent is always given at the company level and above. The platoon leader may give a general intention that defines the purpose of the operation and the relationship among the force, the enemy, and the terrain.

a. Concept of the Operation. Refer to the operation overlay, concept sketch, and/or terrain model. Explain in general terms how the platoon, as a whole, will accomplish the mission. Identify the most important task for the platoon (mission-essential task) and any other essential tasks. If applicable, designate the decisive point, form a maneuver of defensive techniques, and any other significant factors or principles. Attempt to limit this paragraph to about six sentences.

(1) Maneuver. Address all squads and attachments by name, giving each an essential task. Designate the platoon's main effort—that is, who will accomplish the most important task. All other tasks must relate to the main effort. Give mission statements to each subordinate element.

(2) Fires. Refer to the fire support overlay and target list. Describe the concept of fire support to synchronize and complement the scheme of maneuver. If applicable, address priority of fires (include changes), priority targets (who controls fires on them), and any restrictive control measures on the use of fires.

(3) Additional combat support (CS) assets (engineer, air defense artillery [ADA]). State the concept of employment of any CS attachments or who gets priority in their use, how they will be used (priority of effort), how they will be controlled, and by

Operation Order Format

TASK ORGANIZATION
(Explain how the unit is organized for the operation.)

1. SITUATION:
   a. Enemy Forces
   b. Civilians/Noncombatants
   c. NGOs/PVOs, and Neutral Nation Observers, as applicable
   d. Friendly Forces
   e. Attachments/Detachments

2. MISSION:
Written in the directive form, using the third person voice.
   (Example: "2-274th Infantry attacks commencing 05 0625 JAN in zone seize Objective WOLF (LV 815200).)

3. EXECUTION:
Commander's intent *(Succinct definition of what must be done with respect to the enemy and the terrain, and the desired end state.)*
   a. Concept of the Operation *(Summarizes what is to be done to achieve success)*
   b. Subunit Missions
   c. Coordinating Instructions

4. SERVICE AND SUPPORT:
   a. Rations and Water
   b. Equipment/Supplies/Fuel
   c. Maintenance Plan
   d. Casualty Procedures
   e. Evacuation of Captured Personnel and Equipment

5. COMMAND AND SIGNAL:
   a. Command
      (1) Chain of command
      (2) Location of key leaders and radiotelephone operators
   b. Signal

whom. (Do not include information that belongs in the coordinating instructions subparagraph.)

b. Tasks to Maneuver Units. Specify tasks other than those listed in paragraph 3a(1), and the purpose of each for squads and attachments. List each in separate numbered paragraphs. Address the reserve last. State any priority or sequence.

c. Tasks to CS Elements. A platoon may receive an attachment of CS units; for example, an engineer squad. List tasks to CS units in subparagraphs in the order they appear in the Task Organization section. List only those specific tasks that must be accomplished by these units not specified elsewhere.

d. Coordinating Instructions. List the details of coordination and control applicable to two or more units in the platoon or common to all units. Items that may be addressed include:

- Mission-oriented protective posture (MOPP) level
- Priority of intelligence requirements
- Troop safety and operational exposure guidance
- Engagement and disengagement criteria and instructions
- Fire distribution and control measures
- Consolidation and reorganization procedures other than those established in SOP
- Reporting requirements; for example, crossing phase lines or checkpoints
- Terrorism and counterterrorism instructions
- Mission timeline
- Rules of engagement
- Order of march and other movement instructions

Paragraph 4: Service and Support. Include combat service support (CSS) instructions and arrangements supporting the operation that are of primary interest to the platoon, such as:

- Company trains, casualty and damaged equipment collection points, and routes to and from them
- Supply
- Transportation
- Services
- Maintenance
- Medical evacuation
- Enemy prisoner of war (EPW) collection point and instructions on EPW handling
- Miscellaneous instructions for the destruction of supplies and equipment and any other information not covered elsewhere

Paragraph 5: Command and Signal

a. Command.

- Location of the higher unit commander and command post (CP)
- Location of platoon leader and/or CP
- Location of platoon sergeant and/or alternate CP
- Succession of command (if different from SOP)

b. Signal.

- SOI (signal operation instructions) index in effect
- Listening silence, if applicable
- Methods of communication in priority

- Emergency signals and visual signals
- Code words

Annexes. Annexes provide the instructions for conducting specific operations (such as air assaults, boat and truck movements, stream crossings, establishment of patrol bases, and airborne insertions) if they are so detailed that a platoon SOP is insufficient for a particular situation. The format is the same as the five-paragraph OPORD.

Overlays. An operation overlay is a tracing of graphic control measures on a map. It shows boundaries, unit positions, routes, objectives, and other control measures. It helps to clarify the OPORD. Platoons normally trace their overlays from the company operations map. Squad leaders transfer control measures onto their maps as needed. The subordinate's need for higher-unit graphics must be balanced against the risk of the enemy obtaining this information.

When possible, the leader uses the actual terrain model to brief his OPORD. He may also use concept sketches—large, rough drawings of the objective areas—to show the flow of events and actions clearly.

Fragmentary Orders

The leader uses a FRAGO to change an existing order. He normally uses the OPORD format but addresses only those elements that have changed. The leader should make his instructions brief, simple, clear, and specific.

OPERATIONS SECURITY

All measures taken to maintain security and achieve tactical surprise constitute operations security (OPSEC). These measures include countersurveillance, physical security, signal security, and information security. OPSEC also involves the elimination or control of tactical indicators that can be exploited by the enemy. To provide the most effective OPSEC, you must see the enemy before it sees you. The following measures can be used to provide OPSEC:

- Use hide and defilade positions habitually.
- Position observation posts to observe enemy avenues of approach.
- Camouflage positions, vehicles, and equipment against both visual and infrared detection. Break up silhouettes, reduce glare, reduce vehicle signatures caused by dust, exhaust smoke, and tracks.
- Reduce infrared and thermal signatures by parking in shadows, turning off engines and heaters, and using terrain masking.
- Maintain noise and light discipline.

- Patrol aggressively to prevent enemy surveillance and to gather information about the enemy.
- Use smoke to screen movement.
- Enforce proper radio operating procedures: authentication, encoding, limiting transmission time, using low power, and tying down antennas.
- Use radio operators trained in antijam, interference, and deception procedures.
- Overwatch friendly barriers and obstacles.
- Maintain contact with adjacent units.

FRATRICIDE PREVENTION

The underlying principle of fratricide prevention is simple: Leaders who know where their soldiers are, and where they want them to fire, can keep those soldiers alive to kill the enemy. At the same time, leaders must avoid at all costs any reluctance to employ, integrate, and synchronize all required operating systems at the critical time and place. They must avoid becoming tentative out of fear of fratricide; rather, they must strive to eliminate fratricide risk through tough, realistic combined arms training in which each soldier and unit achieves the set standard. Fratricide results in unacceptable losses and increases the risk of mission failure; it almost always affects the unit's ability to survive and function.

Some Causes

Leaders must identify any factors that may affect their units and then strive to eliminate or correct them. These can include:
- Failure in the direct fire control plan, especially designation of target engagement areas
- Land navigation failures
- Failures in combat identification
- Inadequate maneuver control measures
- Failures in reporting and communications
- Weapons errors
- Battlefield hazards, such as unexploded ordnance and unmarked or unrecorded minefields

CONTINUOUS OPERATIONS

U.S. forces execute continuous operations to maintain constant pressure on the enemy without regard to visibility, terrain, or weather conditions. The ability to effectively sustain this pressure is often key to success on the battlefield. It is also the most difficult challenge that Army units face, placing enormous stress on soldiers, vehicles, and equipment. Continuous operations demand that units conduct planning, preparation, and execution activities around the clock while maintaining effective OPSEC at all times.

The leader must understand the demands of continuous operations under all possible conditions. During the planning and preparation phases of an operation, the commander dictates priorities of security, work, and rest. These priorities, in conjunction with readiness condition (REDCON) levels, enable the commander to develop his unit's timeline. He then uses TLPs to outline time requirements and disseminate them to the platoon leaders.

Readiness Conditions
REDCON levels allow quick responses to changing situations and ensure the completion of necessary work and rest plans. The commander uses the REDCON status as a standardized way to adjust the unit's readiness to move and fight.

REDCON-1: full alert; units ready to move and fight
- Nuclear, biological, and chemical (NBC) alarms and hot loop equipment stowed; OPs pulled in.
- All personnel alert and mounted on vehicles or are in final assembly areas; weapons manned and rucks packed.
- Unit is ready to move immediately.

REDCON-2: full alert; units ready to fight
- Equipment stowed (except hot loop and NBC alarms).
- All personnel alert and mounted in vehicles; weapons manned. (Note: Depending on the tactical situation and orders from the commander, dismounted OPs may remain in place.)
- All (100 percent) digital and FM communications links operational.
- Unit is ready to move within 15 minutes of notification.

REDCON-3: reduced alert
- Fifty percent of the unit executes work and rest plans; remainder of the unit executes security plan.
- Unit is ready to move within 30 minutes of notification.

REDCON-4: minimum alert
- OPs manned; one soldier per platoon designated to monitor radio and man turret or crew-served weapons.
- Digital and FM links with task force and other company teams maintained.
- Unit is ready to move within one hour of notification.

Stand-to

Stand-to encompasses all actions taken to bring the unit to a maximum state of preparedness. Times for stand-to are derived from the higher unit's OPORD. Unit SOP should specify stand-to requirements, which usually includes procedures for sending and receiving reports, use of accountability checks for personnel and equipment, and criteria for assuming REDCON levels 1 and 2. (Note: Stand-to procedures for digitized units include the updating of position navigation [POSNAV] systems, the intervehicular information system [IVIS] synchronization, and completion of log-on for SINCGARS [single-channel ground and airborne] radio system.)

Work Plan

The work plan defines tasks and sets milestones for task completion. It enables subordinate leaders and soldiers to focus their efforts in preparing vehicles, equipment, and themselves for operations.

Rest Plan

The rest plan allows some soldiers to sleep while other crewmen conduct priorities of work and maintain security. To be effective in sustained combat, a soldier should get a minimum of 4 hours of uninterrupted sleep every 24 hours. The commander must ensure that subordinate leaders either have rest plans of their own or are following his rest plan as directed.

The unit SOP must provide for an adequate division of duties to allow leaders to sleep. This may require key leaders to share duties. When soldiers are tired, confirmation briefings become critical whenever orders are issued, even for the simplest task.

PRECOMBAT INSPECTIONS

Inspections allow leaders to check the unit's operational readiness. The key goal is to ensure that soldiers, equipment, weapons, and vehicles are fully prepared to execute the upcoming mission. Inspections also contribute to improved morale.

It is essential that all leaders know how to conduct precombat checks (PCCs) and precombat inspections (PCIs) in accordance with applicable unit SOPs and guidelines from appropriate battle doctrine. Leaders should focus on the readiness of mission-essential equipment and ammunition and on the mission understanding of all subordinate leaders and individual soldiers.

Procedures for a comprehensive program of checks and inspections include the following:

Soldier Precombat Inspection (PCI) Checklist
(No more than two minutes is spent inspecting each soldier.)

	GO	NO GO
LBE fits properly		
First-aid pouch w/dressing		
Full canteens w/M-1 drinking cap		
Ammo pouches w/3 loaded magazines each or full SAW drums		
Bayonet		
Helmet w/cover, band, chin strap, and rank		
Dog tags around neck soundproofed and ID card		
Weapon cleaned and zeroed		
Proper MOPP level		
Serviceable mask and hood		
Serviceable overgarments		
Serviceable overboots		
Personal decontamination kit available		
Completed witness statement and casualty feeder card on person		
Proper driver's license		
Understands current mission, commander's intent, situation		
Briefed and understands cold/hot weather injuries and safety		
Understands risk reductions methods for mission		
Flashlight w/colored lens (serviceable)		
Pistol secure w/lanyard		
Night vision serviceable and zeroed		
PAC-4s secure and serviceable/zeroed		
Weapon cleaning kit		
Appropriate inclement weather gear		
Combat lifesaver bag		

- Perform before-operation maintenance checks; report or repair deficiencies.
- Perform prepare-to-fire checks for all weapons. Weapons should be boresighted, and machine guns and individual weapons should be test-fired, if possible.
- Perform communications checks of voice and digital systems.
- Ensure that soldiers in each subordinate element understand the plan, have posted current graphics, and are in the correct uniform and MOPP level.

- Upload vehicles in accordance with unit SOP. Quickly check accountability of equipment.
- Review the supply status of rations, water, fuel, oil, all types of ammunition, pyrotechnics, first-aid kits, combat lifesaver bags, MOPP suits, and batteries; and direct resupply operations as necessary.
- Ensure that vehicles are correctly camouflaged so they match the area of operations.

Each leader should observe his element throughout the process of preparation for combat. The platoon leader or commander should conduct the final inspection of each element once the leader reports that soldiers, vehicles, and equipment are prepared.

For years, leaders have used PCI checklists like the one shown above.

ASSEMBLY AREA PROCEDURES

An assembly area is a location where the unit prepares for future operations. Here the unit receives and issues orders and supplies, services and repairs vehicles and equipment, and feeds and rests soldiers. When an assembly area is used to prepare for an attack, it is usually well forward.

Before occupying an assembly area, the platoon leader designates a quartering party, which reconnoiters the assembly area to ensure that no enemy are present and to establish initial security. Each squad provides two men for the quartering party, with the platoon sergeant or selected NCO in charge. The quartering party determines initial positions for all elements, continues to secure the area, occupies covered and concealed positions, and, as the main body approaches, moves out and guides elements from the release point to their initial positions. The unit occupies its positions in the assembly area and maintains local security. All elements are assigned a sector of the perimeter to ensure mutual support and to cover all gaps by observation and fire. OPs are designated and manned. A priority of work is established to complete the assembly area:

- Position crew-served weapons and chemical-agent alarms and designate principal directions of fire (PDF), final protective line (FPL), and final protective fires (FPF)
- Construct individual and crew-served fighting positions
- Set up wire communications between the elements (radio silence is observed)
- Prepare range cards
- Camouflage positions

- Clear fields of fire
- Distribute ammunition, rations, water, supplies, and special equipment
- Conduct preventive maintenance checks and services on weapons and equipment
- Prepare night sights
- Test-fire small-arms weapons (if the tactical situation permits)
- Conduct personal hygiene and field sanitation
- Institute a rest plan

The platoon leader conducts adjacent unit coordination and assigns security patrols, if applicable. The platoon leader establishes responsibility for overlapping enemy avenues of approach between adjacent squads and platoons, and the leaders ensure that there are no gaps between elements. The platoon leader exchanges information on OP locations and signals and forwards a copy of the sector sketch to the company.

COMMUNICATIONS
Communications are necessary to control subordinate elements, to receive and disseminate information, and to coordinate CS and CSS. The commander is responsible for the discipline of the communications system within his unit and for its operation in the system of the next higher headquarters. Responsibilities for the establishment of communications are as follows:

- Senior unit to subordinate unit
- Supporting unit to supported unit
- Reinforcing unit to reinforced unit
- Left to right and rear to front

Both units take prompt action when communications cannot be established or when they are disrupted.

Five Basic Means of Communications
The commander has five basic means to communicate:

FM Radio
The company commander operates on the company net and monitors the battalion net; the XO operates on the battalion net and monitors the company net; the first sergeant operates on the battalion admin/log net and monitors the company net; platoon leaders operate on platoon nets and monitor the company net. Use of the radio is avoided until enemy contact is made.

Wire

Wire hot loops are established within and between platoons and the company when the unit is stationary. OPs should be included within a hot loop.

Messenger

To reduce electronic signals, messengers are used whenever possible prior to battle. Normally, battalions send messengers to the company, and platoons send messengers to the company commander.

Visual Signals

Visual signals normally include hand and arm signals, flag signals, pyrotechnics, flashlights, and chemical lights. Visual signals should be planned together with, or as a backup to, voice communications. They are normally used either when other communications are lost or to overcome jamming.

Audible Signals

Audible signals are normally used to transmit prearranged messages, to attract attention, and to spread warning alarms. They should be simple to understand, and prearranged meanings should be covered in SOPs.

3

Movement

Infantry's key strength is its ability to cross almost any terrain during all weather conditions. When infantry can move undetected, it gains an advantage over the enemy. Movement fundamentals, formations, and techniques assist the leader in providing security during movement.

FUNDAMENTALS

- Ensure that movement supports a rapid transition to maneuver.
- Conduct reconnaissance of the terrain and the enemy to the extent possible.
- Move on covered and concealed routes and, if the situation permits, during limited visibility.
- Select routes that avoid natural lines of drift, likely ambush sites, and other danger areas.
- Establish security during movement and halts. Avoid moving directly forward from covered positions. All weapons should be prepared to engage targets. Enforce camouflage, noise, and light discipline.
- Designate air guards.
- Make enemy contact with the smallest element possible.

FORMATIONS

Formations are arrangements of elements and soldiers in relation to one another. Squads use formations for control flexibility and security. Leaders choose formations based on their analysis of the factors of METT-TC. Leaders are up front in formations. This allows the fire team leader to lead by example. All soldiers in the team must be able to see their leader.

PLATOON AND SQUAD FORMATION ABBREVIATIONS

PLT LDR	Platoon leader
PSG	Platoon sergeant
SL	Squad leader
TL	Team leader
RATELO	Radio-telephone operator
FO	Forward observer
R	Rifleman
AR	Automatic rifleman
GRN	Grenadier
MG	Machine gun
AIDMAN	Aidman/medic

Fire Team Formations

Wedge

The wedge is the basic formation for the fire team. The interval between soldiers in the wedge formation is normally 10 meters. The wedge expands and contracts, depending on the terrain. When rough terrain, poor visibility, or other factors make control of the wedge difficult, the normal interval is reduced so that all team members can still see their team leader and the team leaders can still see their squad leader. The sides of the wedge can contract to resemble a single file. When moving in less rugged terrain, where control is easier, soldiers expand the wedge or resume their original positions.

File

When the terrain precludes use of the wedge, fire teams use the file formation.

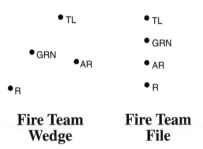

Fire Team Wedge   **Fire Team File**

Squad Formations
Squad formations describe the relationships between fire teams in the squad.

Squad Column
The squad column is the most common formation. It provides good lateral and deep dispersion without sacrificing control, and it facilitates maneuver. The lead fire team is the base fire team. When the squad moves independently or as the rear element of the platoon, the rifleman in the trail fire team provides rear security. Squads can move in normal or modified columns as terrain dictates.

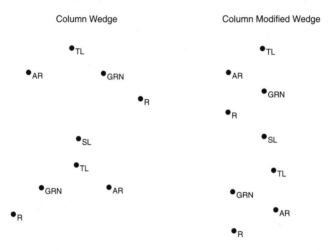

Squad Column Wedge and Modified Wedge

Squad Line
The squad line provides maximum firepower to the front. When a squad is acting as the base squad, the fire team on the right is the base fire team.

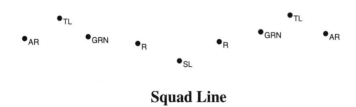

Squad Line

Squad File

When not traveling in a column or line, squads travel in file. The squad file has the same characteristics as the fire team file. If the squad leader wants to increase his control over the formation, enhance morale by leading from the front, and be immediately available to make key decisions, he moves forward to the first or second position. Additional control over the rear of the formation can be provided by moving a team leader to the last position.

Squad File

MOVEMENT FORMATION	WHEN NORMALLY USED	CHARACTERISTICS			
		CONTROL	FLEXIBILITY	FIRE CAPABILITIES/ RESTRICTIONS	SECURITY
SQUAD COLUMN	SQUAD PRIMARY FORMATION	GOOD	FACILITATES MANEUVER, GOOD DISPERSION LATERALLY AND IN DEPTH	ALLOWS LARGE VOLUME OF FIRE TO THE FLANK— LIMITED VOLUME TO THE RIGHT	ALL-ROUND
SQUAD LINE	WHEN MAXIMUM FIREPOWER IS REQUIRED TO THE FRONT	NOT AS GOOD AS SQUAD COLUMN	LIMITED MANEUVER CAPABILITY (BOTH FIRE TEAMS COMMITTED)	ALLOWS MAXIMUM IMMEDIATE FIRE TO THE FRONT	GOOD TO THE FRONT, LITTLE TO THE FLANKS AND REAR
SQUAD FILE	CLOSE TERRAIN VEGETATION, LIMITED VISIBILITY CONDITIONS	EASIEST	MOST DIFFICULT FORMATION FROM WHICH TO MANEUVER	ALLOWS IMMEDIATE FIRE TO THE FLANK, MASKS MOST FIRE TO THE FRONT AND REAR	LEAST

Comparison of Squad Formations

Platoon Formations

Platoon Column

The platoon column is the primary movement formation. It provides good lateral and deep dispersion and simplifies control. The lead squad is the base squad. (Note: METT-TC will determine where crew-served weapons move in the formation. They normally move with the platoon leader so he can quickly establish a base of fire.)

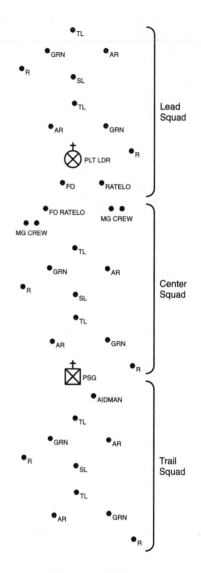

Platoon Column

Platoon Line, Squads on Line

This formation allows the delivery of maximum fire to the front but little fire to the flanks. It is hard to control and does not lend itself well to rapid movement. When two or more platoons are attacking, the company commander chooses one as the base platoon. The base platoon's center squad is its base squad. When the platoon is not acting as the base platoon, its base squad is its flank squad nearest the base platoon. The machine guns can move with the platoon, or they can assume a support position. This is the basic platoon assault formation.

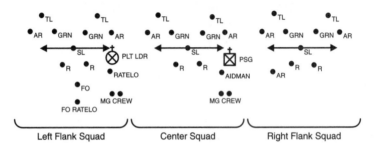

NOTE: The platoon leader (PLT LDR), forward observer (FO), radio-telephone operator
         (RATELO), platoon sergeant (PSG), and the squad leaders (SL) position
         themselves where they can best control the squad.

Platoon Line, Squads on Line

Platoon Line, Squads in Column

The platoon leader uses this formation when he does not want to deploy all personnel on line and when he wants the squads to react to unexpected contact. This formation is easier to control and it lends itself better to rapid

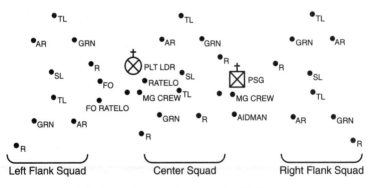

Platoon Line, Squads in Column

movement than the platoon line or squads on line formation; however, it is harder to control than a platoon column and does not facilitate rapid movement as well. When two or more platoons are moving, the company commander chooses one as the base platoon. The base platoon's center squad is its base squad. When the platoon is not the base platoon, its base squad is its flank squad nearest the base platoon.

Platoon Vee
This formation has two squads up front to provide a heavy volume of fire on contact. It also has one squad in the rear that can either overwatch or trail the other squads. This formation is hard to control, and movement is slow. The platoon leader designates one of the front squads as the platoon's base squad.

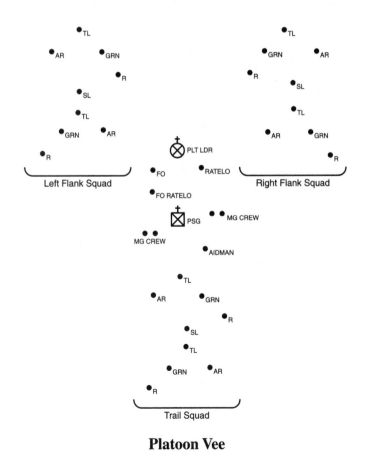

Platoon Vee

Platoon Wedge
This formation has two squads in the rear that can overwatch or trail the lead
squad. It provides a large volume of fire to the front or flanks. It allows the
platoon leader to make contact with a squad and still have one or two squads
to maneuver. The lead squad is the base squad.

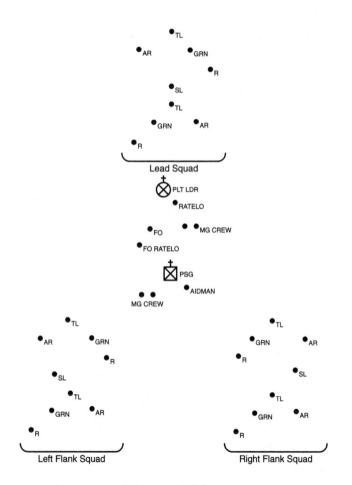

Platoon Wedge

Platoon File

This formation can be set up in several ways. One method is to have three-squad files follow one another using one of the movement techniques. Another method is to have a single platoon file with a front security element (point) and flank security elements. This formation is used when visibility is poor due to terrain, vegetation, or light conditions. The distance between soldiers is less than normal to allow communication by passing messages up and down the file. The platoon file has the same characteristics as the fire team and squad files.

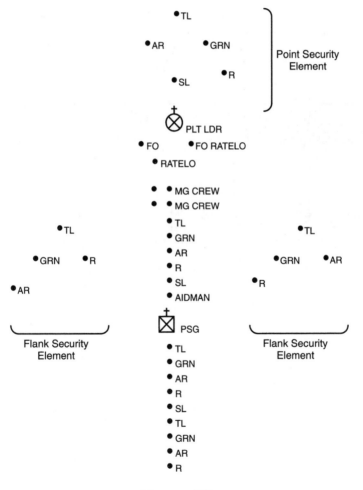

Platoon File

MOVEMENT TECHNIQUES

A movement technique is the manner used to traverse terrain. There are three movement techniques: traveling, traveling overwatch, and bounding overwatch. The selection of a movement technique is based on the likelihood of enemy contact and the need for speed. Factors to consider for each technique are control, dispersion, speed, and security. Movement techniques are not fixed formations. They refer to the distances between soldiers, teams, and squads, which vary based on mission, enemy, terrain, visibility, and other factors that affect control. Soldiers must be able to see their fire team leader. The squad leader must be able to see his fire team leaders. The platoon leader should be able to see his lead squad leader. Leaders control movement with arm and hand signals. They use radios only when needed. Any of the three movement techniques can be used with any formation.

MOVEMENT TECHNIQUES	WHEN NORMALLY USED	CHARACTERISTICS			
		CONTROL	DISPERSION	SPEED	SECURITY
TRAVELING	CONTACT NOT LIKELY	MORE	LESS	FASTEST	LEAST
TRAVELING OVERWATCH	CONTACT POSSIBLE	LESS	MORE	SLOWER	MORE
BOUNDING OVERWATCH	CONTACT EXPECTED	MOST	MOST	SLOWEST	MOST

Movement Techniques

Techniques of Squad Movement
The squad or platoon leader determines and directs which movement technique the squad will use.

Traveling
Traveling is used when contact with the enemy is not likely and speed is needed.

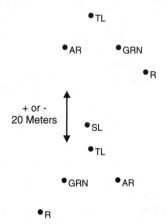

Squad Traveling

Traveling Overwatch
Traveling overwatch is used when contact is possible. Attached weapons move near the squad leader and are under his control so that he can employ them quickly.

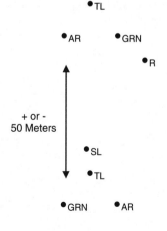

**Squad Traveling
Overwatch**

Bounding Overwatch

Bounding overwatch is used when contact is expected, when the squad leader believes that the enemy is near (based on movement, noise, reflection, trash, fresh tracks, or even a hunch), or when a large, open danger area must be crossed.

The lead fire team overwatches first. Soldiers scan for enemy positions. The squad leader usually stays with the overwatch team.

The trail fire team bounds and signals the squad leader when his team completes its bound and is prepared to overwatch the movement of the other team. Both team leaders must know whether successive or alternate bounds will be used and which team the squad leader will be with. The overwatching team leader must know the route and destination of the bounding team. The bounding team leader must know his team's destination and route, possible enemy locations, and actions to take when he arrives. He must also know where the overwatching team will be and how he will receive his instructions. The cover and concealment on the bounding team's route dictate how its soldiers move. Teams can bound successively or alternately. Successive bounds are easier to control; alternate bounds can be faster.

Alternate Bounds. Covered by the rear element, the lead element moves forward, halts, and assumes overwatch positions. The rear element advances past the lead element and takes up overwatch positions. The sequence continues as necessary, with only one element moving at a time.

Successive Bounds. The lead element, covered by the rear element, advances and takes up overwatch positions. The rear element advances to an overwatch position roughly abreast of the lead element and halts. This sequence continues as necessary. The rear element never advances in forward of the lead element.

Techniques of Platoon Movement
The platoon leader determines and directs which movement technique the platoon will use.

Traveling
Traveling is used when enemy contact is not likely and speed is needed.

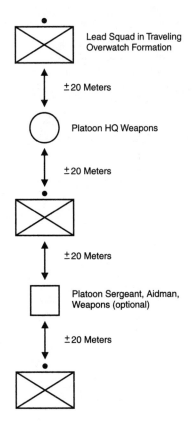

Lead Squad in Traveling Overwatch Formation

±20 Meters

Platoon HQ Weapons

±20 Meters

±20 Meters

Platoon Sergeant, Aidman, Weapons (optional)

±20 Meters

Platoon Traveling

Traveling Overwatch

Traveling overwatch is used when contact is possible but speed is needed. The platoon leader moves where he can best control the platoon. The platoon sergeant travels with the trailing squad, although he is free to move throughout the formation to enforce security, noise and light discipline, and distances between squads. The lead squad uses traveling overwatch, and the trailing squads use traveling.

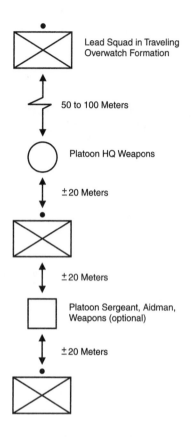

Platoon Traveling Overwatch

Bounding Overwatch

Bounding overwatch is used when contact is expected. Platoons conduct bounding overwatch using successive or alternate bounds. One squad bounds forward to a chosen position; then it becomes the overwatching element unless contact is made enroute. The bounding squad can use traveling overwatch, bounding overwatch, or individual movement techniques (low and high crawl, and short rushes by fire teams or pairs). One squad overwatches the bounding squad from covered positions where it can see and suppress likely enemy positions and view their assigned sector. The platoon leader remains with the overwatching squad. Normally, the platoon's machine guns are located with the overwatching squad. One squad is uncommitted and ready for employment as directed by the platoon leader. The platoon sergeant and the leader of the squad awaiting orders position themselves close to the platoon leader.

Platoon Bounding Overwatch

Considerations. When deciding where to have his bounding squad go, a platoon leader considers:

- The requirements of the mission
- Where the enemy is likely to be
- The routes to the next overwatch position
- The ability of an overwatching element's weapons to cover the bound
- The responsiveness of the rest of the platoon
- The fields of fire at the next overwatch position

Instructions. Before a bound, the platoon leader gives an order to his squad leaders from the overwatch position. He tells and shows them the following:

- The direction or location of the enemy (if known)
- The positions of the overwatching squad
- The next overwatch position
- The route of the bounding squad
- What to do after the bounding squad reaches the next position
- What signal the bounding squad will use to announce that it is prepared to overwatch
- How the squad will receive its next orders

DANGER AREAS

A danger area is any place on the movement route where the unit might be exposed to enemy observation, fire, or both. Units try to avoid danger areas. If a danger area must be crossed, it should be done with great caution and as quickly as possible. Do the following before crossing a danger area:

- Designate near- and far-side rally points.
- Secure the near side (both flanks and rear).
- Reconnoiter and secure the far side.

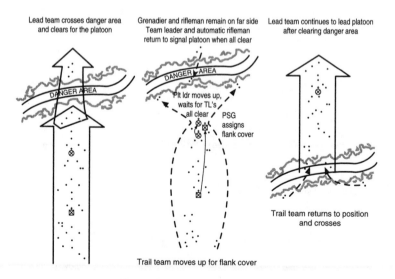

Lead team crosses danger area and clears for the platoon

Grenadier and rifleman remain on far side
Team leader and automatic rifleman return to signal platoon when all clear

Lead team continues to lead platoon after clearing danger area

DANGER AREA

DANGER AREA

Plt ldr moves up, waits for TL's all clear

PSG assigns flank cover

Trail team returns to position and crosses

Trail team moves up for flank cover

Crossing a Danger Area

The unit halts when the lead elements signal "danger area." The leader confirms the danger area, then selects and informs subordinate leaders of near- and far-side rally points. Near-side security is posted to overwatch the crossing. The far-side security team crosses the danger area and clears the far side. Once the far side is cleared, the main body moves quickly and quietly across the danger area. A small unit may cross all at once, in pairs, or one soldier at a time. A large unit normally crosses its elements one at a time. As each element crosses, it moves to an overwatch position or to the far-side rally point. The near-side security element then crosses and resumes its place in the formation as the unit continues its mission.

Crossing Techniques

Open Areas
When crossing an open area, stay concealed and observe carefully from the near side. Post security to give early warning, and send an element across to clear the far side. When cleared, quickly cross the rest of the unit at the shortest exposed distance.

To cross large open areas, a combination of traveling overwatch and bounding overwatch is used. Bounding overwatch is used at any point in the open area where enemy contact may be expected or when the element comes within small-arms range (250 meters) of the far side.

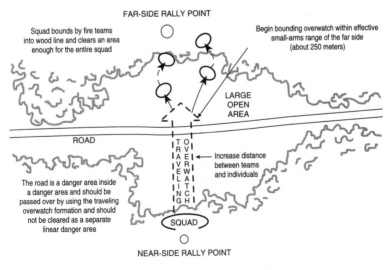

Crossing a Large Open Area

Small open areas may be bypassed, by either using the detour bypass method or contouring around the open area. In the detour bypass method, the force moves around the open area using 90-degree turns to the right or left until the far side is reached. To contour around the open area, the unit uses the wood line and vegetation for cover and concealment as it moves around the open area until reaching the far-side rally point.

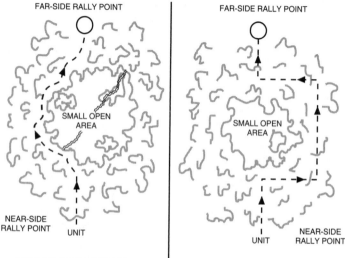

Crossing a Small Open Area

Roads and Trails
Cross a road or trail at or near a bend, at a narrow spot, or on low ground to reduce enemy observation and minimize the unit's exposure.

Villages
Pass on the downwind side and well away from a village. Avoid animals, especially dogs, which might reveal your presence.

Enemy Positions
Pass enemy positions on the downwind side (the enemy might have scout dogs). Be alert for trip wires or other warning devices.

Minefields

Bypass a minefield even if it means changing your route by a great distance. If you *must* pass through a minefield, the lead elements clear a lane for the rest of the unit. Soldiers use their hands to detect trip wires and use sharpened sticks to probe for mines.

Streams

When crossing a stream, select a narrow spot that offers concealment on both banks. Observe the far side carefully, and place security out for early warning. Clear the far side, then cross quickly but quietly.

Wire Obstacles

Avoid crossing wire obstacles if possible; they are normally under observation. If wire must be breached during daytime, use the method that exposes the unit for the shortest amount of time. Check the wire for mines, booby traps, and warning devices. To breach wire at night, either cross over or go under the wire using the following procedures:

To cross over the wire, grasp the first strand lightly, and cautiously lift one leg over. Lower your foot slowly to the ground, feeling carefully for sure footing, then lift the other foot over the wire. Quietly release this wire and feel for the next strand. Cross it in the same way.

To go under the wire, move headfirst. Lie on your back and slide under the bottom strands, pushing forward with your heels. Carry your weapon lengthwise on your body, steadying it with either hand. To prevent the wire from catching on clothing or equipment, let it slide along the weapon. Inch along, holding the wire up with one hand. Do not jerk or pull on the wire. Feel ahead with your free hand for low strands or trip wires.

If the wire must be cut, cut only the lower strands to minimize discovery of the gap. Soldiers should work in a team if possible. Wire should be wrapped with a cloth near a picket, cut partway through, and then bent back and forth until it breaks. The loose end is carefully rolled back to clear the lane. Concertina is hard to control after cutting and can snap back. If concertina must be cut, stake down two loops far enough apart so that a soldier can crawl between them. Then cut partway through and break as previously described.

Enemy Contact at Danger Areas

If the unit makes contact in or around a danger area, the leader determines whether to assault the enemy or break contact, depending on the situation and mission. If the unit becomes disorganized, the near-side and far-side rally points are used to link up and reorganize. Ideally, using movement fundamentals, the unit will see the enemy first, remain undetected, and ambush it.

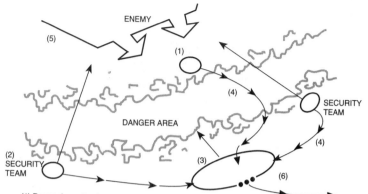

(1) Recon element makes contact.
(2) Flank security fires on enemy.
(3) Main body takes overwatch position and fires on enemy.
(4) Security and recon return to main body.
(5) Smoke and indirect fire used to break contact.
(6) The platoon moves to different place to cross danger area.

Enemy Contact on Far Side

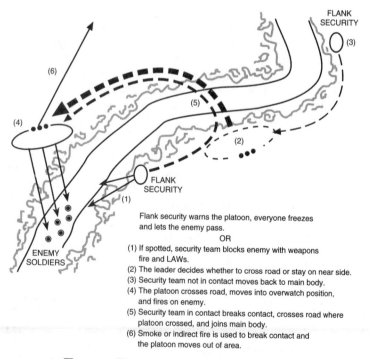

Flank security warns the platoon, everyone freezes
and lets the enemy pass.
OR
(1) If spotted, security team blocks enemy with weapons
fire and LAWs.
(2) The leader decides whether to cross road or stay on near side.
(3) Security team not in contact moves back to main body.
(4) The platoon crosses road, moves into overwatch position,
and fires on enemy.
(5) Security team in contact breaks contact, crosses road where
platoon crossed, and joins main body.
(6) Smoke or indirect fire is used to break contact and
the platoon moves out of area.

Enemy Contact on Road or Trail

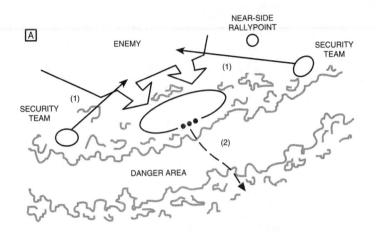

(1) Flank security teams fire in the direction of the enemy.
(2) The platoon moves quickly across danger area.

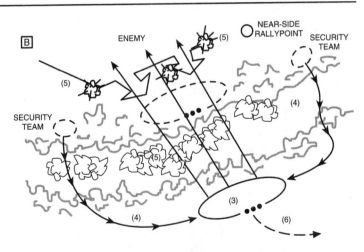

(3) The platoon sets up overwatch position.
(4) Security teams cross danger area and rejoin platoon.
(5) Smoke or artillery used.
(6) The platoon moves out of area.

Enemy Contact on Near Side

SOLDIER'S LOAD
The soldier's load greatly affects movement and is of crucial concern to leaders. Research has shown that a soldier can carry up to 30 percent of his body weight and still retain a high percentage of his agility, stamina, alertness, and mobility. For the average soldier weighing 160 pounds, that would be a 48-pound load. The soldier loses a proportional amount of his functional ability for each pound over 30 percent.

Load Management
Use the following techniques for load management:
- Distribute loads evenly over body and load-bearing equipment (LBE).
- Don't carry anything on the front of the LBE that would prevent the soldier from taking well-aimed shots.
- Distribute loads throughout the unit. If it is necessary to man-pack bulk ammunition, water, rations, or demolitions, divide them into small loads.
- Rotate heavy loads (radios, machine guns, mortars, and antitank weapons) among several soldiers.
- Always consider transportation assets to carry loads.
- Upon enemy contact, drop rucksacks or leave them in an objective rally point (ORP), an assault position, or the assembly area.
- Share or consolidate items. Carry only enough sleeping bags for those who will sleep at the same time. In the same manner, two or three soldiers can share a rucksack and take turns carrying it.
- Consider carrying fewer rations for short operations.
- While carrying rucksacks, use water and rations carried in it first. Then rucksacks can be dropped and soldiers will still have a full supply on their LBE.

Combat Load
The combat load consists of the mission-essential equipment required for soldiers to fight and survive immediate combat operations, plus items needed based on METT–TC. When possible, this load should not exceed 60 pounds. There are two components: fighting load and approach march load.

Fighting Load
The fighting load includes only what is needed to fight and survive immediate combat operations.

Load	Weight (pounds)
Helmet, ballistic	3.4
Pistol belt, suspenders, and first-aid pouch	1.6
Canteen, 1-quart, and cover with water (2 each)	5.6
Case, small arms (2 each)	1.8
Bayonet with scabbard	1.3
Protective mask with decontamination kit	3.0
Rifle, M16A2 with 30 rounds 5.56 Ball	8.8
Magazines (6) with 180 rounds 5.56 Ball	5.4
Grenade, fragmentation (4)	4.0
Total	34.9

Approach March Load

The approach march load contains the items needed for extended combat operations. On long operations, soldiers must carry enough equipment and munitions to fight and exist until a planned resupply can take place. They are dropped at an assault position, an ORP, or other point before or upon enemy contact.

Load	Weight (pounds)
ALICE, medium with frame	6.3
Rations, MRE (2 each)	2.6
Canteen, 2-quart, and cover with water	4.8
Toilet articles	2.0
Towel	0.2
Bag, waterproof	0.8
E-tool with carrier	2.5
Poncho, nylon	1.3
Liner, poncho	1.6
Total	22.1

Sustainment Load

The sustainment load consists of the remaining equipment and material needed for sustained combat operations. This must be carried by company and battalion assets.

FOOT MARCH

Foot marches are the movement of troops and equipment mainly by foot, with limited support by vehicles. They are characterized by combat readiness, ease of control, adaptability to terrain, slow rate of movement, and increased personnel fatigue. Foot marches do not depend on the existence of roads.

A dismounted company moves in a column of twos, a file on each side of the road. Distances: day, 2 to 5 meters between men, 50 meters between platoons; night, 1 to 3 meters between men, 25 meters between platoons. Rates: day, 4 kmph; night, 3.2 kmph (cross country: day, 2.4 kmph; night, 1.6 kmph). Halts: 15 minutes after the first 45 minutes, 10 minutes out of every hour thereafter.

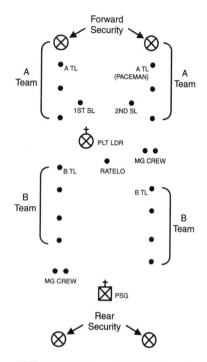

NOTE: 3rd squad can be on either side of the road.

Road March Formation

Road Space, Foot Column

The road space (RS) of a company foot column, used in determining time length of the column, consists of two parts: the space occupied by the men alone (including the distance between them), and the sum of distances between elements of the foot column. (Total RS = RS men + RS platoon distances.)

The RS of the men alone is determined by multiplying the number of men by the appropriate factor selected from the table below:

Formation	2 meters per man	5 meters per man
Single file	2.4	5.4
Column of twos	1.2	2.7

The total RS between platoons is obtained by multiplying the number of platoons (minus one) by the platoon distances.

Time Length (TL), Foot Column

Rate	Formula
4.0 kmph	TL (min.) = RS (meters) $\times$ .0150
3.2 kmph	TL (min.) = RS (meters) $\times$ .0187
2.4 kmph	TL (min.) = RS (meters) $\times$ .0250
1.6 kmph	TL (min.) = RS (meters) $\times$ .0375

Completion Time

The completion time of a foot march is determined by using this formula:
Completion time = SP (start point) time + TL + scheduled halts.

4

Offense

Units undertake offensive operations to destroy the enemy and its will to fight; to seize terrain; to learn enemy strength and disposition; or to deceive, divert, or fix the enemy. Infantry platoons and squads normally conduct offensive operations as part of a larger force. However, they can perform some offensive operations independently. The company commander's application of combat power at the decisive point determines the outcome of the battle. Offensive operations are characterized by surprise, concentration, tempo, and audacity. Offensive operations include movements to contact, attacks, raids, reconnaissance and security operations, and ambushes.

MOVEMENT TO CONTACT
A movement to contact is an offensive action that seeks to gain or regain contact with the enemy. Usually, a unit moving to contact lacks detailed information about the enemy. Upon making contact, a unit identifies the enemy strengths and weaknesses as it develops the situation. A platoon conducts a movement to contact as part of a company.

Planning and Conducting Movements to Contact
Considerations for planning and conducting movements to contact include:
- Make enemy contact with the smallest element possible.
- Prevent detection of elements not in contact until they are in the assault.
- Maintain 360-degree security at all times.
- Report all information quickly and accurately.
- Maintain contact once it is gained.
- Generate combat power rapidly upon contact.
- Fight through at the lowest level possible.

Infantry units use two techniques for conducting a movement to contact—search and attack or approach march.

Search and Attack

Search and attack is used when the enemy is dispersed or is expected to avoid contact or quickly disengage and withdraw, or to deny the enemy movement in an area. The search and attack technique involves the use of multiple squads and fire teams in coordinated actions to make contact with

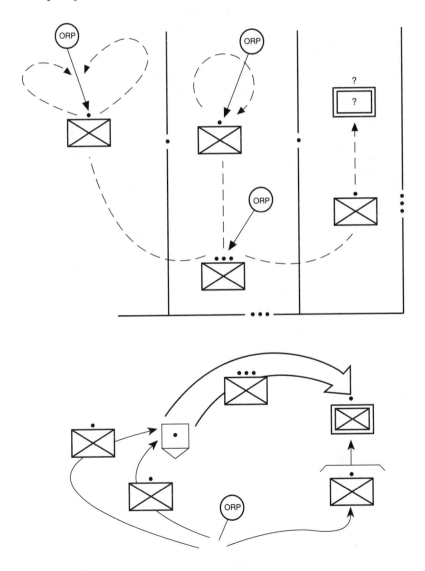

Find, Fix, and Finish the Enemy

the enemy. Platoons attempt to find the enemy and then fix and finish it. They combine patrolling techniques with the requirement to conduct hasty or deliberate attacks once the enemy has been found.

Approach March

The approach march technique may be used when the enemy is expected to deploy using relatively fixed offensive or defensive formations. The concept behind the approach march is to make contact with the smallest element, allowing the commander the flexibility of maneuvering or bypassing the enemy force. As part of a larger unit using the approach march technique, platoons may act as the advance, flank, or rear guard. They may also receive on-order missions as part of the main body.

Advance Guard

As the advance guard, the platoon finds the enemy and locates gaps, flanks, and weaknesses in its defense. The advance guard attempts to make contact on ground of its own choosing, to gain the advantage of surprise, and to develop the situation (either fight through or support the assault of all or part of the main body).

The advance guard operates within the range of the main body's indirect fire support weapons. One rifle squad leads the advance guard. The platoon uses appropriate formations and movement techniques, and the leader rotates the lead squad as necessary to keep soldiers fresh.

Flank or Rear Guard

The entire platoon may act as the flank or rear guard for a battalion conducting a movement to contact using this technique. The platoon moves using the appropriate formation and movement technique; provides early warning; destroys enemy reconnaissance units; and prevents direct fires or observation of the main body.

Main Body

When moving as part of the main body, platoons may be tasked to assault, bypass, or fix an enemy force or to seize, secure, or clear an assigned area. The platoon may also be detailed to provide squads as flank guards, stay-behind ambushes, rear security, or additional security to the front. These squads may come under the direct control of the company commander. Platoons and squads use appropriate formations and movement techniques, assault techniques, and ambush techniques.

ATTACK

An attack is an offensive action characterized by movement supported by fire. There are two types of attack: *hasty* and *deliberate.* They are distinguished chiefly by the time available for preparation.

A hasty attack is conducted with the forces immediately available to maintain momentum or to take advantage of the enemy situation. It does not normally allow for extensive preparation. A deliberate attack is carefully planned and coordinated. More time is available to perform thorough reconnaissance, evaluation of all available intelligence and relative combat strength, analysis of various courses of action, and other factors affecting the situation. It is generally conducted against a well-organized defense when a hasty attack is not possible or has been conducted and failed.

Additionally, special-purpose attacks include *raids* and *ambushes.*

A raid is an operation involving a swift penetration of hostile territory to secure information, to confuse the enemy, or to destroy his installations. It ends with a planned withdrawal after completion of the assigned mission. An ambush is a surprise attack by fire from concealed positions on a moving or temporarily halted enemy unit. It combines the advantages and characteristics of the offense with those of the defense.

Successful attack depends on concentrating the maximum possible shock and violence against the enemy force. Infantry forces combine shock and violence with surprise. The objective is to shatter the enemy's nerve, ruin its synchronization, unravel its plan, and destroy its unit's cohesion and the willingness of its soldiers to fight. A successful attack combines a scheme of maneuver with a coordinated plan of direct and indirect fire support. The focus of an attacking platoon's fire and maneuver is a weak point, a vulnerable flank, or the rear of an enemy. Once he has identified the point of attack, the leader establishes a base of fire to kill, fix, or suppress the enemy at that point. He then maneuvers the rest of his force to a position from which it can assault.

Attack Techniques and Procedures

Seizing and retaining the initiative in the attack involves more than just achieving tactical surprise. It involves a process of planning and preparing for combat operations, finding the enemy first, avoiding detection, fixing the enemy, locating or creating a weakness, and maneuvering to exploit that weakness with a quick and violent assault.

Plan and Prepare

Leaders use troop-leading procedures to ensure that all necessary steps are taken to prepare for an operation. Leaders use the estimate of the situation to analyze the factors of METT-TC, determine the best course of action, and ensure that leaders, soldiers, and their equipment can perform the tasks necessary to accomplish the mission.

Find the Enemy

Platoon leaders find the enemy by knowing how it fights, analyzing the terrain in light of this knowledge, and actively reconnoitering to locate the enemy.

Avoid Detection

Platoons avoid detection by moving along the least expected, generally most difficult route. They use the terrain to mask their movements. They use proper camouflage techniques and move with stealth. This allows platoons to capitalize on surprise. All this requires imagination in leaders and stamina in all soldiers.

Fix the Enemy

Platoons and squads fix enemy forces by employing suppressive fires that kill exposed enemy soldiers and destroy their weapons. At a minimum, they render the volume and accuracy of the enemy's fire ineffective.

Find or Create a Weakness

Leaders look for vulnerable flanks, gaps in lines, or lulls in enemy fire. When they cannot readily find a weakness, they create one with suppressive fire and the surprise of its suddenly coming from an unexpected direction.

Maneuver to Exploit the Weakness

Leaders must exploit this weakness by moving to the best covered and concealed position and then assaulting to destroy, defeat, or capture the enemy.

Consolidate and Reorganize

Finally, platoons and squads must quickly consolidate the position to defend it against an enemy counterattack. Units then reorganize themselves and prepare to continue the mission.

The Deliberate Attack

Platoons and squads conduct deliberate attacks as part of a larger force. The platoon can expect to be a base-of-fire element or an assault element. If the platoon receives the mission to conduct a supporting attack for the company or to attack a separate objective, the platoon leader should constitute a base-of-fire element and an assault element. If the platoon is the supporting effort, the platoon leader may require up to a squad as a reserve. The platoon leader may employ his squads in one of the following ways:

* Two squads and one or both machine guns as the base-of-fire element and one squad (with the remaining machine gun) as the assault element.
* One squad and one or both machine guns as the base-of-fire element and two squads (with the remaining machine gun) as the assault element.
* One squad and one or both machine guns as the base-of-fire element, one squad as the assault element, and one squad (with the remaining machine gun) to follow and support the assault element. This method generally supports the organization of the platoon for breaching obstacles during the assault.

Movement to the Objective

Platoons and squads use the appropriate formations and movement techniques to avoid contact and achieve surprise (see chapter 3). The platoon must remain undetected. If detected early, the platoon concentrates direct and indirect fires, establishes a base of fire, and maneuvers to regain the initiative.

Movement from the Assembly Area to the Line of Departure. The platoon moves forward from the assembly area under company control. When the platoon leader is already forward with the company commander, the platoon sergeant moves the platoon forward. Machine guns and antiarmor weapons can precede the rest of the platoon by moving to an overwatch position on or near the LD. Leaders time the move from the assembly area during reconnaissance or rehearsals to ensure that the lead squad crosses the LD on time and at the right place. The platoon attempts to cross the LD without halting in an attack position. If the platoon must halt in the attack position, it deploys into the initial attack formation, posts security, and takes care of last-minute coordination. Whether or not the platoon halts in the attack position, it must deploy into the attack formation and fix bayonets before crossing the LD.

Movement from the Line of Departure to the Assault Position or Support Position. The platoon moves using the appropriate technique. If it has its own support and assault elements, it may move them together for security, or along separate routes to their respective positions for speed. The base-of-fire element must be in place and ready before the assault element continues beyond the assault position.

The platoon leader's plan must address actions on chance contact. The lead squad executes the battle drill to react to contact. The platoon leader makes an assessment and reports. The company commander may direct the platoon to fight through, fix, and bypass the enemy or establish a hasty defense. If the platoon encounters an obstacle that it cannot bypass, it attempts a breach.

If the company concept calls for decentralized execution, the platoon leader must consider when it is best to initiate his supporting fires. Two factors stand out:

1. *Surprise.* If the attack is not detected, the base-of-fire element may hold fires until the assault element approaches the assault position. This will enhance surprise. The base-of-fire element may initiate fires early to keep the enemy's attention off the assault element as it moves to a flanking or rear position.

2. *Suppression.* The leader must consider the length of time needed to suppress the enemy position and destroy as many weapons and bunkers as possible before the assault.

Movement from the Assault Position to the Objective. The assault position is normally the last covered and concealed position before reaching the objective. As it passes through the assault position, the platoon deploys into its assault formation; that is, its squads and fire teams deploy to place the bulk of their firepower in the front as they assault the objective. A platoon sometimes must halt to complete its deployment and ensure synchronization so that all squads assault at the designated time. The assaulting squads move from the assault position and on to the objective. The platoon must be prepared to breach the enemy's protective obstacles. As the platoon moves beyond the obstacle, supporting fires should begin lifting and shifting away from the objective. Both direct and indirect fires shift to suppress areas adjacent to the objective, destroy enemy forces retreating, or prevent enemy reinforcement of the objective.

Assaulting the Objective. As the platoon or its assault element moves on to the objective, it must increase the volume and accuracy of fires. Squad leaders assign specific targets or objectives for their fire teams. Only when these discreet fires keep the enemy suppressed can the rest of the unit maneuver. As the assault element gets closer to the enemy, there is more emphasis on suppression and less on maneuver. Ultimately, all but one fire team may be suppressing to allow that one fire team to break into the enemy position. Throughout the assault, soldiers use proper individual movement techniques, and fire teams retain their basic shallow wedge formation. The platoon does not get "on-line" to sweep across the objective.

Consolidation and Reorganization. Once enemy resistance on the objective has ceased, the platoon must quickly take steps to consolidate and prepare to defend against a counterattack. Consolidation techniques include:

- *Clock technique.* In this method, the platoon leader designates either a compass direction or the direction of attack as 12 o'clock. He then uses clock positions to identify the left and right boundaries for squads. The platoon leader positions key weapons along the most likely avenue of approach based on his assessment of the terrain.

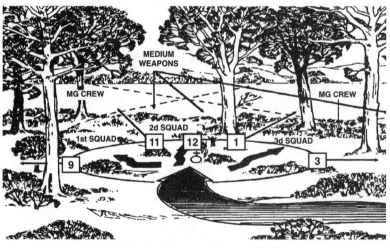

Clock Technique of Consolidation

- *Terrain feature technique.* In a similar manner, the platoon leader identifies obvious terrain features as the left and right limits for squads.

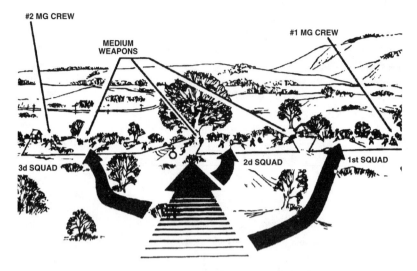

Terrain Technique of Consolidation

In both techniques, the platoon leader ensures that squad sectors of fire overlap each other and provide mutual support for adjacent units.

Reorganization. Once platoons have consolidated on the objective, they begin to reorganize to continue the attack. Reorganization involves:

- Reestablishing command and control
- Remanning key weapons and redistributing ammunition and equipment
- Clearing the objective of casualties and EPWs
- Assessing and reporting the platoon status of personnel, ammunition, supplies, and essential equipment

Limited-Visibility Attacks

Attacks during limited visibility surprise the enemy, cause panic in a weak and disorganized enemy, avoid heavy losses, exploit success, maintain momentum, and keep pressure on the enemy. Platoons and squads attack whenever possible during darkness, fog, heavy rain, and falling snow. Limited-visibility attacks require additional control measures to prevent fratricide and to keep the attack focused on the objective. Boundaries, restrictive fire lines, and limits of advance may assist in control. Limited-visibility attacks require the following fundamentals:

- Well-trained squads
- Enough natural light to employ night vision devices
- A simple plan with sufficient control measures
- Detailed, successful reconnaissance of the objective, routes, passage points, support-by-fire positions, and other key locations (this should be done during daylight and down to the lowest level possible; surveillance of the objective area to report enemy repositioning or additional defensive preparation is part of the reconnaissance plan)

There will be increased difficulty in performing the following:

- Controlling individuals and squads
- Identifying targets and controlling direct and indirect fires
- Navigating and moving
- Identifying friendly and enemy soldiers
- Locating, treating, and evacuating casualties
- Locating and bypassing or breaching enemy obstacles

Control techniques during limited-visibility attacks include the following:

- Fire control techniques. Leaders in the assault element fire all tracers, and their soldiers fire where the tracers impact. A support element tripod-mounted machine gun is positioned on the flank nearest the assault force and fires a burst of tracers every 15 seconds to indicate the near limit of the supporting fires. All other supporting weapons keep their fire on the appropriate side of the tracers.
- No flares, grenades, or smoke should be used on the objective.
- Only certain personnel with night vision devices may engage targets on the objective.
- Use mortar or artillery rounds to orient the attacking elements.
- Place guides from the line of departure to the release points, at the entrance to the assault position, and at points along the probable line of deployment.
- Reduce intervals between soldiers and units.
- Place luminous tape on helmets.

CONTROL MEASURES

Leaders use graphic control measures to regulate or direct the platoon's movements, positions, and fires. Control measures are not intended to restrict the exercise of initiative (the function of command). Leaders use control measures to clarify their intent, focus the platoon or squad effort, and ensure synchronization. Each control measure should have a specific purpose that contributes to mission accomplishment. If a control measure fails the purpose test, leaders should not use it. Control measures can be drawn on a map, overlay, sketch, or terrain model. Leaders should strive to keep control measures easily identifiable and simple. Graphic control measures in the offense include assembly area, attack position, line of departure, boundaries, route, release point, start point, axis of advance, direction of attack, phase line, checkpoint, assault position, objective, contact point, linkup point, infiltration lane, probable line of deployment, and limit of advance.

BATTLE DRILLS
Infantry battle drills describe how platoons and squads apply fire and maneuver to commonly encountered situations. The battle drill is not intended to replace the estimate of the situation but to reduce the estimate of the situation and the decision-making process to the essential elements. (Experience at the Army's combat training centers revealed a deficiency in the action and reaction of small units.) The emphasis on drills is intended to instill an immediate, aggressive response.

Platoon or Squad Attack Drill
The platoon or squad attack drill is a comprehensive exercise that includes actions from planning the action to reorganizing after defeating the enemy. Within the drill, the platoon members may have to execute other drills—for example, the react to enemy contact or break contact drills. These drills can occur in several situations. The discussion of those specific drills also applies to the platoon attack drill, if appropriate situations develop.

    Step 1. **Prepare for combat.** In the assembly area, leaders do the following:

1. Receive the order, issue the warning orders to start preparation, and complete the order or fragmentary order.
2. Check that troops have the right equipment, in sufficient quantities, and that the equipment is serviceable.
3. Check for resupply of ammunition, food, water, and medical supplies in prescribed quantities.
4. Make sure communications equipment is operable and in prescribed quantities.
5. Make sure that soldiers and equipment are camouflaged.
6. Conduct rehearsals and inspections.

    Step 2. **React to enemy contact.** (The platoon is moving as part of a larger unit in a movement to contact or a hasty or deliberate attack.)

COMBAT DRILL STEPS

1. Prepare for combat
2. React to enemy contact
3. Locate the enemy

4. Gain fire superiority
5. Attack (knock out bunker, clear trench line)
6. Consolidate and reorganize

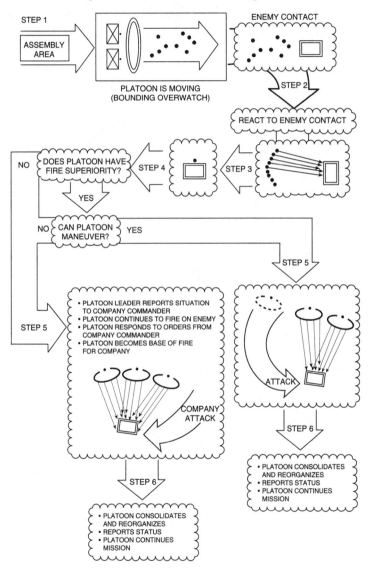

Platoon Attack Drill

1. Seek cover and concealment. Soldiers being fired on take up the closest positions that afford protection from enemy fire (cover) and observation (concealment).
2. Return fire. Automatic riflemen and machine gunners immediately return a heavy volume of suppressive fire on the enemy position. Using all weapons, the lead squad initially places heavy suppressive fires in the direction of the enemy.
3. Position and control soldiers to provide observation, cover and concealment, and fields of fire. Leaders control distribution of fires to place maximum effective, sustained fire on the enemy.

Step 3. **Locate the enemy.**
1. Observe. Squad members use sight and hearing to find known or suspected targets.
2. Reconnoiter by fire. The squad places well-aimed, sustained fire on suspected enemy positions.
3. Employ fire and movement. Squad members move in fire teams, buddy teams, or singly by rushing or crawling. A support element covers the moving element, and the assault element seeks covered firing positions.

Step 4. **Gain fire superiority.** The platoon leader determines whether the lead squad can gain fire superiority over the enemy based on the volume and accuracy of the enemy's return fire.

- If *yes,* he continues to suppress enemy weapons returning the most effective fire, normally crew-served weapons. He uses smoke to conceal the maneuver element's movement from the enemy and prepares to attack.
- If *no,* he deploys another squad and all machine guns to suppress the enemy position and calls for indirect fire.
- If still *no,* he deploys the last squad to provide flank and rear security and to guide the rest of the company forward as necessary. He reports the situation to his commander, continues to place suppressive fire on the enemy, and prepares to become the base-of-fire element for the company's maneuver element.

Step 5. **Attack.** If the squad in contact and the machine guns can suppress the enemy, the platoon leader determines whether the remaining squad(s) not in contact can maneuver.

- If *yes,* the platoon leader maneuvers the other squad(s) into the assault. He determines the enemy weakness based on vulnerable flanks, distance to the enemy, location of enemy positions, and covered and concealed flanking route to the enemy position. Indirect fires and fire from the base-of-fire element are shifted to the opposite side of the enemy position. The assaulting squad(s) fight through the enemy position using fire and maneuver. They try to conduct a flank attack, knocking out bunkers and clearing trench lines.

- If *no,* the platoon leader reports the situation to the company commander. The platoon continues to fire on the enemy and react to orders from the company commander. The platoon may become the support element for the company's assault.

Step 6. **Consolidate and reorganize.**

1. During consolidation, the platoon leader establishes local security, places OPs, positions key weapons, occupies hasty defensive positions, and prepares for counterattack.
2. During reorganization, the platoon reestablishes the chain of command; redistributes ammunition, weapons, and communications equipment; treats casualties; evacuates the wounded; and searches, silences, safeguards, and speeds EPWs to collection points.
3. The platoon leader reports his status and continues the mission.

React to Contact Drill

The react to contact drill takes place when a squad or a platoon is receiving fire from enemy riflemen or an automatic weapon.

Step 1. Soldiers take cover and return fire.

Step 2. Leaders locate known or suspected enemy positions and engage with well-aimed fire. Leaders control fire using the following standard fire commands: alert, direction, description of target, range, method of fire, and command to commence firing.

Step 3. Soldiers maintain contact to left and right, as well as with leaders, and report enemy locations.

Step 4. Leaders check the status of their men.

Step 5. The platoon leader moves to the squad in contact. He brings with him his radiotelephone operator (RATELO), forward observer (FO), the squad leader of the nearest squad, and a machine gun crew. The platoon sergeant moves forward with the second machine gun crew and links up with the platoon leader, ready to assume control of the base-of-fire element.

Step 6. The platoon leader determines whether he must move out of an enemy engagement area. If he is not in an engagement area, he determines whether he can gain and maintain suppressive fire with his element in contact, based on the volume and accuracy of the enemy fire.

Step 7. The platoon leader makes an assessment of the situation, identifying the following:

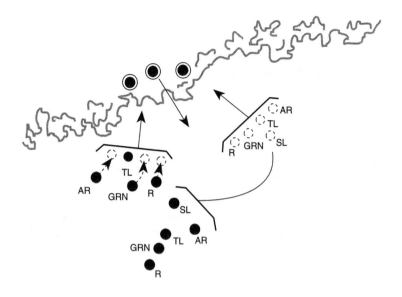

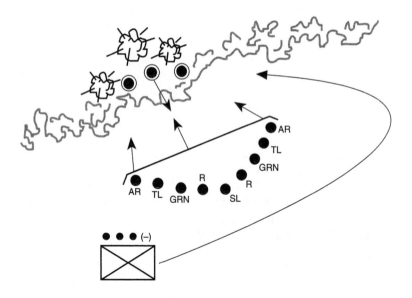

React to Contact Drill

1. Location of the enemy position and obstacles
2. Size of the enemy force (the number of automatic weapons, the presence of vehicles, and the employment of indirect fires are indicators of enemy strength)
3. Vulnerable flanks
4. Covered and concealed flanking routes to the enemy position

   Step 8. The platoon leader then determines his next course of action, such as fire and movement, assault, breach, knock-out bunker, or enter and clear a building or trench.

   Step 9. The platoon leader reports the situation to the company commander and begins to maneuver, calling for and adjusting artillery or mortar fire.

Break Contact Drill

The break contact drill takes place when the squad or platoon is under enemy fire and must break contact.

Step 1. The platoon leader directs one squad in contact to support the disengagement of the remainder of the platoon.

Step 2. The platoon leader orders the first squad to move a certain distance and direction or to a terrain feature or the last objective rally point. Meanwhile, the base-of-fire (supporting) squad continues to suppress the enemy.

Step 3. The moving element uses smoke grenades to mask its movement until it takes up its designated position and engages the enemy position.

Step 4. The platoon leader then directs the base-of-fire squad to move to its next location.

Step 5. While continuing to suppress the enemy, the platoon

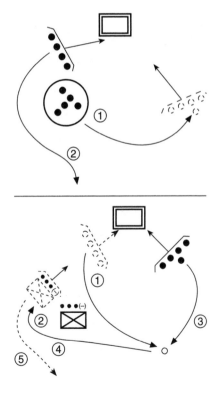

Break Contact Drills

bounds away from the enemy until it either breaks contact or passes through a high-level support-by-fire position.

Step 6. Once contact is broken, the platoon should change direction, if possible, to avoid indirect enemy fire.

Step 7. Leaders account for soldiers, report, reorganize as necessary, and continue the mission.

React to Ambush Drill

In a near ambush (within hand-grenade range), use the following procedures:

Step 1. Immediately return fire.

Step 2. Take up covered positions.

Step 3. Throw fragmentation, concussion, and smoke grenades.

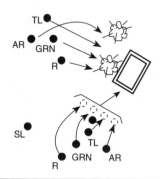

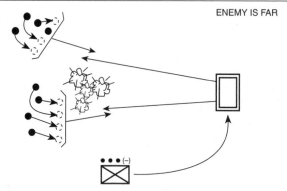

React to Ambush Drills

Step 4. Immediately after the grenades detonate, the soldiers in the kill zone assault through the ambush using fire and movement, while soldiers not in the kill zone identify enemy positions, initiate suppressive fire, take up covered positions, and shift fires as soldiers in the kill zone assault through the ambush.

In a far ambush (beyond hand-grenade range), use the following procedures:

Step 1. Soldiers receiving fire immediately return fire, take up covered positions, and suppress the enemy by destroying or suppressing enemy crew-served weapons first, obscuring the enemy position with smoke, and sustaining suppressive fires.

Step 2. Soldiers not receiving fires move by a covered and concealed route to a vulnerable flank of the enemy position and assault using fire and movement.

Step 3. Soldiers in the kill zone continue suppressive fires and shift fires as the assaulting element fights through the enemy position.

In both near and far ambushes, the platoon leader then calls for mortar or artillery fire to isolate the enemy or to attack as the enemy retreats. Leaders account for soldiers, report, reorganize as necessary, and continue the mission.

Knock-out Bunker Drill

The knock-out bunker drill is used when the platoon identifies enemy in bunkers.

Step 1. The platoon initiates contact.

1. The squad in contact establishes a base of fire.
2. The platoon leader, RATELO, FO, and one machine gun team move to the squad in contact.
3. The platoon sergeant moves the second machine gun team forward and takes charge of the base of fire.

Step 2. The base-of-fire element destroys or suppresses enemy crew-served weapons first and uses smoke to obscure the enemy position. The FO calls for and adjusts indirect fire.

Step 3. The platoon leader determines whether he can maneuver by identifying the following:

1. The enemy bunkers, other supporting positions, and any obstacles
2. The size of the enemy force engaging the platoon
3. A vulnerable flank of at least one bunker
4. A covered and concealed flanking route to the bunker

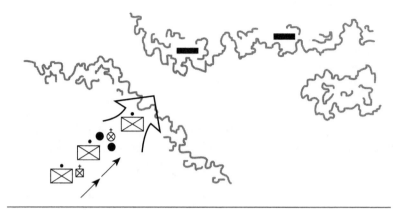

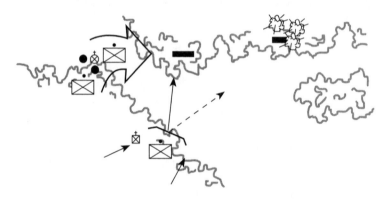

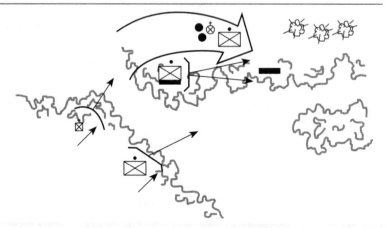

Knock Out a Bunker—Platoon

Step 4. The platoon leader determines which bunker to knock out and directs a squad not in contact to assault it.

Step 5. If necessary, the platoon sergeant repositions elements of the base of fire to isolate the enemy bunker.

Step 6. The assault squad, along with the platoon leader and FO, moves along the covered and concealed route.

1. The squad leader moves with the assaulting fire team.
2. The assaulting fire team approaches the bunker from its blind side.
3. Soldiers constantly watch for other bunkers or enemy positions in support of the known bunker.
4. Upon reaching the last covered and concealed position, the fire team leader and automatic rifleman remain in place and add their fires to suppressing the bunker, while the squad leader positions himself where he can best control his teams.

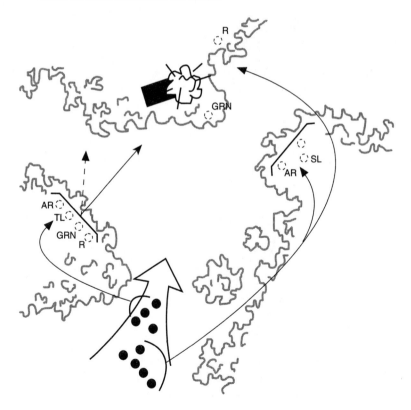

Knock Out a Bunker—Squad

5. On the squad leader's signal, the base-of-fire element lifts or shifts fires to the opposite side of the bunker from the assaulting team's approach.
6. A rifleman and grenadier continue forward to the blind side of the bunker. One soldier takes up a covered position near the exit while the other cooks off (two seconds maximum) a grenade, shouts "Frag out!" and throws it through an aperture.
7. After the grenade detonates, the soldier covering the exit enters the bunker, firing short bursts to destroy the enemy.
8. The squad leader inspects the bunker to ensure that it has been destroyed.
9. The squad leader then reports, reorganizes as needed, and continues the mission.

Step 7. The platoon leader repositions the base-of-fire element as necessary to continue to isolate and suppress the remaining bunkers as squads are maneuvered to knock them out.

Enter and Clear a Trench Drill

The enter and clear a trench drill is used when the platoon is moving and identifies enemy in a trench line, and the platoon leader determines that he can maneuver and assault the trench line.

Step 1. The platoon leader directs one squad to enter the trench and secure a foothold.

Step 2. The platoon leader designates the entry point of the trench line and the direction of movement once the platoon begins clearing.

Step 3. The platoon sergeant positions soldiers and machine guns to suppress the trench and isolate the entry point.

Step 4. The squad leader of the assaulting squad designates one fire team to assault and another fire team to initially support by fire, then follow and support the assaulting team.

1. The squad leader and the assault team move to the last covered and concealed position short of the entry point.
2. The squad leader marks the entry point.
3. The base-of-fire element shifts fires away from the entry point and continues to suppress adjacent enemy positions or isolate the trench as required.
4. The fire team leader and an automatic rifleman remain in a position short of the entry point to add suppressive fire for the initial entry, while the remaining soldiers move by crawling or in rushes to the entry point.

5. The first two soldiers of the assaulting fire team move to the edge of the trench parallel to the trench and on their backs, cook off grenades, shout "Frag out!" and throw grenades into the trench.

6. After ensuring that both grenades detonate, the soldiers roll into the trench, landing on their feet and back to back. They fire their weapons down the trench in opposite directions, then immediately move in opposite directions down the trench, firing three-round bursts. Each soldier continues until he reaches the first corner or intersection. Then both soldiers halt and take up positions to block any enemy movement toward the entry point.

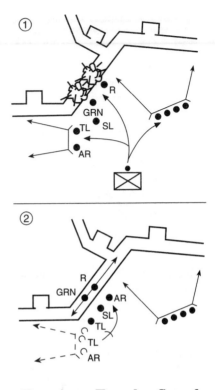

Entering a Trench—Squad

7. After detonation of the grenades, the assault fire team leader and the automatic rifleman enter the trench and relieve the rifleman at one of the secured corners or intersections.

8. The squad leader reports to the platoon leader that he has secured a foothold.

Step 5. The platoon leader now directs one of the base-of-fire squads to move into the trench and begin clearing it.

1. The squad in the trench separates into a lead team and a trail team.

2. The squad leader moves with the lead team to the secure corner or intersection.

3. The lead soldier of the fire team moves abreast of the soldier securing the corner and announces, "Taking the lead." The soldier securing the corner or intersection acknowledges and is bypassed.

4. The lead fire team starts clearing.

Step 6. Using the buddy system, the second soldier cooks off a grenade, yells "Frag out!" and throws a grenade around the corner.

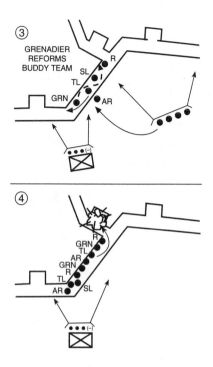

1. Upon detonation of the grenade, the lead soldier moves around the corner firing three-round bursts and advancing as he fires.
2. The entire fire team follows him to the next corner or intersection.

Step 7. At each corner or intersection, the lead fire team performs the same actions described above. The squad leader ensures that the trail team moves and is prepared to take the lead when rotated.

Step 8. The squad leader calls for indirect fire if necessary and reports his progress to the platoon leader.

Step 9. The platoon leader rotates squads to keep soldiers fresh and to maintain the momentum of the assault. He reports to the company commander that the trench line is secure or that he is no longer able to continue clearing.

Clearing a Trench—Squad

Enter Building and Clear Room Drill
This drill is used in urban combat.

Step 1. The fire team initiating contact establishes a base of fire and suppresses the enemy in and around the building.

Step 2. The squad leader determines whether he can maneuver by identifying the building and any obstacles, the size of the enemy force engaging the squad, an entry point, and a covered and concealed route to the entry point.

Step 3. The squad leader directs the fire team in contact to support the entry of the other fire team. He designates the entry point. The platoon and squad shift direct fires and continue to suppress the enemy in adjacent positions and to isolate the building. Indirect fires are lifted or shifted, as necessary.

Step 4. The squad leader and assaulting fire team approach the building and position themselves at either side of the entry point. (Doors and windows should be avoided because they will normally be covered by enemy soldiers inside the building.)

Step 5. The lead soldier of the assaulting fire team cooks off a grenade, shouts "Frag out!" and throws a grenade into the building. (If the building has thin walls and floors, soldiers must take protective measures from grenade fragments.)

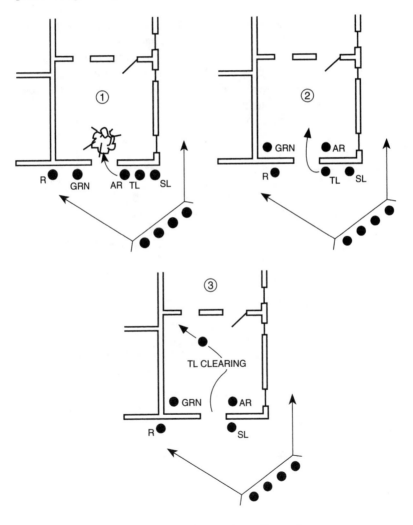

Entering a Building—Squad

Step 6. After the grenade detonates, the next soldier enters the building and positions himself to the left or right of the entrance, up against the wall; engages all identified or likely enemy positions with rapid, short bursts of automatic fire; and scans the room. The soldier may have to move to the left or right because of the size or shape of the room.

1. The first soldier decides where the next man should position himself and gives the command "Next man in!" (left or right).
2. Once in position, the second soldier shouts "Next man in!" (left or right).
3. Depending on the enemy situation and the size of the room, two soldiers may be able to enter the room simultaneously after the grenade detonates. If so, the soldier on the right side enters, fires from left to right, and moves to the right with his back to the wall, while the soldier on the left enters from the left, fires from right to left, and moves to the left with his back to the wall. When both soldiers are in position, the senior soldier shouts "Next man in!" (left or right).

Entering a Room

Step 7. The assaulting fire team leader now shouts "Coming in!" (right or left), enters the building, and positions himself against the wall and where he can control the actions of his fire team. He makes a quick assessment of the room's size and shape and begins to clear the room.

Step 8. Once the room is cleared, the squad leader enters the building and marks the entry point according to the SOP.

Step 9. The squad leader and assault fire team move to the entrance of the next room to be cleared and position themselves on either side. This room and all subsequent rooms are cleared by repeating the procedures described above.

Step 10. The squad consolidates its position in the building and then reorganizes as necessary.

Breach an Obstacle Drill

The breach an obstacle drill is used when the lead squad identifies a wire obstacle, reinforced with mines, that cannot be bypassed and there are enemy positions on the far side of the obstacle.

Step 1. The platoon leader moves forward with his FO and one machine gun team.

Step 2. The platoon leader determines whether he can maneuver.

Step 3. The platoon leader directs one squad to be the base-of-fire element, another to be the breach squad, and a third to be the assault squad once the breach has been made.

Step 4. The base-of-fire squad is joined by the platoon sergeant and the second machine gun team, and together they begin to suppress the enemy and obscure the enemy positions with smoke.

Step 5. The platoon leader leads the breach and assault squads to the breach point

1. The breach squad leader designates a breach fire team and a support fire team.
2. The breaching fire team moves to the breach point using the covered and concealed route. The squad and fire team leader obscure the breach point, using smoke grenades.
3. The breaching fire team leader and an automatic rifleman are positioned on one flank of the breach point to provide security.
4. The grenadier and rifleman of the breaching fire team probe for and mark mines and cut the wire obstacle, marking their path as they proceed. (If available, bangalore torpedoes are preferred for clearing a lane through a minefield.)

Step 6. Once the obstacle has been breached, the fire team leader and the automatic rifleman move to the far side of the obstacle and take up covered and concealed positions with the rifleman and the grenadier.

Step 7. The squad leader signals the supporting fire team to move up and through the breach to the far side, where it takes up covered and concealed positions. The squad leader then moves through the breach and joins the breaching fire team.

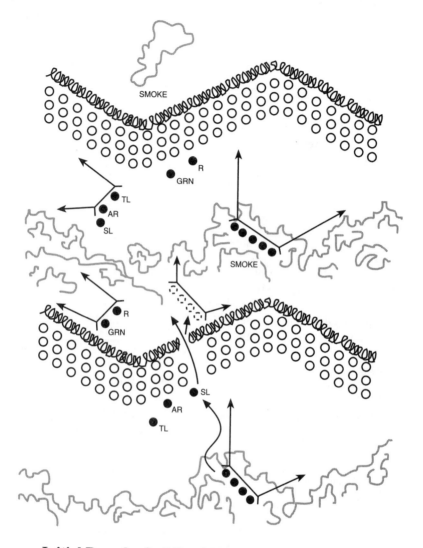

Initial Breach of a Mined Wire Obstacle—Platoon

Step 8. The squad leader reports to the platoon leader and consolidates as needed.

Step 9. The platoon leader leads the assault squad through the breach and positions it to support the movement of the remainder of the platoon or assaults the enemy position covering the obstacle.

Step 10. The platoon leader reports to the company commander.

5

Defense

Platoons and squads normally defend as part of a larger force to disrupt, disorganize, delay, or defeat an attacking enemy, deny an area to an enemy, or protect a flank. They may also defend as part of a larger unit in a retrograde operation. The challenge to the defender is to retain the initiative, that is, to keep the enemy reacting and unable to execute its own plan. The characteristics of the defense are preparation, security, disruption, and flexibility.

Take the Initiative in the Defense. Since the enemy decides the time and place of the attack, leaders seize and retain the initiative in the defense through careful planning, preparation, coordination, and rehearsal. Leaders plan and establish the defense to find the enemy first, without being found. They fix the enemy with obstacles and fires, locate or create a weakness in the enemy's attack plan, and maneuver to exploit that weakness with quick, violent counterattack.

Plan and Prepare. Leaders analyze the factors of METT-TC to determine where best to kill the enemy with fires. They position key weapons to concentrate fires into that area, tie in fires with obstacles, position the remaining platoon and squad weapons to support and protect the key weapons, and reconnoiter and rehearse counterattacks.

Find the Enemy. Platoon leaders find the enemy by knowing how it fights, by analyzing the terrain in light of this knowledge, by positioning OPs along likely avenues of approach, and by actively patrolling to locate the enemy.

Avoid Detection. Platoons avoid detection by concealing their defensive positions or sectors early and continuously, by positioning squads and weapons away from natural lines of drift or obvious terrain features, and by employing effective camouflage and noise and light discipline.

Fix the Enemy. Platoons use a combination of tactical obstacles and direct and indirect fires to disrupt the enemy attack and fix the enemy in a place where the platoon can destroy it with fires.

Find or Create a Weakness. Platoons create a weakness by destroying the enemy's command and control nodes, by isolating the attacking enemy formation from its support, by causing mounted forces to dismount and thereby slowing the attack and making enemy vehicles more vulnerable, by the use of night vision devices to gain a visibility advantage, or by the effective use of illumination to blind or expose the enemy during its attack.

Maneuver to Exploit the Weakness. Having created a weakness, platoons must exploit it with counterattacks against the flank or rear of the enemy attack by fire or maneuver. Platoons must carefully coordinate and rehearse all counterattacks to ensure the proper synchronization in lifting and shifting of direct and indirect fires. They must also consider the threat of follow-on enemy forces against their counterattack.

Reorganize. Platoons and squads must be able to reorganize quickly to continue the defense against follow-on forces.

CONTROL MEASURES

Control measures are used to assign responsibilities, coordinate fires and maneuver, control combat operations, and clarify the concept of the operation. Additionally, control measures ensure the distribution of fires throughout the platoon's area of responsibility and the initial positioning and subsequent maneuvering of squads. Graphic control measures used in the defense include sectors, battle positions, boundaries, contact points, coordination points, forward edge of the battle area (FEBA), strong points, target reference points (TRPs), assembly areas, phase lines, passage points and lanes, release points, and engagement areas.

Fire commands and control measures for individual and key weapons also constitute a type of control measure available to leaders. Weapons control measures include range cards, sectors of fire, principal direction of fire, final protective line, and final protective fires. In addition, antiarmor gunners, machine gun teams, fire teams, squads, and platoons can be given engagement priorities and fire commands.

CONDUCT OF THE DEFENSE

The standard sequence of actions that a platoon takes in defensive operations is as follows:

1. Prepare for combat.
2. Move to defensive positions.
3. Establish defensive positions.
4. Locate the enemy and take action on enemy contact.
5. Fight the defense.
6. Reorganize.

Prepare for Combat

The platoon leader issues a warning order; makes a tentative plan; conducts a reconnaissance of the defensive area; inspects the soldiers for proper equipment, weapons, ammunition, rations, camouflage, and soldier's load; and moves the platoon if not already moving.

Move to Defensive Positions

As with all movement, the platoon applies the fundamentals of movement and uses covered and concealed routes; avoids likely ambush sites; enforces camouflage, noise, and light discipline; maintains all-around security; and uses formations and movement techniques based on METT-TC.

Establish Defensive Positions

The platoon halts in a covered and concealed position to the rear of the defensive area, and the leaders conduct reconnaissance of assigned positions. The platoon moves forward as a whole or by squads, using guides to control movement into positions. A priority of work is established to prepare the defense. The platoon's normal priority of work is as follows:

Establish Local Security

Platoons provide their own security by patrolling, using observation posts (OPs), and detailing a percentage of the platoon to man hasty positions while the rest of the soldiers prepare the defense.

Position Weapons and Soldiers

The success of the defense depends on the positioning of soldiers and weapons. To position their weapons effectively, all leaders must know the characteristics, capabilities, and limitations of their weapons; the effects of terrain; and the tactics used by the enemy. Leaders should position weapons where they have protection, can avoid detection, and can surprise the enemy with accurate, lethal fires. To position the weapon, the leader must know where he wants to destroy the enemy and what effect he wants the weapon to achieve. Additionally, the platoon leader must consider whether his primary threat will be armored vehicles or dismounted infantry and position the appropriate weapons along the most likely avenue of approach first. The platoon leader must consider both mounted and dismounted avenues of approach, and his plan should address both—one as a contingency of the other. Squad leaders position all other weapons to support these key weapons, cover dead space, and provide security.

Machine guns are the platoon's main weapons and are positioned first if the enemy is a dismounted force. Leaders position machine guns to concentrate fires where they want to kill the enemy, fire across the platoon front, cover obstacles by fire, and tie in with adjacent units. They provide a high volume of lethal fire to break up and stop enemy assaults.

Each gun is given a primary and secondary sector of fire. Their sectors of fire should overlap each other and those of adjacent platoons. A gunner fires in his secondary sector only if there are no targets in his primary sector, or when ordered to do so.

Squad leaders position all other weapons to support these key weapons, cover dead space, and provide security. The platoon leader positions antiarmor weapons according to the armored threat. He selects a primary (and supplementary) position and field of fire for each antiarmor weapon. He considers fields of fire, tracking time, and minimum arming range. The antiarmor leader selects alternate positions. Each position should allow flank fire and have cover and concealment. The thermal sights are integrated into the platoon's limited-visibility reconnaissance and surveillance plan.

The M203 grenade launcher is the squad's indirect-fire weapon. It is positioned to cover dead space in the squad sector, especially the dead space for the machine guns. The M203 gunner is also assigned a sector to cover with rifle fire. Each rifleman in the squad is assigned a position and sector of fire. Normally, these positions support the machine guns and antiarmor weapons. They are also positioned to cover obstacles, provide security, cover gaps between units, or provide observation.

Establish the Command Post and Wire Communications
The platoon command post (CP) is set up where the platoon leader can best see and control his platoon. If he cannot see all of the platoon sector from one place, he sets up where he can see and control the main effort. He then sets up an alternate CP where the platoon sergeant can see and control the rest of the platoon.

The platoon CP ties in to the company wire net with a field telephone. Wire is the primary means of communications between the platoon leader and squad leaders. The platoon has its own radio net, and the platoon leader also uses messengers, visual signals, personal contact, or whistles to communicate.

Designate Final Protective Lines and Final Protective Fires
Each machine gun's primary sector includes a final protective line (FPL) or a principal direction of fire (PDF). The gun is laid on the FPL or the PDF unless engaging other targets. When final protective fires (FPFs) are called for, the gunner shifts to and engages on the FPL or PDF. Where terrain

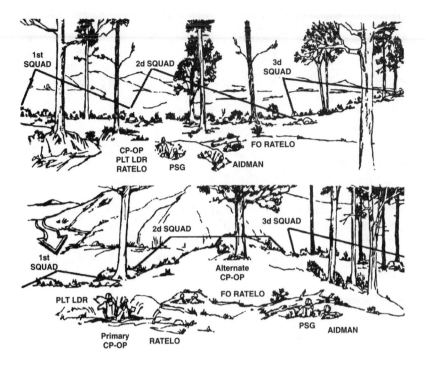

Command Post, Observation Post

Grazing Fire

allows, the platoon leader assigns a machine gun an FPL. The FPL is a line along which grazing fire is placed to stop an assault. Grazing fire is no more than 1 meter above the ground. The FPL is fixed in elevation and direction. A soldier walks the FPL to find dead space. The gunner watches the soldier walking the line and marks spaces that cannot be grazed. The dead space is covered with obstacles, grenade launcher fire, or mines.

When the terrain does not lend itself to an FPL, the platoon leader assigns the machine gun a PDF to cover an area that provides good fields of fire or has a likely avenue of approach. FPFs are a prearranged barrier of indirect fires used to defeat the assaulting enemy unit as soon as possible after it moves into its assault formation. The FPF can be anywhere between the forward position of the friendly unit and the enemy's assault position, which is normally just out of range of the platoon's organic weapons. The FPF should be fired only to stop an enemy assault. On signal, the FPF is fired continuously until the order is given to stop or the mortar or artillery unit runs out of ammunition. All other platoon weapons fire while the FPF is being fired.

Clear Fields of Fire and Prepare Range Cards and Sector Sketches
Fields of fire are cleared far enough out (40 meters) to kill the enemy before it can assault or throw hand grenades into fighting positions. Fields of fire are improved by selective clearing of grass, brush, trees, and rubble. Evidence of clearing is removed or camouflaged.

A range card is a record of the firing data required to engage predetermined targets within a sector of fire during good and limited visibility. Every direct-fire weapon gunner must prepare a range card. Range cards are prepared for primary, alternate, and supplementary positions. Two copies are prepared; one stays at the position, and the other is sent to the platoon leader.

Individual Weapon Range Card. Range cards are prepared immediately upon arrival in a position, regardless of the length of stay, and are updated as necessary. The range card is prepared in accordance with the field manual for the specific weapon. The range card has two sections—a sector sketch section, and a data section. The marginal information at the top of the card is listed as follows:
- SQD, PLT, CO. The squad, platoon, and company designations are listed. Units higher than company are not listed.
- MAGNETIC NORTH. The range card is oriented with the terrain, and the direction of magnetic north arrow is drawn.

The gunner's sector of fire is drawn in the sector sketch section. It is not drawn to scale, but the data referring to the targets must be accurate.

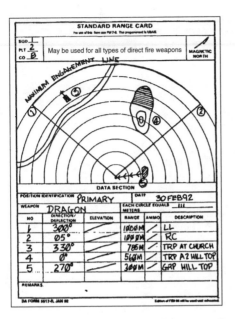

Maximum engagement
line for Dragon

Completed Range Card—Dragon

- The weapon symbol is drawn in the center of the small circle.
- Left and right limits are drawn from the position. A circled "L" and "R" are placed at the end of the left and right limit lines.
- The value of each circle is determined by using a terrain feature farthest from the position that is within the weapon's capability. The distance to the terrain is determined and rounded off to the next even hundredth, if necessary. The maximum number of circles that will divide evenly into the distance is determined and divided. The result is the value for each circle. The terrain feature is then drawn on the appropriate circle.
- All target reference points (TRPs) and reference points are drawn in the sector. They are numbered consecutively and circled.
- Dead space is drawn in the sector.
- A maximum engagement line is drawn on range cards for antiarmor weapons.
- The weapon reference point is numbered last. The location is given a six-digit grid coordinate. When there is no terrain feature to be designated, the location is shown as an eight-digit grid coordinate.

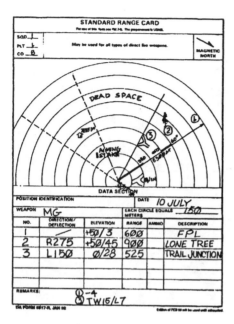

Primary sector with FPL

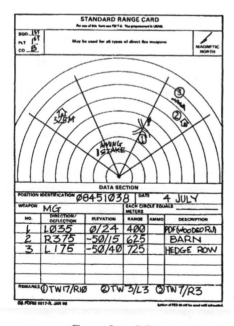

Primary sector with PDF

Completed Range Card—Machine Gun

The data section is filled in as follows:
* Position Identification: The position is identified as primary, alternate, or supplementary.
* Date: The date and time the range card was completed are entered.
* Weapon: The weapon block indicates the weapons used.
* Each circle equals meters. Write in the distance in meters between circles.
* No.: Starting with left and right limits, TRPs and reference points are listed in numerical order.
* Direction/deflection: The direction is listed in degrees. The deflection is listed in mils.
* Elevation: The elevation is listed in mils.
* Range: The distance in meters from the position to the left and right limits and TRPs and reference points.
* Ammo: The type of ammunition used is listed.
* Description: The name of the object is listed, for example, farmhouse, wood line, hilltop.
* Remarks: The weapon reference point data and any additional information are listed.

Leaders prepare sector sketches based on their defensive plan. They use the range card for each crew-served weapon (prepared by the gunners).

Squad Sector Sketch. Each squad leader prepares a sector sketch to help him plan his defense and help him control fire. The squad leader prepares two copies of the sector sketch. He gives one copy to the platoon leader and keeps the second copy at his position. The SOP should state how soon after occupying the position the leader must forward the sketch. The sketch shows the following:
* Squad and platoon identification
* Date/time group
* Magnetic north
* The main terrain features in his sector of fire and the ranges to them
* Each primary fighting position
* Alternate and supplementary positions
* The primary and secondary sectors of fire of each position
* Maximum engagement line
* Machine gun FPLs or PDF
* Dragon positions with sectors of fire
* The type of weapon in each position
* Observation posts and the squad leader's position
* Dead space to include coverage by grenade launchers
* Location of night vision devices (NVDs)
* Obstacles, mines, and booby traps

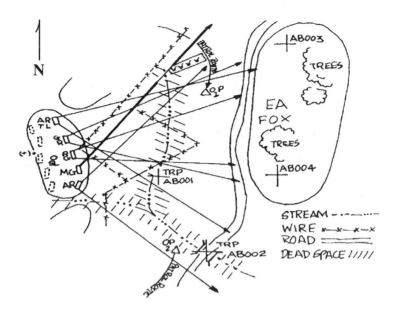

AB003
TREES
EA
FOX
TREES
AB004

STREAM ---·---·····
WIRE x—x—x—x
ROAD ═══
DEAD SPACE /////

Squad Sector Sketch

Platoon Sector Sketch. The platoon leader checks range cards and squad sector sketches. If he finds gaps or other flaws in his fire plan, he adjusts the weapons or sectors as needed. If he finds any dead space, he takes steps to cover it with mines, grenade launcher fire, or indirect fire. He then makes two copies of his platoon sector sketch—one for his use, and the other for the company commander. His sketch shows the following:

- Squad sectors of fire
- Machine gun and antiarmor weapon positions and their sectors of fires, including FPLs and PDFs of the automatic rifles and machine guns and TRPs for the antiarmor weapons
- Maximum engagement lines for antiarmor weapons
- Mines (Claymores) and obstacles
- Indirect fire planned in the platoon's sector of fire (targets and FPF)
- OPs and patrol routes, if any
- Platoon CP
- Platoon/company identification
- Date/time group
- Magnetic north

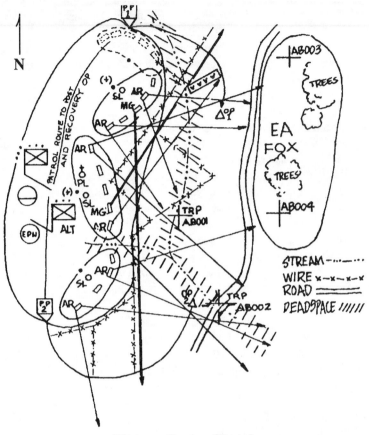

Platoon Sector Sketch

- Location of casualty collection point
- Location of NVDs/thermal sights that are part of the limited-visibility security plan
- Adjustments during limited visibility to maintain coverage of assigned TRPs

Coordinate with Adjacent Units
Coordination between adjacent platoons and squads is normally from left to right and from front to rear. Information exchanged includes the following:

- Location of leaders
- Location of primary, alternate, and supplementary positions and sectors of fire of machine guns, antiarmor weapons, and subunits
- Route to alternate and supplementary positions
- Location of dead space between platoons and squads and how to cover it
- Location of OPs and withdrawal routes back to the platoon's or squad's position
- Location and types of obstacles and how to cover them
- Patrols to be conducted, including their size, type, times of departure and return, and routes
- Location, activities, and passage plans for scouts and other units forward of the platoon's position
- Signals for fire, cease-fire, and any others that may be observed
- Engagement and disengagement criteria

Fire team leaders should also coordinate to ensure that each position knows who and what weapons are to the left and right. This ensures that all positions and all units are mutually supportive and that any gaps between units are covered by fire, observation, patrols, or sensors.

Prepare Primary Fighting Positions

Defensive positions can be classified as primary, alternate, or supplementary. All positions should provide observation and fields of fire within the weapon's or platoon's assigned sector. They should take advantage of natural cover and concealment even before soldiers begin to camouflage them. Soldiers improve their ability to reposition by using covered routes and communications trenches, employing smoke, or planning and rehearsing the repositioning by fire and maneuver.

Primary. A primary position provides a soldier, weapon crew, or unit the best means of accomplishing the assigned mission.

Alternate. Alternate positions allow soldiers, weapon crews, or units to cover the same sector of fire covered from the primary position. Soldiers occupy alternate positions when the primary position becomes untenable or unsuitable for carrying out their tasks. Soldiers may occupy alternate positions before an attack to rest, to perform maintenance, or to add the element of surprise to their defense.

Supplementary. Supplementary positions provide the best means of accomplishing a task that cannot be accomplished from the primary or alternate position. Platoon leaders normally locate supplementary positions to cover additional enemy avenues of approach and to protect the flanks and rear of the platoon position.

As a guideline, a squad can physically occupy a front of about 100 meters. From this position, it can defend 200 to 250 meters of frontage. The frontage distance between two-man fighting positions should be about 20 meters (allowing for a "lazy W" configuration on the ground, which would put fighting positions about 25 meters apart physically). Every position should be observed and supported by the fires of at least two other positions. One-man fighting positions may be located closer together to occupy the same platoon frontage. The distance between fighting positions depends on the leader's analysis of the factors of METT-TC. In determining the best distance between fighting positions, the squad leader must consider:

- The requirement to cover the squad's assigned sector by fire
- The need for security—that is, to prevent infiltrations of the squad position
- The requirement to prevent the enemy from using hand grenades effectively to assault adjacent positions, should it gain a fighting position

The platoon leader assigns primary positions and sectors of fire to his machine guns and antiarmor weapons. He must personally check the lay of each weapon. He assigns primary positions and sectors of fire to his squads. The squad leader normally assigns the alternate position for the squad and has them approved by the platoon leader. Each squad's sector must cover its own sector of fire and overlap into that of the adjacent squad. Flank squad sectors should overlap those of adjacent positions. The platoon leader also assigns supplementary positions if required. The platoon leader may choose to position his squads in depth to gain or enhance mutual support.

Emplace Obstacles and Mines

The platoon leader uses obstacles, mines, wire, and trip flares to improve the defense. The obstacle plan must be tied into the fire and maneuver plan. Obstacles are used to slow the enemy's advance to give the defender more time to mass fires on it, protect defending units, canalize the enemy into places where it can be more easily engaged, separate tanks from infantry, and strengthen areas that are lightly defended. Obstacles disrupt, turn, fix, or block the enemy.

There are two types of obstacles: existing and reinforcing. *Existing obstacles* are those natural or cultural restrictions to movement that are part of the terrain when battle planning begins, such as slopes, gullies, rivers,

Ditch

TREES FELLED TOWARD
ENEMY AT 45˚ ANGLE

ENEMY

75 METERS

TREES NOT DETACHED
FROM TRUNKS

Abatis

ENEMY

Log Crib

swamps, trees, or built-up areas. *Reinforcing obstacles* are those specifically constructed, emplaced, or detonated to tie together, strengthen, and extend existing obstacles. Reinforcing obstacles include road craters, abatis, ditches, log hurdles, cribs, rubble, or wire entanglements.

Wire Obstacles. Wire is classified by its use and location.

- *Tactical wire* is sited parallel to and along the friendly side of the FPL. It breaks up the enemy attack and holds the enemy where its troops can be killed or wounded by automatic rifle fire, Claymores, hand grenades, and machine gun fire.
- *Protective wire* is located to prevent surprise assaults from points close to the defense area. It is close enough for day and night observation but far enough away (40 to 100 meters) to keep the enemy from using hand grenades. Protective wire of adjacent platoons is connected by supplementary wire; this encloses the entire defensive

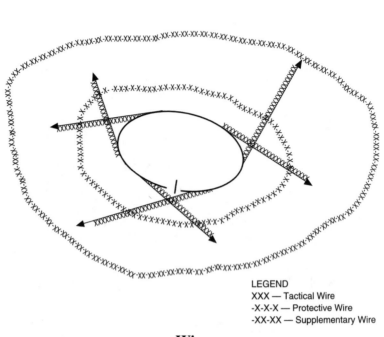

LEGEND
XXX — Tactical Wire
-X-X-X — Protective Wire
-XX-XX — Supplementary Wire

Wire

position. Gaps must be provided, however, to allow patrols to exit and enter the position.

- *Supplementary wire* is used to disguise the exact lines of the tactical wire. It prevents the enemy from locating the unit's perimeter and machine guns by following the wire.

Minefields. Mines are one of the most effective tank destroyers and personnel killers on the battlefield. Minefields the infantry platoon most commonly emplaces are the hasty protective, point, and phony.

- *Hasty protective minefields* are used to supplement weapons, prevent surprise, and give early warning of enemy advance. The platoon can lay this type of minefield, but only with company commander authorization. These minefields are placed across likely avenues of approach, within range of and covered by the platoon's organic weapons. The mines can be laid in a random pattern on top of the ground if time does not permit burying them. Only metallic mines are used; booby traps are not used in a hasty protective minefield because they delay removal of the mines. The minefield location must be recorded and reported to the company commander and adjacent platoons. When the platoon leaves the area (except when forced to withdraw by enemy action), the minefield must be removed or transferred to the relieving platoon leader.

- *Point minefields* disorganize enemy forces and hinder their use of key areas. Point minefields are of irregular shape and size; they include all types of antitank, antipersonnel, and antihandling devices. They are used to add to the effect of existing and reinforcing obstacles or to rapidly block an enemy counterattack along a flank of approach.
- *Phony minefields* simulate live minefields and deceive the enemy. They are used to degrade enemy mobility and preserve friendly mobility. They are used when lack of time or material prevents the use of actual mines. Phony minefields may be used as gaps in live minefields. To be effective, a phony minefield must look like a live one; metallic objects must be buried, or the ground made to look as though objects are buried.

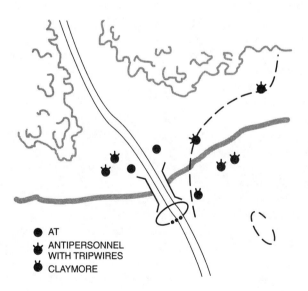

Minefield

Establish Target Reference Points and Other Fire Control Measures
TRPs are easily identifiable manmade or natural objects used to reference enemy locations. Fire control measures ensure the proper concentration and distribution of fires. Antiarmor weapons normally are part of the company or battalion plan. One leader controls all antiarmor weapons firing from a single position or into a single engagement area. Platoon leaders usually control the fires of machine guns. Squad leaders and fire team leaders control automatic rifles, grenade launchers, and rifle fire.

Sectors of fire are used to assign responsibility and ensure distribution of fires across the platoon and squad front. Sectors should always overlap with adjacent sectors.

Engagement areas are used to concentrate all available fires into an area where it is desired to kill the enemy.

Fire distribution is controlled by two methods: point fire and area fire. When firing *point fire,* the platoon's fires are directed at one target, usually marked by tracer fire or by M203 fire. When firing *area fire,* the platoon covers an area from left to right and in depth using frontal fire, cross fire, depth fire, or a combination.

Frontal fire is used when the enemy is moving perpendicular to the platoon's direction of fire. Each squad engages targets to its immediate front. As targets are destroyed, fires are shifted toward the center of the enemy.

Cross fire is used when the enemy is moving perpendicular to the platoon's direction of fire and terrain does not allow frontal fire. It is also used when the enemy is moving oblique to the platoon's direction of fire. When using cross fire, the squads engage targets from left to right or from right to left, depending on their location

Depth fire is used when the enemy is moving parallel to the platoon's direction of fire. Squads engage targets from front to rear or from rear to front. As targets are destroyed, fires are shifted toward the center of the enemy. Depending on the situation, the platoon may use any combination of the above techniques.

Fire Commands. Leaders use fire commands to direct fires of the unit. A fire command has six parts:

1. Alert. The leader alerts the soldiers by name or unit designation, by some type of visual or sound signal, by personal contact, or in any other practical way.
2. Direction. The leader tells the soldiers the general direction or pinpoint location of the target.
3. Description. The leader describes the target briefly but accurately. The formation of enemy soldiers is always given.

4. Range. The leader tells the range to the target in meters.
5. Method of fire. The leader designates the weapons to fire. He can also tell the type and amount of ammunition to fire and the rate of fire.
6. Command to fire. The leader tells soldiers when to fire. He can use an oral command, a sound, or a visual signal. When he wants to control the exact moment, he says, "At my command." When he wants firing to start at the completion of the command, he just says, "Fire."

Targets appear in random order at different times and locations throughout the battlefield. *Engagement priorities* allow the leader to designate which target he wants destroyed first. Engagement priorities are usually done by weapons systems. For example, Dragon gunners would fire first at the most threatening armored vehicle and then at any armored vehicle in the kill zone or primary sector. Machine guns would fire at groups of five or more in the primary sector and then at automatic weapons. Riflemen would fire in their primary and secondary sectors from nearest to farthest, starting on the flank and working toward the center. Any number of priorities can be assigned to any weapon system.

Prepare Alternate and Supplementary Positions
Soldiers prepare their primary positions first. Once both alternate and supplementary positions have been assigned, the leader decides which of the two to prepare after the primary position.

Establish a Sleep and Rest Plan
The leader must ensure that his soldiers can conduct both sustained and continuous operations; to do so, it is essential that both soldiers and leaders get enough rest. The plan should allow soldiers at least 4 to 5 hours of sleep each 24 hours; this will sustain performance for several days; 6 to 8 hours of sleep can sustain performance indefinitely.

Reconnoiter Routes
The platoon leader and squad leaders must reconnoiter routes to and from alternate and supplementary positions and routes used on a counterattack.

Rehearse Engagements, Disengagements, and Counterattack Plans
If security permits, the platoon must rehearse movement to and from alternate and supplementary positions and the counterattack plan. Leaders use rehearsals to practice essential tasks, reveal weaknesses or problems in the plan, coordinate the actions of subordinate elements, and improve soldier understanding of the concept of operations.

Stockpile Ammunition, Food, and Water
The platoon requests and allocates pioneer tools, barrier material, rations, water, batteries, and ammunition. Ammunition and water resupply points are set up.

Dig Trenches to Connect Positions
Based on available time, trenches are dug to connect fighting positions so soldiers can move by covered routes. The trench should zigzag so the enemy will not be able to fire down a long section.

Improve or Adjust Positions as Required
As time allows, the platoon's positions are continually improved.

Locate the Enemy
In the defense, platoons and squads use both active and passive measures to enhance security. Active measures include patrolling, OPs, specific levels of alert, and stand-to times. Passive measures include camouflage, movement control, noise and light discipline, proper radiotelephone procedures, ground sensors, night vision devices, and thermal sights. These measures are all designed to find the enemy before it finds you.

Once the enemy is detected, the platoon leader:
- Alerts the squad leaders, platoon sergeant, and his forward observer
- Reports the situation to the company commander
- Calls in OPs (the squad leader or platoon leader may decide to leave the OPs in place if the soldiers manning them can provide effective flanking fires, their positions afford them adequate protection, or their return would compromise the platoon's position)
- Calls for and adjusts indirect fire when the enemy is at maximum range
- Initiates the long-range direct fires of his platoon on command from the company commander

Leaders and individual soldiers return to their positions and prepare to fire on command from the platoon leader.

Fight the Defense
Forces defend aggressively, continually seeking opportunities to take advantage of the enemy's errors or failures. Defense includes maneuver and counterattack, as well as keeping key positions secure. The battle begins when the planned signal or event for beginning fire occurs. The platoon leader

determines whether the platoon can destroy the enemy from its assigned positions. If the answer is *yes,* the platoon continues to fight the defense. The platoon leader or FO continues to call for indirect fires as the enemy approaches. The platoon normally begins engaging the enemy at maximum effective range. It attempts to mass fires and initiate them simultaneously to achieve surprise. Long-range fires tied in with obstacles should disrupt enemy formations, channelize the enemy toward engagement areas, prevent or severely limit its ability to observe the location of friendly positions, and destroy the enemy as it attempts to breach tactical obstacles.

Leaders control fires using standard commands, pyrotechnics, and other prearranged signals. The platoon increases the intensity of fires as the enemy closes within range of additional weapons. Squad leaders work to achieve a sustained rate of fire from their positions by having buddy teams fire their weapons so that both are not reloading at the same time. In controlling and distributing fires, the platoon and squad leaders consider:

- Range to the enemy
- Priority targets (what to fire at, when to fire, and why)
- Nearest or most dangerous targets
- Shifting to concentrate fires on their own initiative or as directed by higher headquarters
- Ability of the platoon to engage dismounted enemy with enfilading, grazing fires
- Ability of the platoon's antiarmor weapon to achieve flank shots against enemy vehicles

As the enemy closes on the platoon's protective wire, the platoon leader initiates FPFs.

- Machine guns and automatic weapons fire along interlocking PDFs or FPLs as previously designated and planned. Other weapons fire at designated PDFs. M203 grenade launchers engage the enemy in dead space or against enemy attempts to breach protective wire.
- The platoon continues to fight with Claymores and hand grenades.
- If applicable, the platoon leader requests indirect FPFs if they have been assigned in support of his positions.

The platoon continues to defend until the enemy is repelled or the platoon is ordered to disengage.

If the answer is *no,* and the platoon cannot stop or destroy the enemy from its current position, the platoon leader reports the situation to the company commander and continues to engage the enemy or repositions the platoon (or squads of the platoon). In this situation—and when directed by the company commander—the platoon leader may:

- Continue fires into the platoon sector (engagement area).
- Occupy supplementary positions.
- Reinforce other parts of the company.
- Counterattack locally to retake lost fighting positions.
- Withdraw from an untenable position using fire and movement to break contact (the platoon leader will not be ordered to move his platoon out of position if it will destroy the integrity of the company defense). In any movement out of a defensive position, the platoon must employ all direct and indirect fire means available to suppress the enemy long enough for the unit to move.

Reverse Slope Defense

The reverse slope defense is an alternative to defending on the forward slope. This defense takes place on the part of a hill or ridge that is masked by the crest from enemy direct fire and ground observation. The platoon must control the crest by fire. The advantages of defending from a reverse slope are as follows:

- Enemy ground observation of the position is masked.
- Because of this, there is more freedom of movement in the position.
- Enemy direct-fire weapons cannot hit the position.
- Enemy indirect fire is less effective due to the lack of ground observation.
- The defender gains the element of surprise.
- If the enemy attacks over the crest, it will isolate itself from its supporting elements.

The disadvantages are:

- It is more difficult to observe the enemy. Soldiers can see no farther forward than the crest, so it is difficult to determine just where the enemy is as it advances. This is especially true during periods of limited visibility. OPs must be placed well forward of the crest for early warning and long-range observation.
- Moving out of the position under pressure may be more difficult.
- Fields of fire are normally short. Grazing fire may be less than 600 meters.
- Obstacles on the forward slope can be covered only with indirect fire or by units on the flanks, unless some weapons are initially placed forward.
- If the enemy gets to the crest, it can assault down the hill. This may give the enemy a psychological advantage.

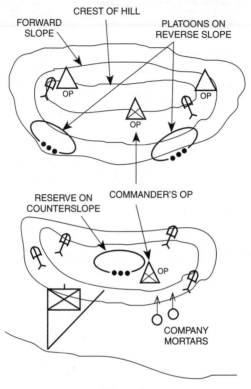

CREST OF HILL
FORWARD
SLOPE
PLATOONS ON
REVERSE SLOPE
OP
OP
OP
RESERVE ON
COUNTERSLOPE
COMMANDER'S OP
OP
COMPANY
MORTARS

Reverse Slope Defense

- If not enough OPs are put out or if they are not put in the right positions, the enemy may suddenly appear at close range without sufficient warning.

Preparing the Reverse Slope Defense. The forward platoons are 200 to 500 meters from the crest of the hills, where they can have the best fields of fire and still have the advantages of the reverse slope. If it places them in supporting distance, the overwatching platoon may be positioned on the forward slope of the next high ground to the rear (counterslope). The following are the tasks of the overwatching platoon:

- Protect the flanks and rear of the forward positions
- Reinforce the fires of the forward elements
- Block penetrations of the forward positions

- Cover the withdrawal of forward units
- Counterattack

Platoon leaders plan indirect-fire FPFs on or short of the crest of the hill to deny that area to the enemy and to help break up the enemy's assault as it crosses the hill. OPs are positioned on or just forward of the crest to watch the entire platoon sector of fire. The OPs can vary in size from two soldiers to a squad reinforced with machine guns and antiarmor weapons. Leaders place obstacles below the crest of the hill on the friendly side. Tied in with the FPF, this can be effective in stopping or slowing an assault.

Fighting the Reverse Slope Defense. The conduct of the defense from a reverse slope is the same as from a forward slope; however, the OPs forward of the position not only warn of the enemy's advance but also delay, deceive, and disorganize the enemy by fire. OPs withdraw before they become engaged by the enemy. If machine guns are with the OPs, they withdraw first so they can occupy their primary fighting positions before the enemy reaches the crest.

As the OPs withdraw, indirect fire is placed on the forward slope and on the crest of the hill to slow the enemy's advance. Soldiers in primary positions hold their fire until the enemy crosses the crest. Then, as the enemy moves over the crest of the hill, the defenders hit the enemy with all available fire.

When the enemy assaults across the crest and is defeated, it will try to turn, bypass, or envelop the defense. To counter this, the overwatch element orients its fires to the flanks of the forward slope. Also, the defense must have appropriate supplementary positions and obstacles, as well as security elements, to warn if the enemy tries to envelop or bypass the position. Against armored, motorized, or road-bound attack, position antiarmor weapons and machine guns so their primary sectors are to the flanks of the reverse slope.

Perimeter Defense

The major advantage of the perimeter defense is the preparedness of the platoon to defend against an attack from any direction. The main disadvantage is that combat power is not concentrated at first against an enemy avenue of approach. A perimeter defense differs from other defense in the following respects:

- The trace of the platoon is circular or triangular rather than linear.
- Unoccupied areas between squads are smaller.
- The flanks of the squads are bent back to conform to the plan.
- The bulk of combat power is in the perimeter.
- The reserve is centrally located.

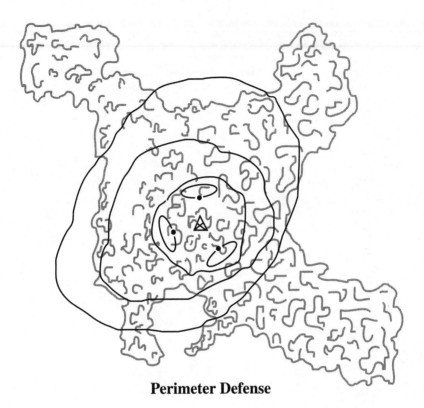

Perimeter Defense

Defense in Sector

Defense in sector maximizes the combat abilities of the infantry. It allows the platoon to fight throughout the depth of the sector using dispersed small-unit tactics.

Preparing to Defend in Sector. The platoon is usually assigned a sector within the company sector. The platoon leader may in turn assign sectors to individual squads to permit maximum freedom of action. (A sector is delineated by boundaries, and a unit assigned a sector can maneuver and fire within that sector without coordinating with neighboring units. A squad has no way to call for fire, and normally its movement is restricted by the platoon leader. These limitations argue against squad sectors.) Each squad conducts detailed reconnaissance of its sector (or position) and identifies all likely enemy avenues of approach, choke points, kill zones, and obstacles, as well as all tentative positions. The platoon leader confirms the selected tentative sites and incorporates them into his concept. He designates initial positions and the sequence in which successive positions are to be occupied. He gives each squad specific guidance concerning contingency plans, rally points, and other coordinating instructions. Squads then prepare the defense in the sequence designated by the platoon leader. They initially prepare the primary position, then a hasty supplementary position, and finally they select an alternate position. Squads improve positions as time permits.

Fighting the Sector Defense. When security warns of approaching enemy, the squad occupies its primary positions and prepares to engage the enemy. As the enemy moves into the choke point or kill zone, the squad initiates an ambush. It engages the enemy targets only as long as squads do not become decisively engaged. Squads then move to their next position and repeat the same process. The leader must plan the disengagement. Supporting positions, the use of smoke, and rehearsals are key to effective disengagement. Casualty evacuation and resupply are difficult when defending this way.

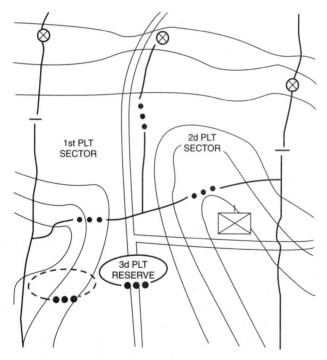

Sector Defense

Mutually Supporting Battle Positions

This technique concentrates firepower into a given engagement area and prevents the attacker from isolating one part of the company and concentrating its combat power in that area.

Preparing to Defend from Mutually Supporting Battle Positions. Platoons are assigned mutual supporting battle positions that cover the likely enemy avenue of approach. Each position must be supported by another position that can deliver fires into the flank or rear of the enemy attacking it. Battle positions (BP) should be positioned to achieve surprise and to allow maneuver within and between BPs. The BPs are located on terrain that provides cover and concealment and restricts vehicular movement. The fire plan includes obstacles with extensive use of mines to slow and stop the enemy in the engagement area. Aggressive counterreconnaissance by squad-size patrols provides security and confuses the enemy as to the location of the main defenses.

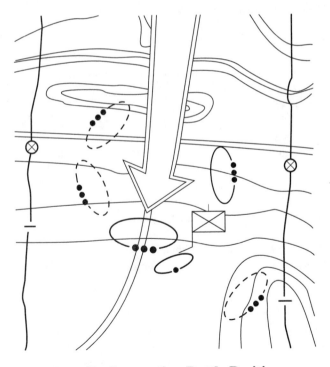

Mutually Supporting Battle Positions

Fighting the Battle Position Defense. Fighting the battle position defense relies on achieving surprise from each of the BPs. If the counter-reconnaissance effort has been successful in keeping the enemy from locating the BPs, when the obstacles and indirect fire trap the enemy in the engagement area, one platoon initiates fires. As the enemy orients on this platoon and begins to maneuver against it, other BPs open fire; once the original platoon is no longer receiving enemy fire, it withdraws and maneuvers to an alternate BP to continue destruction of the enemy or to a rally point.

A variation is engaging with massed fires from all BPs. A disadvantage to this technique is that if there are still uncommitted enemy forces outside the engagement area, they will know the location of the BPs and will attempt to isolate and concentrate against them.

Reorganization in Combat

Reorganization begins automatically at team and squad levels during the battle to prepare for the next battle. To prepare for the next attack, the platoon should accomplish the following:

Man Key Weapons

Replace key soldiers lost during battle; for example, ensure that crew-served weapons are manned and new team leaders are designated.

Reestablish Security

If soldiers withdrew from the OPs to their fighting positions, return them to their OPs. If some did not get back to their positions, check their status and replace casualties. As soon as possible, reestablish the sleep-alert system.

Treat and/or Evacuate Casualties

Treat casualties as far forward as possible. Return those who can continue to fight to their positions; evacuate the others.

Redistribute Ammunition and Supplies

Distribute remaining ammunition and supplies equally among the soldiers, including ammunition from the casualties.

Relocate Fighting Positions and Weapons Positions

During the assault, the enemy may have pinpointed some of the fighting and weapons positions. If certain positions are in danger, move soldiers and weapons (especially crew-served weapons) to their alternate positions.

Reestablish Communications
If a phone line was cut during the attack, soldiers on each end of the line try to find and repair the break or lay new wire. If a signal, such as a green star cluster, was used to cease fire, consider changing the signal, since its meaning may now be known by the enemy.

Repair Fighting Positions
Each soldier checks and replaces the camouflage, overhead cover, and sandbags on existing positions and camouflages new positions.

Repair and/or Replace Obstacles
Repair and/or replace damaged or breached obstacles, mines, and booby traps only if enemy soldiers are far enough away that it can be done safely. Otherwise, wait for poor visibility to do so, or use smoke to hinder observation.

6

Other Tactical Operations

Other tactical operations include retrograde, relief in place, linkup, and stay-behind. Platoons participate in these operations as part of a larger force and employ the tactics and techniques discussed in other chapters. These operations require special planning and considerations in their execution.

RETROGRADE

A retrograde operation is an organized movement to the rear or away from the enemy. Forces conduct these operations to harass, exhaust, resist, delay, and destroy the enemy. Retrograde operations gain time, avoid combat under unfavorable conditions, or draw the enemy into an unfavorable position. The three types of retrograde operations are withdrawal, delay, and retirement.

Withdrawal

In a withdrawal, all or part of a deployed force voluntarily disengages from the enemy to free itself for a new mission. The mission might be to defend another position or to attack someplace else. Units withdraw either under pressure or not under pressure. Platoons have three basic methods of disengaging from the enemy: They can thin their lines or move out either by fire team or by squad.

- To disengage by thinning the lines, squad and team leaders direct soldiers to move rearward in buddy teams, with each soldier covering the other as they move back in turn. Smoke must be used for concealment if the soldiers are moving across open areas.
- To disengage by fire teams, one team fires while the other one moves, alternating roles. This method can be used if thinning the lines is not

needed because enemy fire is light or teams have already moved back
far enough.
* To disengage by squads, the platoon leader has each squad move
  back in turn, covered by the fire of the others. The platoon moves
  back by squads if thinning the lines or maneuver by fire teams is not
  needed because enemy fire is light or squads have already moved
  back sufficiently.

Disengagement by Individuals (Thinning the Lines)

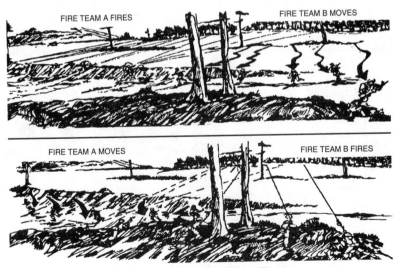

Disengagement by Fire Teams

Withdrawal Not under Pressure

Withdrawal not under pressure is conducted with speed, secrecy, and deception and is best performed at night or during periods of reduced visibility. The company disengages and moves to the rear while the enemy is not attacking. The company leaves a detachment left in contact (DLIC) as a security force to cover the withdrawal by deception, fire, or maneuver. A platoon or one squad from each platoon serves as the DLIC. The composite platoon is normally the best method because there is less repositioning involved. As the DLIC, platoons perform the following:

- Reposition squads and weapons to cover the company's withdrawal.
- Reposition a squad in each of the other platoon positions to cover the most dangerous avenue of approach into the area.
- Continue the normal operating pattern of the company.
- Cover the company withdrawal by fire if the company is attacked during withdrawal.
- Withdraw once the company is at its next position. If under contact, the DLIC might have to maneuver to the rear until contact is broken, then assemble to move to the company.

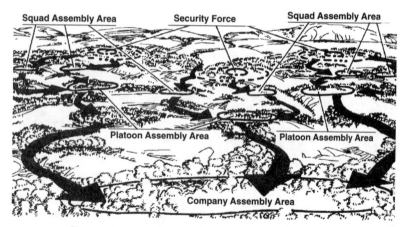

Company Withdrawl Not Under Pressure

Withdrawal under Pressure

The amount of enemy pressure determines how the withdrawal is conducted. If it is not possible to prepare and position the security force, the platoon conducts a fighting withdrawal. The platoon disengages from the enemy by maneuvering to the rear. Soldiers, fire teams, and squads not in contact are withdrawn first so they can provide suppressive fires to allow the soldiers, team, or squad in contact to withdraw. If enemy pressure is light

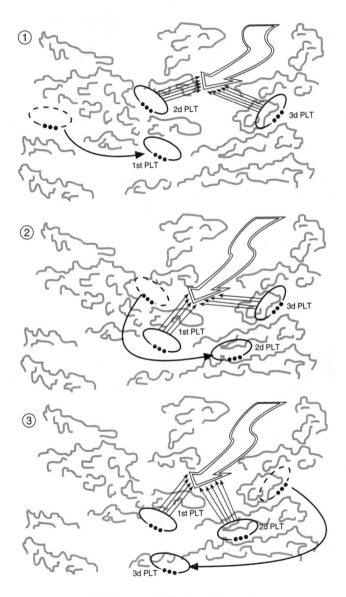

Withdrawl Under Pressure

enough to permit a security force, a platoon (or a composite platoon) repositions itself to fight the enemy as the rest of the company withdraws.

Delay

Units conduct delaying operations when there are too few forces to attack or defend or when the defensive plan calls for drawing the attacker into an unfavorable situation. The enemy is made to slow its movement by being forced to repeatedly deploy for the attack. Before the enemy assaults, the delaying force withdraws to a new position. The basics of a delay require the following of the delaying force:

- Have mobility equal to that of the enemy, or reduce the mobility of the enemy to a level the delaying force can contend with.
- Maintain contact with the enemy to avoid being outmaneuvered.
- Preserve the freedom to maneuver.

The squads and platoons disengage from the enemy as in a withdrawal. Once disengaged, the platoon moves to its next position and defends again, forcing the enemy to deploy. These tactics slow the advance of the enemy, causing casualties and equipment losses. The platoon can employ ambushes, snipers, obstacles, minefields, and artillery and mortar fire.

Retirement

Retirements are rearward movements conducted by units not in contact. Platoons and squads participate in a retirement as part of a larger force and move using standard movement techniques. Typically, another unit's security force covers their movement. Retiring units move at night if possible and conduct daylight movement only if the mission requires it or if the enemy is incapable of interfering. Operational security is emphasized during the entire movement.

RELIEF IN PLACE

A relief in place may be needed to maintain combat effectiveness during prolonged combat operations. A relief in place is an operation in which a platoon is replaced in combat by another platoon. The incoming platoon assumes responsibility for the combat mission and assigned sector or zone of action of the outgoing platoon.

Coordination

Platoon responsibility is usually limited to the detailed coordination between key personnel and their counterparts.

Leaders must reconnoiter different routes into and out of the position; assembly area; logistics points; primary, alternate, and supplementary positions; obstacles; immediate terrain; and, when possible, patrol routes and OP locations. The outgoing leader must provide copies of the platoon sector sketch, fire plan, range cards for all weapons, barrier plan, minefield records, counterattack plans, and plans for any other tasks the platoon may have been tasked to perform.

Both leaders must know which method and sequence of relief has been prescribed in the higher unit order and how they will execute the plan. They are responsible for the following:

- Knowing whether their platoons will execute the relief by squads or as a complete platoon (method). Platoons may also execute the relief by occupying adjacent terrain or terrain in depth (to the rear) rather than by relieving soldiers in position.
- Knowing the order of relief (sequence) for platoons within the company.
- Coordinating the use of guides (outgoing unit places guides to move incoming unit to positions), signals, challenge and password, and passage of responsibility for the mission and control of the platoon (normally when the majority of the incoming platoon is in place).
- Coordinating the exchange of tripods for crew-served weapons, phones or switchboards, and emplaced munitions. Platoons do not exchange radios.
- Identifying numbers, types, and location of supplies to be left behind, including sensors, construction materiel, wire, and any supplies that might slow down the movement of the outgoing platoon.

Execution
During the execution, both leaders should co-locate at the outgoing platoon leader's CP. The leader of the outgoing platoon remains responsible for the defense of the area until the majority of the incoming platoon is in position. If the enemy attacks during the relief, the leader who has responsibility at the time is in control. The other leader assists with assets under his control as directed.

Squad leaders physically walk soldiers to positions and trade them out on a one-for-one basis. They allow time for outgoing soldiers to brief their reliefs on their position, range cards, and other pertinent information. Both the relieved and relieving platoons must maintain security to deny the enemy knowledge of the relief. The relieved platoon keeps local security elements in place. These elements are the last soldiers to be relieved. Both platoons observe strict communications security and maintain normal movement and activity. All leaders report completion of their portion of the relief as soon as possible.

LINKUP

Linkups normally occur in enemy-controlled areas and are meetings of friendly ground forces. Linkups depend on control, detailed planning, and stealth.

Site Selection

Sites must be easy to find at night, have cover and concealment, be off the natural lines of drift, be easily defensible for a short period, and offer access and escape routes.

Recognition Signals

Far and near recognition signals are needed to keep friendly units from firing at each other. Although units conducting a linkup exchange radio frequencies and call signs, radio is used only to ensure control and prevent fratricide. Visual and voice recognition signals are planned. A near signal could be a sign and countersign exchange, using either words or number combinations. A far signal could use flashlights, chemical lights, infrared lights, or VS-17 panels. Signals are also placed on the linkup point, such as stones placed in a prearranged pattern, markings on trees, and arrangements of wood or tree limbs. The first unit to the linkup point places the signal and positions the contact team to watch it. The next unit to the site then stops at the signal and initiates the far recognition signal.

Indirect Fire

Leaders plan use of indirect fires to support linkup operations. Indirect fires can mask noise, deceive the enemy of friendly intent by placing fire at other locations, and distract the enemy. Plan indirect fires along the routes and at the linkup point for support in case chance contact is made.

Contingency Plans

Contingency plans should be made for enemy contact before linkup, during linkup, and after linkup; how long to wait at the linkup point; and what to do if some elements do not make it to the linkup point. Alternate linkup points and rally points need to be designated.

Execution

The unit stops and sets up a linkup rally point about 300 meters away from the linkup point. A contact team is sent to the linkup point; it pinpoints the site and observes the area. If it is the first at the site, it clears the immediate area and marks the linkup point, using the prearranged signal. It then takes up a covered and concealed position to watch the linkup point. The next unit approaching also sets up a rally point and sends out a contact team. When this contact team arrives at the linkup point and spots the recognition signal, it initiates the far recognition signal, which is answered by the first team, and they exchange near recognition signals. The contact teams coordinate the actions required to link up the units.

STAY-BEHIND OPERATIONS

Stay-behind operations can be used as part of defense or delay missions. If the enemy bypasses the friendly unit, this offers an opportunity to attack the enemy's weakest point (CS and CSS units). The unit that stays behind can inflict casualties on the enemy; disrupt its offensive cohesion by attacking key command, control, and communications elements; and detract from the enemy's main effort by making it necessary to allocate forces for rear area operations. The stay-behind force can furnish intelligence on the enemy in the area and call for and adjust indirect fires.

Stay-behind operations are either unplanned or deliberate. An *unplanned* stay-behind operation is one in which the platoon finds itself cut off from other friendly elements for an indefinite time without specific planning or targets. A *deliberate* stay-behind operation is one in which the platoon plans to operate in enemy-controlled areas as a separate element for a certain amount of time or until a specific event occurs. Squads and platoons conduct this type of operation as part of larger units.

Planning

Planners must pay strict attention to task organization, reconnaissance, combat service support, and a deception plan.

Task Organization

The stay-behind unit includes only the soldiers and equipment needed for the mission. It needs only minimal logistics support and provides for its own security. It must be able to hide easily and move through restrictive terrain.

Reconnaissance
Reconnaissance is conducted to locate suitable sites for patrol bases, OPs, caches, water sources, dismounted and mounted avenues of approach, kill zones, engagement areas, and covered and concealed approach routes.

Combat Service Support
Because the stay-behind unit will not be in physical contact with its supporting unit, water, rations, ammunition, radio batteries, and medical supplies are cached.

Deception Plan
Most stay-behind operations are set up covertly. The enemy must be misled during this effort to cause it to act in a manner favorable to the unit's plan.

Execution
While other friendly forces keep the enemy occupied, the unit moves its elements from defensive positions by clandestine techniques to avoid detection. The unit allows the enemy to bypass it without making contact. Once the stay-behind units are positioned and other friendly forces have withdrawn, combat operations are begun. These include reconnaissance, raids, and ambushes against targets of opportunity or against a set of priority targets assigned by higher headquarters. The stay-behind unit can either wait in place until friendly forces counterattack to their locations or infiltrate small units through the enemy to friendly positions.

7

Patrolling

Patrols are missions to gather information or to conduct combat operations. There are three types of patrols: reconnaissance, combat, and tracking. This chapter describes the planning of, preparation for, and conduct of patrols, along with the establishment of and actions taken in the patrol base.

ORGANIZATION AND PLANNING

To accomplish its mission, a patrol must perform specific tasks—for example, secure itself, cross danger areas; establish rally points; reconnoiter the patrol objective; and breach, support, or assault. When possible, in assigning tasks, the leader should maintain squad and fire team integrity. The chain of command continues to lead its elements during a patrol. Some squads and fire teams may perform more than one task in an assigned sequence; others may perform only one task. The leader must plan carefully to ensure that he has identified and assigned all required tasks in the most efficient way. Elements and teams for platoons conducting patrols include the common and specific elements for each type of patrol. The following elements are common to all patrols.

Headquarters Element. The headquarters consists of the platoon leader, RATELO, platoon sergeant, FO, and FO RATELO. It may consist of any attachments that the platoon leader or the platoon sergeant must control directly.

Surveillance Team. The surveillance team keeps watch on the objective from the time the leader's reconnaissance ends until the unit deploys for actions on the objective. It then joins its element.

Enroute Recorder. The enroute recorder records all information collected during the mission.

Compass Man. The compass man assists in navigation by ensuring that the lead fire team leader remains on course at all times. Instructions to the compass man must include an initial azimuth, with subsequent azimuths provided as necessary. The compass man should preset his compass on the initial azimuth before moving out, especially if the move will be during limited-visibility conditions. The platoon or squad leader should designate an alternate compass man.

Pace Man. The pace man maintains an accurate pace at all times and reports the pace at intervals designated by the platoon or squad leader and at the end of each leg. The leader should designate an alternate pace man.

Aid and Litter Team. Aid and litter teams are responsible for treating and evacuating casualties.

Enemy Prisoner of War Team. EPW teams are responsible for controlling enemy prisoners in accordance with the five S's (search, silence, segregate, safeguard, and speed to the rear) and the leader's guidance.

Initial Planning and Coordination

Leaders plan and prepare for patrols using TLPs and the estimate of the situation. Leaders identify required actions on the objective, then plan backward to the departure from friendly lines and forward to the reentry of friendly lines. They normally receive the OPORD in the battalion or company CP, where communications are good and key personnel are available. Because patrols act independently, move beyond the direct-fire support of the parent unit, and operate forward of friendly units, coordination must be thorough and detailed. Leaders normally coordinate directly with three different elements: higher headquarters (usually battalion staff or the company commander), the unit through which the platoon or squad will conduct its forward and rearward passage of lines, and the leaders of other units that will be patrolling in adjacent areas at the same time. Patrol leaders use checklists to preclude the omission of any items vital to the accomplishment of the mission.

Higher Headquarters Coordination

Items coordinated between the leader and the battalion staff or company commander include:

- Changes or updates in the enemy situation
- Best use of terrain for routes, rally points, and patrol bases
- Light and weather data
- Changes in the friendly situation
- The attachment of soldiers with special skills or equipment; for example, engineers, sniper teams, scout dog teams, FOs, or interpreters
- Use and location of landing zones
- Departure and reentry of friendly lines

- Fire support on the objective and along the planned routes, including alternate routes
- Rehearsal areas and times
- Special equipment requirements
- Transportation support, including transportation to and from the rehearsal site
- Signal plan—call sign frequencies, code words, pyrotechnics, and challenge and password.

Forward Unit Coordination

The departure from friendly lines must be thoroughly planned and coordinated. The leader should consider the following sequence of actions:

- Make contact with friendly guides at the contact point.
- Move to the coordinated initial rally point.
- Complete final coordination.
- Move to and through the passage point.
- Establish a security-listening halt beyond the friendly unit's final protective fires.

The coordination includes SOI information, signal plan, fire plan, running password, procedures for departure and reentry lines, dismount points, initial rally points, departure and reentry points, and information about the enemy. The platoon leader provides the forward unit leader with the unit identification, size of the patrol, departure and return times, and area of operation. The forward unit leader provides the patrol leader with the following:

- Additional information on terrain
- Known or suspected enemy positions
- Likely enemy ambush sites
- Latest enemy activity
- Detailed information on friendly positions and obstacle locations, including the location of OPs
- Friendly unit fire plan
- Support that the unit can provide; for example, fire support, litter teams, guides, communications, and reaction force

Completion of the Plan

As the platoon leader completes his plan, he considers the following.

Essential and Supporting Tasks. The leader ensures that he has assigned all essential tasks to be performed on the objective, at rally points, at danger areas, at security or surveillance locations, along the route(s), and at passage lanes.

Key Travel and Execution Times. The leader estimates time requirements for movement to the objective, the leader's reconnaissance of the objective, the establishment of security and surveillance, the completion of all assigned tasks on the objective, the movement to an objective rally point to debrief the platoon, and the return to and through friendly lines.

Primary and Alternate Routes. The leader selects primary and alternate routes to and from the objective. The return routes should differ from the routes to the objective.

Signals. The leader should consider the use of special signals, such as arm and hand signals, flares, voice, whistles, radios, and infrared equipment. All signals must be rehearsed so that all soldiers know what they mean.

Challenge and Password Forward of Friendly Lines. The challenge and password from the SOI must not be used beyond the forward edge of the battle area (FEBA). In the odd-number system, the leader specifies an odd number. The challenge can be any number less than the specified number. The password is the number that must be added to it to equal the specified number.

The platoon leader can also designate a running password. This code word alerts a unit that friendly soldiers are approaching in a less than organized manner and possibly under pressure. This may be used to get soldiers quickly through a compromised passage of friendly lines. The running password is followed by the number of soldiers approaching (for example, "Moosebreath five"). This prevents the enemy from joining a group in an attempt to penetrate a friendly unit.

Location of Leaders. The leader considers where he and the platoon sergeant and other key leaders should be located for each phase of the patrol mission. The platoon sergeant is normally with the following elements for each type of patrol:

- On a raid or ambush, he normally controls the support element.
- On an area reconnaissance, he normally stays in the ORP.
- On a zone reconnaissance, he normally moves with the reconnaissance element that sets up the linkup point.

Actions on Enemy Contact. Unless required by the mission, the platoon avoids enemy contact. The leader's plan must address actions on chance contact at each phase of the patrol mission. The platoon's ability to continue the mission will depend on how early contact is made, whether the platoon is able to break contact successfully (so that its subsequent direction of movement is undetected), and whether the platoon receives any casualties as a result of the contact.

The plan must also address the handling of seriously wounded soldiers and those killed in action (KIAs), as well as the handling of prisoners who are captured as a result of chance contact and are not part of the planned mission.

    Contingency Plans. The leader leaves for many reasons throughout the planning, coordination, preparation, and execution of his patrol mission. Each time the leader departs without radio or wire communications, he must issue a five-point contingency plan that covers:

    1. Where the leader is going.
    2. Who he is taking with him.
    3. The amount of time he plans to be gone.
    4. The actions taken if the leader does not return.
    5. The unit's and the leader's actions on chance contact while the leader is gone.

RALLY POINTS

The leader considers the use and locations of rally points. A rally point is a place designated by the leader where the platoon moves to reassemble and reorganize if it becomes dispersed.

Selection of Rally Points

The leader physically reconnoiters routes to select rally points whenever possible. He selects tentative points if he can conduct only a map reconnaissance. He confirms them by actual inspection as the platoon moves through them. Rally points must:

- Be easy to find
- Have cover and concealment
- Be away from natural lines of drift
- Be defendable for short periods

Types of Rally Points

The most common types of rally points are initial, enroute, objective, reentry, and near- and far-side rally points. Soldiers must know which rally point to move to at each phase of the patrol mission. They should know what actions are required there and how long they are to wait at each rally point before moving to another.

Initial Rally Point (IRP)

An IRP is a place inside friendly lines where a unit may assemble and reorganize if it makes enemy contact during the departure of friendly lines or before reaching the first enroute rally point.

Enroute rally point (ERP)

The leader designates ERPs every 100 to 400 meters (based on the terrain, vegetation, and visibility). When the leader designates a new ERP, the previously designated one goes into effect. This precludes uncertainty over which one soldiers should move to if contact is made immediately after the leader designates a new rally point. There are three ways to designate a rally point:

1. Physically occupy it for a short period. This is the preferred method.
2. Pass by at a distance and designate using arm and hand signals.
3. Walk through and designate using arm and hand signals.

Objective Rally Point (ORP)

The ORP is a point out of sight, sound, and small-arms range of the objective area. It is normally located in the direction that the platoon plans to move after completing its actions on the objective. The ORP is tentative until the objective is pinpointed. Actions at or from the ORP include:

- Reconnoitering the objective
- Issuing a FRAGO
- Disseminating information from reconnaissance if contact was not made
- Making final preparations before continuing operations; for example, recamouflaging; preparing demolitions; lining up rucksacks for quick recovery; preparing EPW bindings, first-aid kits, and litters; and inspecting weapons
- Accounting for soldiers and equipment after actions at the objective are complete
- Reestablishing the chain of command after actions at the objective are complete

Occupation of an ORP by a Squad. In planning the occupation of an ORP, the squad leader follows this sequence:

- Halt beyond sight, sound, and small-arms weapons range of the tentative ORP (200 to 400 meters in good visibility; 100 to 200 meters in limited visibility).
- Position security.
- Move forward with a compass man and one member of each fire team to confirm the location of the ORP and determine its suitability. Issue a five-point contingency plan before departure.
- Position the Team A soldier at 12 o'clock and the Team B soldier at 6 o'clock in the ORP. Issue them a contingency plan and return with the compass man.

- Lead the squad into the ORP; position Team A from 9 to 3 o'clock and Team B from 3 to 9 o'clock.

The squad may also occupy the ORP by force. This requires more precise navigation but eliminates separating the squad.

Occupation of an ORP by a Platoon. The platoon leader should consider the same sequence in planning the occupation of an ORP. He brings a soldier from each squad on his reconnaissance of the ORP and positions them at the 10, 2, and 6 o'clock positions. The first squad in the order of march establishes the base leg (10 to 2 o'clock). The trailing squads occupy from 2 to 6 o'clock and 6 to 10 o'clock positions, respectively.

Reentry Rally Point (RRP)
The RRP is located out of sight, sound, and small-arms weapons range of the friendly unit through which the platoon will return. This also means that the RRP should be outside the final protective fires of the friendly unit. The platoon occupies the RRP as a security perimeter.

Near-and Far-Side Rally Points
These rally points are on the near and far sides of danger areas. If the platoon makes contact while crossing the danger area and control is lost, soldiers on either side move to the rally point nearest them. They establish security; reestablish the chain of command; determine their personnel and equipment status; and continue the patrol mission, link up at the ORP, or complete their last instructions.

LEADER'S RECONNAISSANCE OF THE OBJECTIVE
The plan must include the leader's reconnaissance of the objective once the platoon or squad establishes the ORP. During his reconnaissance, the leader pinpoints the objective; selects security, support, and assault positions for his squads and fire teams; and adjusts his plan based on his observation of the objective. Each type of patrol requires different tasks during the leader's reconnaissance. The platoon leader takes different elements with him. The leader must plan time to return to the ORP, complete his plan, disseminate information, issue orders and instructions, and allow his squads to make any additional preparations.

REENTRY OF FRIENDLY LINES
The platoon leader's initial planning and coordination must include the reentry of friendly lines and should follow this sequence:

- The platoon halts in the RRP and establishes security.
- The platoon leader radios the code word advising the friendly unit of its location and that it is ready to return. The friendly unit must acknowledge the message and confirm that guides are waiting before the platoon moves from the RRP.
- If radio communications are not possible, the platoon leader, RATELO, and a two-man (buddy team) security element move forward and attempt to contact an OP using the challenge and password. The OP notifies the friendly unit that the platoon is ready to return and requests a guide.
- If the platoon leader cannot find an OP, he moves with the RATELO and security element to locate the coordinated reentry point. He must move straight toward (and away from) friendly lines, never parallel to them. All lateral movement should be outside of small-arms weapons range. (Note: The platoon leader should attempt this procedure only during daylight. At night, he should use other backup signals to make contact with friendly units. The preferred method is to wait until daylight if contact with the friendly unit cannot be made as planned.)
- Once the friendly unit acknowledges the return of the platoon, the platoon leader issues a five-point contingency plan and moves with his RATELO and a two-man (buddy team) security element on a determined azimuth and pace to the reentry point.
- The platoon leader uses far and near recognition signals to establish contact with the guide.
- The platoon leader signals the platoon forward (radio) or returns and leads it to the reentry point. He may post the security element with the guide at the enemy side of the reentry point.
- The platoon sergeant counts and identifies each soldier as he passes through the reentry point.
- The guide leads the platoon to the assembly area.
- The platoon leader reports to the command post of the friendly unit. He tells the commander everything of tactical value concerning the friendly unit's area of responsibility.

RECONNAISSANCE PATROLS

The three types of reconnaissance patrols are area, zone, and route. Reconnaissance patrols provide timely and accurate information on the enemy and terrain. The commander must inform the patrol leader of the specific information requirements for each mission.

Organization

Besides the common elements, reconnaissance patrols use a reconnaissance team and/or a reconnaissance and security (R&S) team. Reconnaissance teams reconnoiter the objective area once the security teams are in position. Normally these are two-man (buddy) teams to reduce the possibility of detection. R&S teams are normally used in a zone reconnaissance but may be useful in any situation when it is impractical to separate the responsibilities for reconnaissance and security.

Area Reconnaissance

An area reconnaissance is conducted to obtain information about a specified location and the area around it. The location may be given as a grid coordinate or an objective on an overlay. In an area reconnaissance, the platoon or squad uses surveillance or vantage points around the objective from which to observe it and the surrounding area. After observing the objective for a specified time, all elements return to the ORP and report their observations to the leader or the recorder. Once all information is collected, it is disseminated to every soldier.

Zone Reconnaissance

A zone reconnaissance is conducted to obtain information on enemy, terrain, and routes within a specified zone. Zone reconnaissance techniques include the use of moving elements, stationary teams, or a series of area reconnaissance actions.

Moving Elements

The leader plans the use of squads or fire teams moving along multiple routes to cover the entire zone. Methods for planning the movement of multiple elements through a zone include the fan, the box, converging routes, and successive sectors.

Fan Method. The leader first selects a series of ORPs throughout the zone. The platoon establishes security at the first ORP. Each R&S team moves from the ORP along a different fan-shaped route that overlaps with others to ensure reconnaissance of the entire area. The leader maintains a reserve at the ORP. When all R&S teams have returned to the ORP, the

platoon collects the information and disseminates it to every soldier before
moving on to the next ORP.

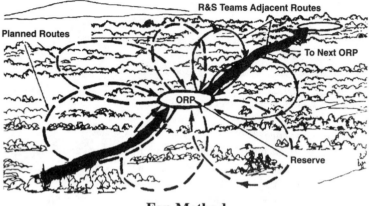

Fan Method

Box Method. The leader sends his R&S teams from the ORP along
routes that form a boxed-in area. He sends other teams along routes through
the area within the box. All teams meet at a linkup point at the far side of the
box from the ORP.

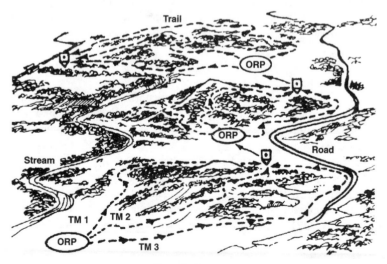

Box Method

Converging Routes Method. The leader selects routes from the ORP through the zone to a linkup point at the far side of the zone from the ORP. Each R&S team moves along a specified route and uses the fan method to reconnoiter the area between routes. The leader designates a time for all teams to linkup.

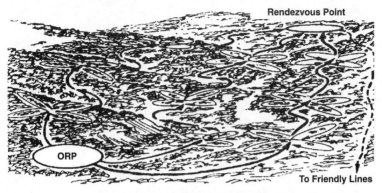

Converging Routes Method
Using Fans Enroute

Successive Sector Method. The leader divides the zone into a series of sectors. Within each sector, the platoon uses the converging routes method to reconnoiter to an intermediate linkup point, where it collects and disseminates the information gathered so far before reconnoitering the next sector.

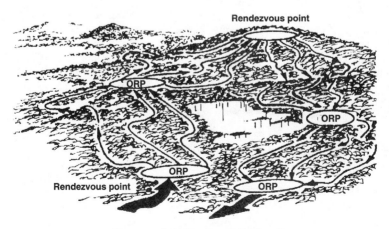

Successive Sector Method

Stationary Teams
Using this technique, the leader positions surveillance teams in locations where they can collectively observe the entire zone for long-term, continuous information gathering. He must consider sustainment requirements when developing his soldiers' load plan.

Multiple Area Reconnaissance
The leader tasks each of his squads to conduct a series of area reconnaissance actions along a specified route.

Route Reconnaissance
A route reconnaissance is conducted to obtain detailed information about one route and all the adjacent terrain or to locate sites for emplacing obstacles. A route reconnaissance is oriented on a road; a narrow axis, such as an infiltration lane; or a general direction of attack. Normally, engineers are attached to the infantry unit for a complete route reconnaissance. Infantry can conduct a hasty route reconnaissance without engineer support. A route reconnaissance results in detailed information about trafficability, enemy activity, NBC contamination, and aspects of adjacent terrain from both the enemy and the friendly viewpoint. In planning a route reconnaissance the leader considers the following:

- The preferred method for conducting a route reconnaissance is the fan method described above. The leader must ensure that the fans are extensive enough to reconnoiter intersecting routes beyond direct-fire range of the main route.
- If all or part of the proposed route is a road, the leader must treat the road as a danger area. The platoon moves parallel to the road using a covered and concealed route. When required, R&S teams move close to the road to reconnoiter key areas.

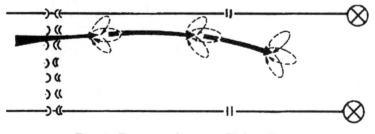

Route Reconnaissance Using Fans

COMBAT PATROL

Combat patrols are conducted to destroy or capture enemy soldiers or equipment; destroy installations, facilities, or key points; or harass enemy forces. They also provide security for larger units. The two types of combat patrol missions are ambush and raid.

Organization

Besides the common elements, combat patrols also have the following elements and teams.

Assault Element

The assault element seizes and secures the objective and protects special teams as they complete their assigned actions on the objective.

Security Element

The security element provides security at danger areas, secures the ORP, isolates the objective, and supports the withdrawal of the rest of the platoon once it completes its assigned actions on the objective.

Support Element

The support element provides direct fire support and may control indirect fires for the platoon.

Breach Element

The breach element breaches the enemy's obstacles when required.

Demolition Team

Demolition teams are responsible for preparing and exploding the charges to destroy equipment, vehicles, or facilities on the objective.

Search Team

The assault element may comprise two-man (buddy) teams or four-man (fire team) search teams to search bunkers, buildings, or tunnels on the objective. These teams may search the objective or kill zone for casualties, documents, or equipment.

Leader's Reconnaissance of the Objective

In a combat patrol, the leader has additional considerations when conducting his reconnaissance of the objective from the ORP. He is normally the assault element leader, and should also take the support element leader, the security element leader, and a surveillance team (a two-man team from the assault element) with him. The leader designates a release point halfway between the ORP and the objective. Squads and fire teams separate at the release point and move to their assigned positions. The platoon leader confirms the location of the objective and determines that it is suitable for the assault or ambush. He notes the terrain and identifies where he can place mines or Claymores to cover dead space. He notes any other features of the objective that may cause him to alter his plan. If the objective is the kill zone for an ambush, the leader's reconnaissance party should not cross the objective—doing so would leave tracks that might compromise the mission. The platoon leader confirms the suitability of the assault and support positions and routes from them back to the ORP. The platoon leader posts the surveillance team and issues a five-point contingency plan before returning to the ORP.

Ambush

An ambush is a surprise attack from a concealed position on a moving or temporarily halted target. Antiarmor ambushes are established when the mission is to destroy enemy armored or mechanized forces. Ambushes are classified by category—hasty or deliberate; type—point or area; and formation—linear or L-shaped. The leader uses a combination of category, type, and formation in developing his ambush plan. The key planning considerations include:

- Covering the entire kill zone by fire
- Using existing or reinforcing obstacles (Claymores and other mines) to keep the enemy in the kill zone
- Protecting the assault and support elements with mines, Claymores, or explosives
- Using security elements or teams to isolate the kill zone
- Assaulting into the kill zone to search dead and wounded, assemble prisoners, and collect equipment (the assault element must be able to move quickly through its own protective obstacles)
- Timing the actions of all elements of the platoon to preclude loss of surprise
- Using only one squad to conduct the entire ambush and rotating squads over time from the ORP (this technique is useful when the ambush must be manned for a long time)

Linear Ambush

In an ambush using a linear formation, the assault and support elements deploy parallel to the enemy's route. This positions both elements on the long axis of the kill zone and subjects the enemy to flanking fire. This formation can be used in close terrain that restricts the enemy's ability to maneuver against the platoon or in open terrain, provided a means of keeping the enemy in the kill zone can be effected.

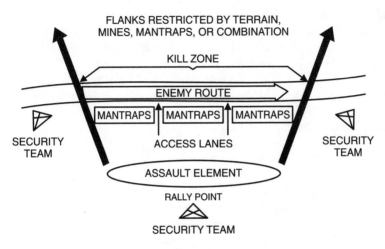

Linear Ambush Formation

L-shaped Ambush

In an L-shaped ambush, the assault element forms the long leg parallel to the enemy's direction of movement along the kill zone. The support element forms the short leg at one end of and at right angles to the assault element.

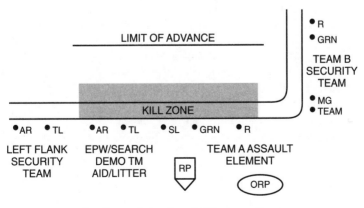

L-shaped Ambush Formation

This provides both flanking (long leg) and enfilading (short leg) fires against the enemy. The L-shaped ambush can be used at a sharp bend in a trail, road, or stream. It should not be used where the short leg would have to cross a straight road or trail.

Hasty Ambush

A platoon or squad conducts a hasty ambush when it makes visual contact with an enemy force and has time to establish an ambush without being detected. The actions for a hasty ambush must be well rehearsed so that soldiers know what to do on the leader's signal. They must also know what action to take if detected before they are ready to initiate the ambush.

Deliberate Ambush

A deliberate ambush is conducted against a specific target at a predetermined location. The leader requires detailed information in planning a deliberate ambush, including:
- Size and composition of the targeted enemy unit
- Weapons and equipment available to the enemy
- The enemy's route and direction of movement
- Times that the targeted unit will reach or pass specified points along the route

Point Ambush

In a point ambush, soldiers deploy to attack an enemy in a single kill zone. The security or surveillance teams should be positioned first, and the support element should be in position before the assault element moves forward of the release point. The support element must overwatch the movement of the assault element into position.

The platoon leader is the leader of the assault element. He must check each soldier once the assault position has been established. He signals the surveillance team to rejoin the assault element.

Actions of the *assault element* include:
- Identify individual sectors of fire as assigned by the platoon leader. Emplace aiming stakes.
- Emplace Claymores and other protective devices.
- Emplace Claymores, mines, or other explosives in dead space within the kill zone.
- Camouflage positions.
- Take weapons off "SAFE." Moving the selection lever on the weapon causes a metallic click that could compromise the ambush if soldiers

wait until the enemy is in the kill zone. This must be the last action performed by all soldiers before waiting to initiate the ambush.

Actions of the *support element* include:

• Identify sectors of fire for all weapons, especially machine guns. Emplace limiting stakes to prevent friendly fires from hitting the assault element in an L-shaped ambush.

• Emplace Claymores and other protective devices.

Instructions to security teams must include how to notify the platoon leader of the enemy's approach into the kill zone (SALUTE [size, activity, location, unit, time, equipment] report). The security element must also keep the platoon leader informed if any enemy forces are following the lead force.

The platoon leader must determine how large an element his ambush can engage successfully. He must be prepared to let units pass that are too large and report to higher headquarters any units that pass his ambush unengaged.

The platoon leader initiates the ambush. He may use a command-detonated Claymore and should also plan a backup method for initiating the ambush should the primary means fail. This should also be a casualty-producing device such as a machine gun. This information must be passed out to all soldiers and practiced during rehearsals.

Soldiers must have a means of engaging the enemy in the kill zone during periods of limited visibility if it becomes necessary to initiate the ambush then. Use of tracers must be weighed against how it might help the enemy identify friendly positions. The platoon leader may use handheld or indirect illumination flares.

The platoon leader should include indirect fire support as part of his plan. Indirect fires can cover the flanks of the kill zone to help isolate it. They can also help the platoon disengage if the ambush is compromised or the platoon must depart the ambush site under pressure.

The platoon leader must have a good plan to signal the advance of the assault element into the kill zone to begin its search and collection activities. Smoke may not be visible to the support element. All soldiers must know and practice relaying this signal during rehearsals.

The assault element must be prepared to move across the kill zone using individual movement techniques if there is any return fire once they begin to search. Otherwise, the assault element moves across by bounding fire teams. Other actions in the kill zone include the following.

• Collect and secure all EPWs and move them out of the kill zone before searching bodies. Establish a location for EPWs and enemy wounded who will not be taken back that provides them cover yet allows them to be found easily by their units.

- Search from one side to the other and mark bodies that have been searched to ensure that the area is thoroughly covered.
- Use the two-man search technique. As the search team approaches a dead enemy soldier, one man guards while the other man searches.
- Identify and collect equipment to be carried back and prepare it for transport. (Clear all weapons and place them on "SAFE.")
- Identify and collect remaining equipment for destruction. The demolition team prepares dual-primed explosives (C4 with two M60 fuse lighters and time fuse) and awaits the signal to initiate. This is normally the last action performed before departing the objective and may signal the security elements to return to the ORP.

The platoon leader must plan the withdrawal from the ambush site:
- Elements normally withdraw in the reverse order that they established their positions.
- The elements may return first to the release point, then to the ORP, depending on the distance between elements.
- The security element at the ORP must be alert to assist the platoon's return to the ORP. It maintains security for the ORP while the rest of the platoon prepares to leave.

Area Ambush

In an area ambush, soldiers deploy in two or more related point ambushes. A platoon is the smallest unit to conduct an area ambush. Platoons conduct area ambushes where enemy movement is largely restricted to trails or streams.

The platoon leader selects one principal ambush site around which he organizes outlying ambushes. These secondary sites are located along the enemy's most likely approach to and escape from the principal ambush site. Squad-sized elements are normally responsible for each ambush site. They establish an area ambush as described above.

The platoon leader must determine the best employment of his machine guns. He normally positions them both with the support element of the principal site.

Squads responsible for outlying ambushes do not initiate their ambushes until after the principal one is initiated. They then engage to prevent enemy forces from escaping or reinforcing.

Squad Antiarmor Ambush

The purpose of an antiarmor ambush is to destroy armored vehicles. A squad can conduct a dismounted antiarmor ambush, organizing into an armor-killer team and a support-and-security team. The armor-killer team fires into the kill zone. Normally, the Dragon is the main weapon of this team. Where fields of fire are less than 100 meters, light antitank weapons (LAWs) may be the main antiarmor weapon. In that case, the armor-killer team must mass LAW fires into the kill zone to make sure the enemy vehicle is destroyed. The support-and-security team provides security and should be positioned where it can cover the withdrawal of the armor-killer team.

At the Ambush Site. When the squad arrives at the ambush site, the leader reconnoiters and picks the kill zone. Good positions have the following attributes:

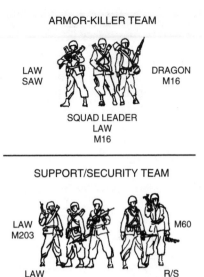

Squad Antiarmor Ambush

- Good fields of fire
- Cover and concealment
- An obstacle between the teams and the kill zone
- Covered and concealed withdrawal routes

Establishing an Antiarmor Ambush. Position a support-and-security team first, and provide security on both flanks. Position the Dragon and then the machine gun so they can cover the kill zone.

The leader initiates the ambush when the enemy enters the kill zone. A command-detonated antiarmor mine is an excellent means of initiating the ambush. The Dragon may be used to initiate the ambush, but it has a slow rate of fire, gives off a signature, and may not hit the target. When possible, the first and last vehicles of a column should be destroyed to keep other vehicles from escaping.

The rest of the squad opens fire when the ambush is initiated. Indirect fires should fall into the kill zone as soon as possible. If the kill zone is in range, squad members fire a LAW.

If enemy dismounted troops precede the armored vehicles, the squad leader must decide whether they pose a threat to the ambush. If they can outflank his squad before the enemy armor can be hit, he may decide to withdraw and set up another ambush somewhere else.

Raid

A raid is a combat operation to attack a position or installation followed by a planned withdrawal. Squads do not execute raids. The sequence of platoon actions for a raid is similar to that for an ambush. Additionally, the assault element of the platoon may have to conduct a breach of an obstacle. It may have additional tasks to perform on the objective; for example, demolition of fixed facilities.

TRACKING PATROL

Platoons and squads may receive the mission to follow the trail of an enemy unit. Even while tracking, they still gather information about the enemy, the route, and surrounding terrain.

Training

Soldiers must be taught to move stealthily and well trained in tracking techniques. Once soldiers are deployed into an area of operations, training continues so that the platoon can learn about local soil, climate, vegetation, animals, vehicles, footwear, and other factors.

Organization

When the platoon receives the mission to conduct a tracking patrol, it assigns the task of tracking to only one squad. The remaining squads and attachments provide security.

Trail Signs

Men, machines, and animals leave signs of their presence as they move through an area. These signs can be as subtle as an odor or as obvious as a well-worn path. All soldiers can read obvious signs such as roads, worn trails, or tracks in sand and snow; however, attention to detail, common sense, alertness, logic, and knowledge of the environment and enemy habits

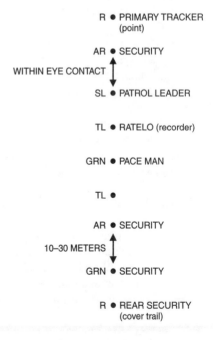

Tracking Patrol

enable soldiers to obtain better information from signs they find in the battle area.

Trail and Sign Analysis

Once the first sign is discovered, it must not be disturbed or covered and should be analyzed carefully before the patrol follows the enemy. If the sign is found at the site of enemy activity, the exact occurrence can often be reconstructed. If a trail is the first sign found, the tracker can still determine such facts as the size and composition of the groups being tracked, their direction, and their general condition. The tracker must determine as much as possible about the enemy before following it, and his knowledge of the enemy continues to grow as he finds additional signs.

Finding the Trail

Finding the trail is the first task of the tracking team. The tracking team can reconnoiter around a known location of enemy activity when the trail cannot be found in the immediate area. There are two ways to hunt for a trail:

1. The tracking team can locate and follow the enemy's trail from a specific area or location where the enemy has been seen. This can be a camp or base or the site of an enemy attack or enemy contact.
2. The route of a friendly unit may cross a trail left by an enemy group. This can be by chance, or the team can deliberately take a route it believes will cut across one or more probable enemy routes.

Regaining a Lost Trail

If the tracker loses the trail, he immediately stops. The tracking team then retraces its path to the last enemy sign and marks this point. The team studies the sign and the area around it for any clue as to where the enemy went. It looks for signs that the enemy scattered, backtracked, doglegged, or used any other countertracking method. If the trail still cannot be found, the team establishes security in a spot that avoids destroying any sign. Then the tracker and an assistant look for the trail by "boxing" the area around the last sign. The tracking team always returns to the same path, away from the last sign, to create as few trails as possible.

PATROL BASES

A patrol base is a position set up when a squad or platoon conducting a patrol halts for an extended period. When the unit must halt for a long time in a place not protected by friendly troops, it takes both active and passive security measures. Patrol bases should be occupied no longer than 24 hours,

and the same patrol base is never used twice. Patrol bases are used for the following purposes:
- To avoid detection by stopping all movement
- For hiding during a long, detailed reconnaissance of an objective area
- To eat, clean weapons and equipment, and rest
- To plan and issue orders
- To reorganize after infiltrating an enemy area
- As a base from which to conduct several consecutive or concurrent operations such as ambush, raid, reconnaissance, or security

Site Selection
A tentative site is normally selected from a map or by aerial reconnaissance. Its suitability must be confirmed before occupation. An alternate site is selected in the event the first site is unsuitable or must be evacuated unexpectedly. The site should be on terrain of little tactical value to the enemy, off natural lines of drift, difficult for foot movement, and near a source of water; offer cover and concealment; and be defensible for a short period of time.

Occupation of the Patrol Base
The area is reconnoitered, and when it is determined to be secure, the patrol enters from a 90-degree turn. The platoon sergeant and the last fire team get

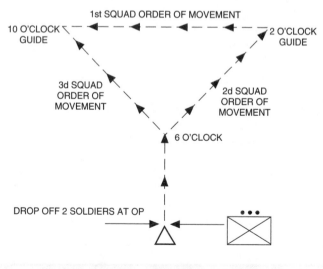

Occupation of the Patrol Base

rid of any tracks from the turn. A two-man OP is left at the turn. The platoon moves into the position with squad leaders moving to the left flank of their squad sector. The platoon leader checks the position, starting at 6 o'clock and moving in a clockwise direction. He meets each squad leader at the squad's left flank, adjusts the perimeter as needed, and repositions machine guns if he finds better locations.

When the perimeter is secure, the platoon leader directs each squad to conduct a reconnaissance to the front of its sector. Each squad sends out a team from the left flank of the squad sector, which moves a distance away from the position as directed by the platoon leader (200 to 400 meters, depending on terrain and vegetation). It then moves clockwise and reenters the patrol base at the right flank of the squad sector. The team looks for enemy, water, built-up areas, human habitat, roads, or trails. The platoon leader gathers information from the reconnaissance teams and determines the suitability of the area as a patrol base.

Patrol Base Activities

The considerations for a perimeter defense apply to establishing a patrol base. The leader assigns a priority of work, including the following.

Security

Each squad establishes an OP, and the soldiers quietly dig hasty fighting positions. Priorities of work can be accomplished by two-man positions, with one soldier on guard while the other soldier digs, conducts personal hygiene and maintenance, and eats. Noise and light discipline is enforced. Claymores are put out. Sector sketches and range cards are prepared. Soldiers should use only one point of entry and exit.

Alert Plan

The platoon leader states the alert posture (for example, 50 percent or 33 percent awake) and stand-to time for day and night. He prepares a roster for periodic checks of fighting positions and OPs and ensures that OPs are relieved periodically and that at least one leader is awake at all times. No more than half of the platoon eats at one time.

Withdrawal Plan

The platoon leader prepares a contingency plan for enemy contact, including a signal (for example, star cluster) to withdraw, order of withdrawal (squads not in contact move out first), and rendezvous point.

Maintenance

Leaders ensure that weapons and equipment are cleaned and maintained. Machine guns, radios, and night vision devices are not broken down at the same time. Weapons are not disassembled at night.

Field Sanitation and Personal Hygiene

Latrines are dug and trash points designated. Soldiers shave, wash, and brush teeth daily. A water party is organized to fill all canteens. No trash is left behind, and the position is sterilized upon departure.

8

Air Assault and
Airborne Operations

AIR ASSAULT OPERATIONS

Air assault operations are those in which assault forces using the firepower and mobility of helicopters maneuver on the battlefield to engage and destroy enemy forces or to seize and hold key terrain. They are deliberate and precisely planned combat operations designed to allow friendly forces to strike over extended distances and terrain barriers.

Ground Tactical Plan

The foundation of an air assault operation is the commander's ground tactical plan, around which subsequent planning is based. The ground tactical plan for an air assault operation contains essentially the same elements as any other infantry attack but differs in that it is prepared to capitalize on speed and mobility in order to achieve surprise. Assault echelons are placed on or near the objective and organized so as to be capable of immediate seizure of objectives and rapid consolidation for subsequent operations. The plan depends on the commander's evaluation of METT-TC, including, in particular, the availability of landing zones (LZs) in the area. The plan should include the following:

- Missions of all subordinate elements and methods for employment
- Zones of attack, sectors, or areas of operations with graphic control measures
- Task organization, including command relationships
- Location and size of reserves
- Fire support
- Combat service support

It is important that aircrews know the ground tactical plan and the ground commander's intent.

Landing Plan
The landing plan must support the ground tactical plan. This plan sequences elements into the area of operations, ensuring that elements arrive at designated locations and times and are prepared to execute the tactical plan. The following should be taken into account in the landing plan:
- The availability, location, and size of potential LZs are overriding factors.
- The company is most vulnerable during landing.
- Elements must land with tactical integrity.
- Troops are easily disoriented if the landing direction changes and they are not kept informed.
- The company must be prepared to fight in any direction after landing, since there may be no other friendly troops in the area.
- The landing plan should offer flexibility so that a variety of options is available in developing a scheme of maneuver.
- Supporting fires (artillery, attack helicopters, close air support, naval gunfire) must be planned in and around each LZ.
- Although the objective may be beyond the range of supporting artillery fire, artillery or mortars can be brought into the LZs early to provide fire support for maneuver troops.
- Resupply and medical evacuation by air must be provided for.

Selection of Landing Zones
Each LZ is selected using the following criteria:
- *Location.* It can be located on, near, or away from the objective, depending on METT-TC.
- *Capacity.* The size determines how much combat power can be landed at one time. Size also determines the need for additional LZs or separation between serials.
- *Alternates.* An alternate LZ should be planned for each primary LZ to ensure flexibility.
- *Enemy disposition and capabilities.* Enemy troop concentrations, air defenses, and their capability to react are considered when selecting an LZ.
- *Cover and concealment.* LZs are selected that deny enemy observation and acquisition of friendly ground and air elements while they are enroute to or from (and in) the LZ. Depending on METT-TC, the LZ and approaches should be masked from the enemy by terrain features.

- *Obstacles.* If possible, the company should land on the enemy side of obstacles when attacking, and at other times use the obstacles to protect LZs from the enemy. LZs must be free of obstacles. Engineers must be part of the task organization for contingency breaching of obstacles.
- *Identification from the air.* LZs should be easily identifiable from the air. If pathfinder support or friendly reconnaissance units are present, they should mark the LZ with chemical lights, preferably of the infrared type, if the assault troops wear night vision goggles.
- *Approach and departure routes.* Approach and departure routes should avoid continued flank exposure of aircraft to the enemy.
- *Weather.* Reduced visibility or strong winds may preclude or limit the use of marginal LZs.

Single versus Multiple Landing Zones
In addition to deciding where to land in relation to the objective, consideration is given to the use of a single LZ or multiple LZs. The following are the advantages of using a single LZ:
- Allows concentration of combat power
- Facilitates control of the operation
- Concentrates supporting fire
- Provides better ground security for subsequent lifts
- Requires fewer attack helicopters for security
- Makes it more difficult for the enemy to detect the operation by the reduced number of flight routes in the operation area
- Centralizes any required resupply efforts
- Concentrates efforts of limited LZ control personnel and engineers on one LZ
- Requires less planning and rehearsal time

The following are the advantages of using multiple LZs:
- Avoids grouping assets in one location and creating a lucrative target for enemy fire
- Allows rapid dispersal of ground elements to accomplish tasks in separate areas
- Reduces the enemy's ability to detect and react to the initial lift
- Forces the enemy to fight in more than one direction
- Reduces the troop and aircraft congestion that can occur on one LZ
- Makes it difficult for the enemy to determine the size of the air assault force and the location of supporting weapons

Air Movement Plan

The air movement plan is based on the ground tactical and landing plans. It specifies the schedule and provides instruction for air movement of troops, equipment, and supplies from pickup zone (PZ) to LZ. It also provides coordinating instructions regarding air routes, air control points, and aircraft speeds, altitudes, and formations.

Loading Plan

The loading plan is based on the air movement plan. It ensures that troops, equipment, and supplies are loaded on the correct aircraft. Unit integrity is maintained when aircraft loads are planned; however, assault forces and equipment may be cross-loaded so that command and control personnel, all types of combat power, and a mix of weapons arrive at the LZ ready to fight. Aircraft loads are also planned in priority to establish a bump plan (see below).

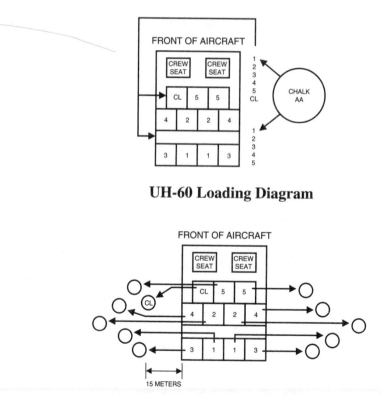

UH-60 Loading Diagram

UH-60 Unloading Diagram

Planning must cover the organization and operation of the PZ, including load positions, day and night markings, and communications. The loading plan is most important when mixing aircraft types. Ground and aviation unit movement to the PZ is scheduled so that only the troops to load and the helicopter to be loaded arrive at the PZ at the same time. To coordinate movement of units to the PZ, assembly areas, holding areas, and routes of movement are selected.

At company and lower levels, each man and major items of equipment or supplies are assigned to specific aircraft by an airloading table. The airloading table is an accountability tool, a loading manifest for each aircraft. When time is limited, the table can be a sheet of paper from the squad leader's notebook. These lists are left with a specified person in the PZ. This procedure ensures that if an aircraft is lost, a list of personnel and equipment on board is available.

During load planning, unit leaders attempt to maintain the following:
- Tactical integrity of units. Fire teams and squads are loaded intact on the same aircraft, and platoons in the same serial. This ensures integrity as a fighting unit upon landing.
- Self-sufficiency of loads. Each load should be functional by itself whenever possible. Every towed item is accompanied by its prime mover. Crews are loaded with their vehicle or weapon. Ammunition is carried with the weapon. Component parts accompany the major items of equipment. Sufficient personnel are on board to unload the cargo.
- Tactical cross-loading. Loads should be planned so that all leaders, or all crew-served weapons, are not loaded on the same aircraft. Thus if an aircraft is lost, the mission is not seriously hampered.

Aircraft Bump Plan

Each aircraft load has a bump sequence designated on its airloading table. Bump priority ensures that the most essential personnel and equipment arrive at the objective area first. It specifies personnel and equipment that may be bumped and delivered later. If all personnel within the load cannot be lifted, individuals must know who is to off-load and in what sequence. This ensures that key personnel are not bumped arbitrarily.

Also, bump sequence is designated for aircraft within each serial or flight. This ensures that key aircraft loads are not left in the PZ. When an aircraft within a serial or flight cannot lift off and key personnel are on board, they off-load and reboard another aircraft that has priority. A PZ bump and straggler collection point is established to account for, regroup, and reschedule these personnel and/or loads for later delivery.

Lifts, Serials, and Loads

To maximize operational control, aviation assets are designated as lifts, serials, or loads.

A *lift* is one sortie of all utility and cargo aircraft assigned to a mission. Each time all assigned aircraft pick up troops and/or equipment and set them down on the LZ, one lift is completed. The second lift is completed when all lift aircraft place their second loads on the LZ.

When a lift is too large to fly in one formation, it is organized into a number of *serials*. A serial is a tactical grouping of two or more aircraft under the control of a serial commander and separated from other tactical groupings within the lift by time or space. Serials also may be organized when the capacity of available PZs or LZs is limited or to take advantage of available flight routes.

A *load* is personnel or equipment designated to be moved by a specific aircraft. Each aircraft within the lift is termed a load. For example, within a lift of ten, there are aircraft loads one through ten.

Staging Plan

The staging plan is based on the loading plan and prescribes the arrival time of ground units (troops, equipment, and supplies) at the PZ in the proper order for movement. Loads must be ready before aircraft arrive at the PZ; usually, ground units are expected to be in PZ posture 15 minutes before aircraft arrive.

Helicopters

Several types of helicopters may be used in air assault operations: observation, utility, cargo, and attack.

Observation Helicopters (OHs)

The OHs are organic to aviation units found within the division. They are used to provide command and control, aerial observation and reconnaissance, and aerial target acquisition.

Utility Helicopters (UHs)

The UHs are the most versatile of all helicopters, performing a variety of tasks. As such, they are available in almost every unit possessing helicopters. UHs are used to conduct combat assaults and provide transportation, command and control, and resupply. When rigged with special equipment, they also may be used to provide aeromedical evacuations, conduct radiological surveys, and dispense scatterable mines.

Cargo Helicopters (CHs)
These aircraft are organic to corps aviation units. They normally provide transportation, resupply, and recovery of downed aircraft.

Attack Helicopters (AHs)
AHs are organized in groups varying in size from company to battalion and can also be task organized to meet mission needs. They are used to provide overwatch, destroy point targets, provide security, and suppress air defense weapons.

Capabilities
Under normal conditions, helicopters can ascend and descend at relatively steep angles; this enables them to operate from confined and unimproved areas. Troops and their combat equipment can be unloaded from a helicopter hovering a short distance above the ground with troop ladders and rappelling means, or if the helicopter can hover low enough, the troops may jump to the ground. The troop ladder can also be used to load personnel when the helicopter cannot land. Cargo can be transported as an external load and delivered to areas inaccessible to other types of aircraft or to ground transportation.

Because of a wide speed range and high maneuverability at slow speeds, helicopters can fly safely and efficiently at low altitudes, using terrain and trees for cover and concealment. Because of their ability to fly at high or low altitudes, decelerate rapidly, maintain slow forward speed, and land nearly vertically, helicopters can operate under marginal weather conditions. Helicopters can land on the objective area in a tactical formation, LZs permitting. Night and/or limited-visibility landings and liftoffs can be made with a minimum of light. Helicopters flying at low levels are capable of achieving surprise, deceiving the enemy at the LZs, and employing shock effect through the use of suppressive fires. Engine and rotor noise may deceive the enemy as to the direction of approach and intended flight path.

Limitations
The high fuel consumption of helicopters imposes limitations on range and allowable cargo load (ACL). Helicopters may reduce fuel loads to permit an increased ACL, but reducing the fuel load also reduces the range and flexibility. The load-carrying capability of helicopters decreases with increases in altitude, humidity, and temperature. This limitation may be compensated for through reduction of fuel load. Weight and balance affect flight control. Loads must be properly distributed to keep the center of gravity within allowable limits.

Hail, sleet, icing, heavy rains, and gusty winds (30 knots or more) limit or preclude the use of helicopters. Crosswind velocities above 15 knots for utility helicopters and 10 knots for cargo helicopters, and downwind velocities above 5 knots for either type of helicopter, affect the selection of the direction of landing and liftoff.

Engine and rotor noise may compromise secrecy. Aviator fatigue requires greater consideration in the operation of rotary-wing aircraft than in the operation of fixed-wing aircraft.

Loads

The type-load method is the most efficient method used in the conduct of air assault operations and in operational planning. Army aviation units are frequently required to support numerous major units operating over expansive tactical zones. Standardization of type loads within the theater of operations ensures responsive and effective air mobility with a minimum of time required for planning.

The use of type loads does not limit the flexibility of a ground tactical unit to be airlifted. The type-load method is very useful at battalion and company levels to plan and conduct air assault operations.

Sample Type Loads

UH-1. Maximum ACL for the UH-1 is 2,000 pounds. As fuel is reduced following the initial airlift, the troop load may be increased to eight or nine for subsequent liftoffs.

Cargo	Weight	Total
1) 7 personnel	1,680	1,680
2) Bulk cargo	2,000	2,000
3) 1 ea $1/4$ ton trailer	565	
Load on trailer (external load)	500	1,065

UH-60. Maximum ACL is 11 to 13 troops, depending on seating configuration.

Cargo	Weight	Total
1) 11 personnel	2,640	
1 ea $^1/_4$-ton truck w/trailer	3,500	6,140
(external)		
2) 7 personnel	1,680	
1 ea M102 howitzer	3,195	
40 rds ammo (A-22)	2,400	7,275
3) 1 ea M99B	7,700	7,700
(HMMWV-loaded) (external)		

CH-47. Type-load data are based on an aircraft maximum gross weight of 33,000 pounds on a standard day at mean sea level. As density altitude increases, or when the aircraft is required to operate at higher altitudes, the payload is reduced accordingly.

Cargo	Weight	Total
1) 20 personnel	4,800	
1 ea A-22 container (slingload)	3,000	7,800
2) 8 personnel	1,920	
3) 22 personnel	5,280	
3 ea 81-mm mortars	282	
150 rds ammo (slingload)	2,250	7,812
4) 16 personnel	3,840	
2 ea mortars, 4.2-in.	1,200	
100 rds ammo (slingload)	3,000	8,040
5) 5 personnel	1,200	
1 ea M998 (loaded) (slingload)	7,700	8,900
6) 3 personnel	720	
1 M101A1 howitzer	4,680	
with sec equip		
40 rds ammo	2,400	7,800
7) 1 M102 howitzer	3,195	
60 rds 105-mm ammo	3,600	
Equip	430	7,225
8) 33 personnel	7,920	7,920

CH-54. Type-load data are based on an aircraft maximum gross weight of 38,000 pounds on a standard day at mean sea level. As density increases, or when the aircraft is required to operate at higher altitudes, the payload is reduced accordingly.

Sample pod loads	Weight
1) Mixed cargo	10,000
2) 1 ³/₄-ton truck with trailer	8,000
3) 150 rds 105-mm ammo (boxed)	17,000
4) 67 troops at 240 lbs ea	16,080

Sample 4-point slingloads	Weight
1) 2¹/₂-ton truck	13,000
2) Road grader (front sec)	9,000
3) Road grader (rear sec)	14,000
4) HD6 bulldozer	16,000
5) APC, M113	18,000

Sample single-point slingloads	Weight
1) 4 ea 500-gal fuel bags	13,200
2) CH-47 helicopter minus engines and blades	16,000
3) 155-mm howitzer	14,000
4) 100 rds 155-mm ammo	14,000

Seats-out Operation

With the UH-60, if the troop seats are removed, 22 combat-loaded soldiers and their rucksacks can be loaded. Conducting combat operations with seats out reduces the number of aircraft needed for each mission. The aircraft can

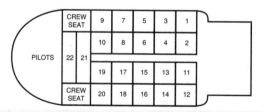

UH-60 Seats-out Loading Diagram

be loaded from either or both sides. Loading is quicker if both sides are used. Before the soldiers enter the aircraft, each soldier's rucksack is placed on the floor of the aircraft where the soldier will sit. Once all rucksacks are loaded, the soldiers are loaded from rear to front. Soldiers in the aircraft help by pulling the others in tightly until they are all loaded and the doors are closed. The aircraft doors should be opened as the helicopter approaches the LZ. Soldiers hold on to each other until time to unload. They should unload from both sides if the ground slope permits. (*Caution:* The seats-out technique is used in combat only—never in training.)

AIRBORNE OPERATIONS
Airborne forces may be strategically, operationally, or tactically deployed on short notice to drop zones (DZs) anywhere in the world. The primary advantages of airborne operations are their abilities to respond quickly on short notice, to bypass all land or sea obstacles, to surprise, and to mass rapidly on critical targets.

Missions
Airborne forces execute parachute assaults to destroy the enemy and to seize and hold important objectives until linkup is accomplished.

Strategic Missions
Simply alerting airborne forces for employment is a show of force that is politically significant in a strategic context. Airborne forces have strategic mobility and can move from distant bases to strike at important targets deep in enemy-held territory with little warning.

Operational Missions
Airborne forces can be employed anywhere in the theater of war. They attack deep to achieve operational-level objectives.

Tactical Missions
Airborne forces assault in the rear or to the flank of the enemy, preferably where few fixed defenses exist and where well-organized enemy combat units are not initially present.

Fundamentals
Airborne forces require specially selected, trained, and highly disciplined soldiers and leaders. Airborne operations must capitalize on surprise, and they require centralized, detailed planning and aggressive, decentralized

execution. The ground tactical plan must drive all other plans through the reverse-planning process.

Echelons
Army combat forces within an airborne force are organized into three echelons: the assault, the follow-on, and the rear.

Assault Echelon
The assault echelon consists of those forces required to seize the assault objectives and the initial airhead, reserves, and supporting units.

Follow-on Echelon
The follow-on echelon consists of forces required for subsequent operations. It enters the objective area by air or surface movement when required.

Rear Echelon
The rear echelon consists of administrative and service elements that remain in the departure area. These elements may be brought forward to support the airhead, as required.

Phases
An airborne operation is conducted in four closely related phases: marshaling, air movement, landing, and ground tactical.

Marshaling Phase
The marshaling phase begins with the receipt of the warning order and ends when the transport aircraft departs.

Air Movement Phase
The air movement phase begins with aircraft takeoff and ends with unit delivery to the DZ or LZ.

Landing Phase
The landing phase begins when paratroopers and equipment exit the aircraft by parachute or are airlanded and ends when all elements of the relevant echelons are delivered to the objective area.

Ground Tactical Phase
The ground tactical phase begins with the landing of units and extends through the seizure and consolidation of the initial objectives. It ends when the mission is completed or the airborne force is extracted or relieved.

Reverse-Planning Process
The reverse-planning process is accomplished as follows.

Ground Tactical Plan
The ground tactical operation phase of an airborne operation can include, but is not limited to, raids, linkup, relief, withdrawal, exfiltration, recovery, and airfield seizure. As with air assault operations, the ground tactical plan is the basis for development of all other plans. Special consideration is given to the reassembly and reorganization of the assault forces and to the decentralized nature of initial operations in the objective area. The ground tactical plan includes the following:

Assault objectives and airhead line. The initial goal of airborne operations is the establishment of an airhead and its subsequent defense. An appropriate assault objective is one that the force must control early in the assault to accomplish the mission or enhance security of the airborne unit during the establishment of the airhead. The airborne unit is vulnerable from the time it lands until follow-on forces can be delivered to the airhead. A mobile enemy unit attacking the airhead during these early moments can completely disrupt the operations; therefore, the commander selects as assault objectives places where high-speed enemy avenues of approach enter the airhead. These are secured before the defense is set up in the airhead line. The airhead is then cleared of organized enemy resistance and forces are positioned to secure the airhead line.

Reconnaissance and security forces including OPs. Security in all directions is an overriding consideration early in any airborne operation, since an airhead is essentially a perimeter defense. Security forces are landed early in the assault echelon. The reconnaissance and security line is established immediately 4 to 6 kilometers from the airhead to afford security to the airborne force during its landing and reorganization. The security force includes scouts, AT weapons, engineers, Army aviation, and (sometimes) light armor.

Boundaries. Boundaries assign sectors of responsibility to combat elements. Each unit should be able to clear its assigned area of enemy forces. Boundaries should be selected that can serve during the assault and later operations.

Task organization. Once commanders have determined the scheme of maneuver and fire support features of the ground plan, they task-organize units (e.g., group different types of units) to execute assigned missions. Infantry units usually form the nucleus of the tactical groupings. Attachments are made before the move to or on arrival in the marshaling area. Units are organized into assault, follow-on, and rear echelons. Infantry platoons are normally in the assault echelon.

Designation of reserve. The employment of the reserve elements follows the normal employment of a reserve unit in ground operations. At battalion level, a platoon is normally assigned a reserve mission and enters the airhead with the assault echelon.

Supply. There are three supply phases: accompanying, follow-on, and routine. *Accompanying* supplies are taken into the airhead by assault forces. They are issued to units before marshaling. At platoon level they include each soldier's combat load, basic loads of ammunition, and other supplies. *Follow-on* supplies include all classes of supply. They are air-delivered after the assault to help the unit operate until normal supply procedures can be set up. *Routine* supplies are requested and delivered by normal procedures, depending on the tactical situation.

Landing Plan

The landing plan links the air movement plan to the ground tactical plan. The landing plan includes the following:

Locations and descriptions of DZ, LZ, and/or extraction zone (EZ). DZs and LZs can be on top of the objective, near the objective, or at a distance from the objective. Single or multiple DZs can be used. Factors such as surprise, strength of enemy force, complexity of the objective area, and time are considered in selecting DZs and LZs. EZs support low-altitude parachute extraction system (LAPES) delivery of supplies. In this system, a parachute is deployed behind the aircraft and attached to a platform that is extracted from the aircraft. Using LAPES, loads up to 37,175 pounds can be delivered into a small EZ. The impact and slide-out zone should be clear of obstructions and relatively flat.

Sequence of delivery. The sequence of delivery is based on the ground commander's priorities and not on the allocation or availability of aircraft.

Method of delivery. Personnel can arrive by parachute drop or can be airlanded. Equipment and supplies can be airlanded or delivered by free drop, high-velocity drop, low-velocity drop, high-altitude low-opening (HALO); or LAPES.

Place of delivery. At higher echelons, zones are assigned in broad general terms. At lower levels, locations must be described more specifically and only after a detailed analysis. Factors to be considered are ease of identification, straight-line approach, range of enemy suppressive fires, proximity to the objective, weather and terrain, mutual support, and configuration.

Time of delivery. The timing varies with each operation; however, the airborne force tries to conduct assaults during limited visibility to protect the force and to surprise the enemy. If the airborne assault is a supporting attack, it can be committed in advance of, during, or after the main effort. *Assembly plan.* The sooner soldiers assemble and reorganize as squads and platoons, the sooner they can de-rig their equipment and start fighting as cohesive units. Cross-loading of key personnel, weapons, and equipment is important in rapid assembly. The assault force may assemble on the objective (if it is lightly defended or the enemy can be suppressed); on the DZ when the DZ will not be used by follow-on forces, speed is not essential, and dismounted avenues of approach from the DZ to the objective are available; or adjacent to the DZ when the DZ is to be used by follow-on forces or is compromised during the airborne assault. Units both assemble and leave the assembly area (AA) as quickly as possible. They stay in the AA only long enough to establish CPs and communications, organize into combat groupings, and determine their status.

Movement Plan

The air movement plan provides the information required to move the airborne force from the departure airfields to the objective area. The air movement plan includes departure airfields, aircraft by serial, parking diagram, aircraft mission (air movement tables and routes), and unit providing the aircraft.

The air component commander is responsible for execution of the air movement phase, but the planning is done jointly. It ensures the efficient loading and delivery of units to the objective area. Army planners consider tactical integrity, cross-loading, and self-sufficiency of each load.

Tactical integrity. Squads are kept together on the same aircraft if possible; fire teams are never split. Fire support teams and their RATELOs are on the same aircraft with the commander they support. Platoon leaders (and platoon sergeants on a different aircraft) should have their FO, RATELO, and at least one machine gun crew and one Dragon (Javelin) gunner on the same aircraft.

Cross-loading. Cross-loading distributes leaders, key weapons, and key equipment among the aircraft of the formation to preclude total loss of command and control or unit effectiveness if an aircraft is lost.

Self-sufficiency. Each aircraft load should be self-sufficient so its personnel can operate effectively by themselves if any other aircraft misses the DZ. A weapons system should have the complete crew for the system on the same aircraft, along with sufficient ammunition. Squads and/or fire teams should jump both aircraft doors to reduce the amount of separation on the DZ.

Marshaling Plan

The marshaling plan provides the needed information and procedures for units of the airborne force to prepare for combat, move to departure airfields, and load aircraft. It includes movement to the marshaling area, passive defensive measures, dispersal procedures, departure airfields, marshaling camp operations, briefback schedule, preparation for combat (inspection, supervision, rehearsal, and rest), and communications.

The marshaling plan is developed by higher headquarters and includes all the details to move the platoon and get it loaded onto aircraft. During this phase, leaders brief personnel, inspect, prepare airdrop containers, issue rations and ammunition, rehearse, perform maintenance, and store unneeded items.

9

Operations in
Special Environments

The infantry platoon can be expected to operate in all types of environments. This chapter describes the characteristics, tactics, techniques, and special considerations of operations in built-up areas, jungles, deserts, and mountains. Remember, however, that the principles and fundamentals of combat do not change in different environments. Priorities may alter and techniques may vary, but fit and trained soldiers and units can quickly adjust to different conditions.

OPERATIONS IN BUILT-UP AREAS
Urban growth in all parts of the world has changed the face of the battlefield. Built-up areas include all manmade features, cities, towns, and villages, as well as some natural terrain. Combat in built-up areas focuses on fighting for and in cities, towns, and villages.

Built-up areas are classified into four categories.
1. Large cities: population in the millions, with associated urban sprawl, covering hundreds of square kilometers
2. Towns or small cities: population up to 100,000 and not part of a major urban complex
3. Villages: population of 3,000 or less
4. Strip areas built along roads connecting towns or cities

Characteristics
Built-up areas consist mainly of manmade features, such as buildings. Buildings provide cover and concealment, limit fields of observation and fire, and block movement of troops. Thick-walled buildings provide ready-made, fortified positions.

Underground Systems

Streets are usually avenues of approach. However, forces moving along streets are often canalized by buildings and have little space for off-road maneuver. Thus, obstacles on streets in towns are usually more effective than those on roads in open terrain, since they are more difficult to bypass.

Subterranean systems found in some built-up areas, including subways, sewers, cellars, and utility systems, are easily overlooked but can be important to the outcome of operations.

Special Considerations

Target Engagement
In the city, the ranges of observation and fields of fire are reduced by structures. Targets are usually briefly exposed at ranges of 100 meters or less. Fighting in built-up areas consists mostly of close, violent combat. Infantry

troops use mostly light antitank (AT) weapons, automatic rifles, machine guns, and hand grenades. Antitank guided missiles (ATGMs) are seldom used because of the short ranges involved and the many obstructions that interfere with missile flight.

Small-Unit Battles
Units fighting in built-up areas often become isolated, making combat a series of small-unit battles. The defender has tactical advantages over the attacker, occupying strong positions, whereas the attacker must be exposed in order to advance. Greatly reduced line-of-sight ranges, built-in obstacles, and compartmented terrain require the commitment of more troops for a given frontage. The troop density for both an attack and a defense can be three to five times greater than for an attack or defense in open areas.

Munitions and Special Equipment
Forces engaged in fighting in built-up areas use large quantities of munitions because of the need for reconnaissance fire, which is due to short ranges, limited visibility, and the intensity of urban battle. LAWs or AT-4s, rifle and machine gun ammunition, 40-mm grenades, hand grenades, and explosives are high-use items. Units must also have special equipment such as grappling hooks, rope, snap links, collapsible pole ladders, rope ladders, construction material, axes, and sandbags.

Communications
Wire is the primary means of communications for units defending in built-up areas. Radio communications sometimes encounter problems because of tall structures and electrical power lines. Visual signals are limited to fields of observation. Messengers can be used as a means of communications.

Stress
Continuous close combat, intense pressure, high casualties, fleeting targets, and concealed enemy fire produce psychological strain and physical fatigue for soldiers.

Offensive Operations
The offense takes the form of either a hasty attack or a deliberate attack.

Hasty Attacks
Hasty attacks occur as a result of a movement to contact or a meeting engagement. A hasty attack in a built-up area is different from a hasty attack

in open terrain, because the close nature of the built-up area makes command, control, and communications difficult. Also, massing fires to suppress the enemy may be difficult.

Deliberate Attacks
Deliberate attacks are fully coordinated operations that employ all assets against the enemy's defense. Attacking the enemy's main strength is avoided, and combat power is focused on the weakest point of its defense. A deliberate attack is usually conducted in the following phases:
1. Reconnoiter the objective.
2. Move to the objective.
3. Isolate the objective. This involves seizing terrain that dominates the area so the enemy cannot supply or reinforce the defenders.
4. Secure a foothold. This involves seizing an intermediate objective that provides cover from enemy fire and a place from which attacking troops can enter the built-up area.
5. Clear the built-up area. A clearing unit must enter, search, and clear each building in its zone. A single building may be an objective for a squad or, if the building is large, for a platoon.

Technique for Looking Around a Corner

Attack of a Building

The most common platoon offensive mission is the attack of a building. The platoon must kill the defenders and secure the building. The assault has three steps:

1. Isolate the building.
2. Enter the building.
3. Clear the building methodically, room by room and floor by floor.

An attacking platoon is organized with an assault element, a support element, and a security element. Close coordination is required between the assault and support elements, and all means of communications are used between them.

The attack involves isolating the building to prevent the escape or reinforcement of its defenders, suppressing the defenders with supporting direct and indirect fires, entering the building at the least defended point, and

Attack of a Building

clearing the building. To clear it, troops normally go quickly to the top floor and clear from the top down. The clearing is performed by the rifle squads, which pass successively through each other (leapfrogging) as rooms and floors are secured. Platoons should be supported by engineers to help with demolition clearing.

Defensive Operations
A defender can inflict heavy losses on a larger attacking force by taking advantage of the abundant cover and concealment, using the terrain, and fighting from well-prepared and mutually supporting fighting positions.

Defensive Area
The defense of a built-up area should be organized around key terrain features, buildings, and areas that provide cover and concealment, fields of fire and observation, and impediments to the enemy attack. Likely avenues of approach should be blocked by obstacles and covered by fire. A platoon is normally tasked to defend a building, part of a building, or a group of small buildings. The platoon should be organized into a series of firing positions, located to cover avenues of approach and obstacles and to provide mutual support. Snipers may be placed on the upper floors.

Considerations in Preparing the Defense
- **Dispersion.** It is better to have defensive positions in two mutually supporting buildings than in one building that can be bypassed.
- **Concealment.** City buildings provide excellent concealment. Obvious positions, especially at the edge of a built-up area, should be avoided, since they are most likely to receive the heaviest enemy fire.
- **Fields of fire.** Positions should have good fields of fire in all directions. Broad streets and open areas, such as parks, offer excellent fields of fire.
- **Observation.** Select buildings that permit observation into the adjacent sectors. Higher stories offer the best observation but attract enemy fire.
- **Covered routes.** Routes for movement of personnel and supplies should go through or behind buildings.
- **Fire hazards.** Buildings that burn easily should be avoided.
- **Time.** Buildings that need extensive preparation are undesirable when time is a factor.

JUNGLE OPERATIONS
The jungle environment includes densely forested areas, grasslands, cultivated areas, and swamps. Jungles in their various forms are common in tropical areas of the world, mainly Southeast Asia, Africa, and Latin America. Jungles are classified as primary or secondary jungles based on the terrain and vegetation.

Primary Jungles
Primary jungles are the tropical forests. Depending on the types of trees growing in these forests, primary jungles are further classified as either tropical rain forests or deciduous forests.

Tropical Rain Forests
Tropical rain forests consist mostly of large trees whose branches spread and lock together to form canopies. These canopies, which can exist at two or three different levels, may form as low as 10 meters from the ground. The canopies prevent sunlight from reaching the ground, causing a lack of undergrowth on the jungle floor. Extensive above-ground root systems and hanging vines are common. These conditions, combined with a wet, soggy surface, make vehicular traffic difficult, although foot movement is easier in tropical rain forests than in other types of jungle. Observation from the air is nearly impossible, and ground observation is generally limited to about 50 meters.

Deciduous Forests
Deciduous forests are found in semitropical zones where there are both wet and dry seasons. In the wet season, trees are fully leaved; in the dry season, much of the foliage dies. Trees are generally less dense than in rain forests, allowing more rain and sunlight to filter to the ground; this produces thick undergrowth. In the wet season, when the trees are in full leaf, observation from the air and on the ground is limited and movement is more difficult than in rain forests. In the dry season, however, both observation and trafficability improve.

Secondary Jungles
Secondary jungles are found at the edges of rain forests and of deciduous forests and in areas where jungles have been cleared and abandoned. Secondary jungles appear when the ground has been repeatedly exposed to sunlight. These areas are typically overgrown with weeds, grasses, thorns, ferns, canes, and shrubs. Foot movement is extremely slow and difficult.

Vegetation may reach a height of 2 meters, limiting observation to the front to a few meters.

Characteristics of Jungle Operations

Jungle battles are most often ambushes, raids, and meeting engagements; battles are not fought for high ground as frequently as in conventional battles. Orientation is on the enemy rather than on the terrain. Hills in the jungle are often too thickly vegetated to permit observation and fire. In the jungle, roads, rivers and streams, fording sites, and LZs are more likely to be key terrain features. The following limitations may restrict fire and movement:

- Lack of line of sight and clearance may prevent visual contact between units, interlocking fires, and the use of optically tracked, wire-guided missiles or Dragon missiles.
- Tree limbs may block mortars, flame weapons, 40-mm grenades, and hand grenades.
- Machine guns may not be able to attain grazing fire.
- Adjustment of indirect fire support is difficult due to limited visibility and may have to be accomplished by sound.
- Sounds do not carry as far in the jungle as on the conventional battlefield because of the amount of foliage.
- Movement through the heat, thick vegetation, and rugged terrain tires soldiers rapidly, and a lack of roads hinders resupply and evacuation.
- Command and control is difficult because, with the dense foliage, leaders can see and control only a portion of their units.
- Thick foliage and heavy monsoon rains often weaken radio communications.

Jungle Movement

Map and aerial reconnaissance should be conducted before making a move in the jungle. Leaders should consider the following:

- Lines of drift, such as ridgelines, are easy to guide on because they avoid streams and gullies and are usually less vegetated.
- Danger areas, such as streambeds and draws, are usually more thickly vegetated. They offer excellent concealment, but travel along them is slow and difficult.
- Roads and trails should be avoided. Although they are easy to move on, they offer little concealment and are most likely to be under enemy observation, are easily ambushed, and may well be mined or booby-trapped.

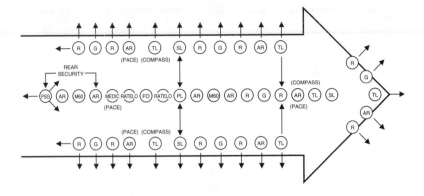

Jungle Movement Formation

Jungle Movement Technique

The jungle movement technique is basically a formation of mutually supporting multiple columns. This technique should be used only by platoons and is most effective during daylight. The lead fire team is always in a wedge (modified). Each squad maintains an azimuth and a pace. Support elements may move with the headquarters element or be attached to a squad or squads. Traveling overwatch and bounding overwatch may be used when necessary. The file formation should be avoided in all but the most thickly vegetated areas.

Halts

Halts should be planned on terrain that lends itself to all-around defense. During short halts, soldiers drop to one knee and face outward, their weapons at the ready. If halted at a trail crossing, security elements should be sent out along the trail. During longer halts, a perimeter defense should be established; run security patrols around the position and emplace Claymore mines and early-warning devices. Before an overnight halt, stop while there is still enough daylight to establish a secure perimeter defense, prepare ambushes, and dispatch patrols, as necessary.

Night Movement

The following points can be of assistance during a night movement:

- Attach two luminous tape strips, about the size of a lieutenant's bar, side by side to the back of each soldier's headgear. Having two strips aids depth perception and reduces the hypnotic effect that one strip can cause.

* Reduce distance between soldiers. When necessary, each soldier should hold on to the belt or pack of the man in front of him.
* The leading man should carry a long stick to probe for sudden drop-offs or obstacles.
* Listening may become more important to security than observing. When a strange noise is heard, halt and listen for at least one minute. If the noise is repeated or cannot be identified, send out patrols to investigate. Smells likewise can be an indication of enemy presence in an area.
* All available night vision devices should be used.

Lost or Disoriented Soldiers

Few soldiers have ever been permanently lost in the jungle, although many have taken longer to reach their destination than they should have. Disoriented soldiers should ask themselves the following questions:

* What was the last known location?
* Did we go too far and pass the objective? (Compare estimates of time and distance traveled.)
* Does the terrain look the way it should? (Compare the surroundings with the map.)
* What features in the area will help fix the location? (Try to find these features.)

If still unable to determine location, the leader can call for an air or artillery orienting round. (This may cause a loss of security.) An Army or Air Force aircraft can be contacted and guided to the general location by radio and the pilot signaled by a mirror, smoke, or panels. The pilot will determine and report the lost soldier's location. (This also causes a loss of security and should be a last resort.)

DESERT OPERATIONS

Deserts are arid, barren regions of the earth incapable of supporting normal life due to a lack of water. Temperatures vary according to latitude and season, from 136° Fahrenheit and above in Mexico and Libya to the bitter cold winter of the Gobi in East Asia. There are three types of deserts: mountain, rocky plateau, and sandy or dune deserts.

Mountain Deserts
Mountain deserts are characterized by scattered ranges or areas of barren hills or mountains, separated by dry, flat basins. High ground may rise gradually or abruptly from flat areas to several thousand feet above sea level. The deserts of Yemen are examples of mountain deserts.

Rocky Plateau Deserts
Rocky plateau deserts have a relatively slight relief interspersed by extensive flat areas, with quantities of solid or broken rock at or near the surface. They may be cut or dry, steep-walled, eroded valleys known as wadis in the Middle East and arroyos or canyons in the United States and Mexico. The Golan Heights is an example of rocky plateau desert.

Sandy or Dune Deserts
Sandy or dune deserts are extensive flat areas covered with sand or gravel, the products of ancient deposits or of modern wind erosion. Flat is relative in this case, as some areas may contain sand dunes that are more than 300 meters high and 6 to 10 kilometers long. Other areas, however, may be totally flat for distances of 3,000 meters or more. Areas of California, New Mexico, and the western Sahara are examples of dune deserts.

Manmade Features in Deserts

Roads and Trails
Roads and trails are scarce in the open desert. Some surfaces, such as lava beds or salt marsh, may preclude any form of routine vehicular movement. Ground transportation often can travel in any direction necessary, but speed of movement varies, depending on surface texture. Rudimentary trails exist in many deserts for use by minor caravans and nomadic tribesmen, with wells or oases approximately every 12 to 20 kilometers, although there are some waterless stretches of over 60 kilometers.

Structures
Apart from nomadic tribesmen who live in tents, desert inhabitants live in thick-walled structures with small windows, usually built of masonry or a mud and straw mixture (adobe). The ruins of earlier civilizations are scattered across the deserts. Ancient posts and forts, usually in ruins, invariably command important avenues of approach and frequently dominate the only available passes in difficult terrain.

Mineral Extraction
Exploration for and exploitation of minerals or oil occur in many desert areas, especially in the Middle East. Wells, pipelines, refineries, quarrying, and crushing plants may be of strategic and tactical importance. Pipelines are often raised 1 meter off the ground and can inhibit movement.

Agriculture
Many desert areas are fertile when irrigated, and a number of desert villages depend on irrigation canals. Agriculture in these areas has little effect on military operations, except that canals may hamper surface mobility.

Environmental Effects on Personnel
The desert is essentially neutral, affecting both sides equally; the side whose personnel are best prepared for desert operations has a distinct advantage. Desert operations need to take into account the following:

- Acclimatization to heat is necessary to permit the body to reach and maintain efficiency in its cooling process. A period of approximately two weeks should be allowed for acclimatization, with progressive degrees of heat exposure and physical exertion. Situations may arise in which it is not possible for men to become fully acclimatized before being required to do heavy labor; then, heavy activity should be limited to cooler hours, and soldiers should be allowed to rest more frequently than normal.

- The sun's rays, either direct or reflected off the ground, affect the skin and can also produce eyestrain and temporarily impaired vision. Overexposure causes sunburn. Soldiers should acquire a suntan in gradual stages, in the early morning or late afternoon, to gain some protection against sunburn. In all operational conditions, soldiers should be fully clothed in loose garments.

- The combination of wind and dust or sand can cause extreme irritation to the mucous membranes and chap the lips and other exposed skin surfaces. Irritative conjunctivitis, caused by fine particles entering the eyes, is a frequent complaint of vehicle crews, even if wearing goggles.

- Climatic stress on the human body in the hot desert can be caused by any combination of air temperature, humidity, air movement, and radiant heat. The body is also adversely affected by such factors as a lack of acclimatization, obesity, dehydration, alcoholic excess, lack of sleep, old age, and poor health.

- Sandstorms can be extremely painful on bare skin, which is one reason why soldiers must always be fully clothed. When visibility is reduced by sandstorms to the extent that military operations are impossible, soldiers should not be allowed to leave their group unless secured by a line for recovery.

Tactical Operations
The desert environment and its effects on personnel and equipment require some modification to tactics, techniques, and procedures.

Objective
The objective of unit operations in desert warfare is destruction of the enemy. Because key terrain features are scarce in many desert areas (although they do exist in some, such as the passes of Sinai), units are seldom tasked to seize or retain specific terrain features. It may be necessary to secure terrain for water sources, routes, or communication sites, or to control positions that permit observation even though they may be only a few meters higher than the surrounding area.

Mobility
Most deserts permit movement by ground troops. Speed of execution is essential and requires self-contained all-mechanized or air assault forces with excellent communications. Dismounted infantry is used in areas where vehicular movement is limited, such as mountains, and sometimes is also used to establish strong points and blocking positions.

Observation and Field of Fire
The normally flat desert terrain permits direct-fire weapons to be used out to their maximum range. The desert is not absolutely flat, however, so weapons are sited to provide mutual support. When preparing defensive positions, it is important to inspect the positions from the enemy side to ensure that available cover and concealment are maximized. Observation of fires, especially direct fires, may be difficult. Considerable dust clouds can be thrown up by high-velocity direct-fire weapons. Use flank observers to report elevation and azimuth errors.

Maneuver
Small units use proper movement techniques and whatever cover is available. To surprise the enemy, it is almost always necessary to maneuver in

conditions that preclude observation—at night, behind smoke, or during dust- or sandstorms.

Reconnaissance and Security
Aggressive and continuous reconnaissance and constant all-around security are required because of the almost complete freedom of maneuver on desert terrain, together with the ability to observe great distances. Many desert maps are inaccurate, making up-to-date terrain reconnaissance necessary. Observation posts should be sited in pairs, as far apart as possible to permit accurate resection, and at different heights to avoid the possibility of dust clouds blocking the vision of both simultaneously. Patrols are most often mounted, dismounting only when necessary to accomplish a mission.

Cover and Concealment
When moving in the desert, cover can be achieved only by terrain masking, because of the lack of heavy vegetation or manmade objects. Total conceal-ment is rarely attained, but properly used camouflage can make it difficult for the enemy to perceive what an object is. Any form of desert movement creates dust; to reduce dust clouds, movement should be on the hardest ground available. Light and noise at night may be seen or heard from miles away, so strict discipline in those areas is necessary.

Special Operations
Because of the wide areas involved in desert operations, gaps can almost always be found in enemy defenses. Small units can slip through to conduct raids, sabotage installations and pipelines, gather intelligence, and effect liai-son with friendly irregular forces.

MOUNTAIN OPERATIONS
As in other unique environments, units operating in mountainous terrain will find it necessary to apply different planning considerations than in less restrictive terrain. Mountain ranges are grouped for military purposes into three basic categories: alpine, interior, and coastal ranges.

Alpine Ranges
Alpine ranges have high, rugged peaks and meadows or plateaus that extend well above the regional snow line. Frequently, glacial ice and snow remain on the ground throughout the year. Abrupt slopes, sharp peaks and ridges, exposed bedrock, numerous lakes, and large masses of rock and gravel deposited by glaciers are common. Valleys, separated by impenetrable

masses of high, steep cliffs, generally rise to narrow passes that allow lines of communications. These passes are often closed by snow during the winter, however. The battle is fought along these valleys and on the terrain that allows access to the passes. The intervening highlands can fragment major units. Alpine ranges are typified by the Alps of central Europe.

Interior Ranges

Interior or inland ranges are less formidable than alpine systems and may cover large areas. They are normally complex and incorporate a variety of landforms. They may include large upland plains as well as regions of high peaks that rise above the snow line. The valleys in interior ranges are generally below the timberline, and in some ranges they have historically served as invasion routes. Above the timberline are steep slopes and vertical cliffs. Valleys and upland meadows are usually covered with vegetation. During winter, valleys and mountain slopes may be blanketed with snow, making movement difficult. During spring thaws or heavy rains, the rivers and streams may become deep and swift. Roads are few and normally follow the valleys. Units in interior ranges may be fragmented in many cases by rugged terrain on the heights separating natural communication corridors. Examples of interior ranges are the Appalachian Mountains of the United States, the Harz Mountains of central Germany, and the Pyrenees of Spain.

Coastal Ranges

Coastal ranges border expanses of water and have been sculpted by erosion of glaciers, wind, and water. Most peaks do not rise above the timberline, but many slopes are devoid of vegetation because of their steepness and rocky surfaces. Roads are normally limited, and during the winter, there may be sufficient snowfall to close the few that exist. Examples include the fjords of Norway and the mountains of southern Alaska, British Columbia, southern Chile, and the Pacific Northwest.

Mountain Characteristics

Certain characteristics apply to most mountain ranges.

- There is normally a temperature drop of 3° to 6° Fahrenheit for each 300-meter gain in elevation.
- In higher elevations, there may be a 40° to 50° Fahrenheit difference between the temperature in the shade and in the sun.
- Fog generally occurs more frequently in mountainous terrain than at lower elevations.
- On clear days, the temperature rises quickly after sunrise and falls quickly after sunset.

Effects on Weapons

Although mountainous terrain generally permits excellent long-range observation and fields of fire, steep slopes and rugged terrain frequently produce significant areas hidden from observation. To reduce the amount of dead space and to prevent low-hanging clouds from adding to the visibility problem, observation posts can be echeloned in depth and in height.

To provide fire into dead space, alternate firing positions for direct-fire weapons are prepared, and indirect fire is planned in these areas. A great amount of dead space gives added importance to weapons with a high angle of fire, as well as to hand grenades and grenade launchers. Grenade launchers are useful for covering close-in dead space and supplementing indirect fires. Machine guns and automatic weapons provide long-range fire along avenues of approach. Grazing fire can rarely be achieved because of the radical changes in elevation.

The slopes of the terrain affect range estimation. An observer looking down from a height tends to underestimate the range, while someone looking upward from low ground is likely to overestimate the range. The steepness of the slope and irregularities of the terrain limit the extent of grazing fire from automatic weapons. The difficulties of ammunition resupply make it necessary to enforce strict fire control and discipline. Terrain features may separate adjacent units, precluding mutual support.

The effectiveness of rifle fire is increased by splintering and ricocheting effects when a bullet impacts on rock. Expert marksmen should be identified to take advantage of opportunities to engage targets to the maximum effective range of weapons. Soldiers have a tendency to shoot high when firing downhill and low when firing uphill.

LAW, Flash, and recoilless rifles are ideally suited for direct fire against enemy weapon emplacement. The 90-mm recoilless rifle is more effective than the LAW or M202 Flash against bunkers and dismounted infantry.

ATGMs are portable but may be a hindrance in dismounted operations because of bulk and weight. Their employment may be limited by a lack of armored avenues of approach and suitable targets.

Mortars are suitable for supporting dismounted infantry because of their high angle of fire and rapidity of fire. The 60-mm mortar is an ideal weapon because of its portability, its ease of concealment, and the light weight of its ammunition, which eases resupply. The 81-mm mortar provides longer range and delivers more explosives. The 4.2-inch mortar (107-mm) can fire either white phosphorus (WP) or high explosives (HE) at greater ranges than smaller mortars. The weight of this mortar and its ammunition may necessitate employing fewer mortars and using the extra gun crews to transport ammunition.

Movement

In mountain operations, platoons can use any of the three movement techniques, keeping in mind the following considerations:

- When moving from one ridge to another (cross-compartment), use bounding overwatch with the lead element securing the high ground before the rest of the unit crosses the low ground.
- When moving along a compartment, move on the high ground (not on a ridge) or place an element there to secure the flanks.
- Because of the narrow routes, squads and fire team wedges may be compressed to files.
- When the danger of rockslides or avalanches exists, the distances between soldiers and units should be increased.
- Movement in the mountains is slow. A good estimate of the ground distance is the map distance plus one-third.
- While existing roads and trails offer the easiest routes for foot movement, the tactical situation may require that other routes be used. The enemy knows that the roads and trails exist and will be watching them. (In 1982, the Israeli Defense Force consistently moved on single-lane mountain roads in eastern Lebanon with tanks and armored personnel carriers. Time after time, they were ambushed by Syrian antitank gunners and infantrymen.) Infantry must secure the high ground controlling trails.

10

Combat Support and Combat Service Support

Combat support is any external support provided by the battalion antitank (AT) and mortar platoons, field artillery (FA), close air support (CAS), air defense artillery (ADA), military intelligence (MI), and combat engineers.

INDIRECT FIRE

Normally, the company plans most of the indirect fires and assigns platoons specific responsibilities. The platoon is limited by its ability to observe and initiate fires.

Field Artillery

FA can provide indirect fires to suppress, neutralize, or destroy enemy targets. Because it can mass fire quickly, FA produces more devastating effects on targets than mortars do.

Mortars

Mortars are organic to the battalion and the company and at times may be attached to or in direct support of platoons. They provide responsive fire against closer and smaller targets. Mortars can be used to do the following:
- Attack infantry in the open
- Attack infantry in positions without overhead cover (using variable time [VT] fuses) or with light overhead cover (using delay fuses).
- Suppress enemy positions and armored vehicles
- Obscure the enemy's vision (using white phosphorus)
- Engage the enemy on reverse slopes and in gullies, ditches, built-up areas, and other defilade areas
- Provide continuous battlefield illumination

- Provide obscuring smoke (smoke on the enemy positions) or screening smoke (smoke between the enemy and friendly units)
- Mark enemy locations for direct fire or CAS

DIRECT FIRE

Direct-fire support can be provided by tanks and antitank weapons (TOW, Dragon/Javelin, MK19). Leaders can direct tank or antitank and MK19 fires by radio, by phone, or face-to-face. They can identify the target location by TRP or tracer fire, or give the direction, description, and range. Another technique uses the gun barrel or TOW launcher with the clock method as a baseline for direction—for example, "Enemy tank, 10 o'clock, 1,200 meters." The gun barrel is at 12 o'clock when pointing directly forward from the vehicle or launcher, and it is at 6 o'clock when pointing directly to the rear.

Attack Helicopters

Attack helicopters are mainly antiarmor weapons, but they do have antipersonnel ability with rockets. Aeroscouts usually arrive ahead of the attack aircraft and set up communication with the ground force.

Close Air Support

The U.S. Air Force provides CAS on a preplanned or immediate-need basis. A forward air controller (FAC), on the ground or in the air, acts as a link between the ground force and the aircraft. Friendly positions must always be marked during close air strikes. Smoke grenades, flares, signal mirrors, strobe lights, vehicle lights, and thermal sources are commonly used as markers.

AIR DEFENSE ARTILLERY

Divisional air defense weapons may support and be positioned with infantry units. All ADA fires are controlled by orders and procedures established by higher headquarters.

MILITARY INTELLIGENCE

Ground surveillance radar and remote sensor teams from the division MI battalion may be attached to or support infantry units.

COMBAT ENGINEERS

Engineers are a valuable asset, and higher commanders determine their priority. Engineers can help the infantry prepare obstacles or positions by providing technical advice or the skills to do work beyond the ability of infantry units.

COMBAT SERVICE SUPPORT AT PLATOON LEVEL

Combat service support (CSS) operations at platoon level are a vital part of infantry operations. They consist of logistical, personnel, and health service functions. CSS is integrated into the tactical planning process from the starting phases of operations. Well-planned and -executed CSS is a large part of mission accomplishment and success of combat operations. Like CS, CSS is a combat multiplier. Soldiers well supplied with food, water, ammunition, shelter, and medical care are more successful in accomplishing their missions than those who are not. At platoon level, the platoon sergeant is the key CSS operator. He consolidates information and needs from the squad leaders, requests support from the XO or first sergeant, and assigns responsibilities to squads.

Resupply Operations

Platoon resupply is mainly a "push" system. The platoon receives a standard package of supplies based on past usage factors and planning estimates. Whatever supply technique is directed, leaders must ensure security. This involves security at the resupply point and rotating personnel to ensure continuous manning of crew-served weapons and OPs, leader availability, and unit preparedness in case of enemy attack. Platoons use backhauling to remove residue, casualties, damaged equipment, or excess ammunition to the rear. During each resupply operation, the platoon must plan for backhauling of excess items. Backhauling can be by manpack, vehicles, or aircraft. Effective backhauling lessens the platoon's need to bury, camouflage, or otherwise dispose of unneeded material.

In-Position or Tailgate Technique

The company brings forward supplies, equipment, or both to individual fighting positions. This technique is used when an immediate need exists to resupply single classes of supplies during contact or when contact is imminent. It enables leaders to keep squad members in their fighting positions.

Out-of-Position or Service Station Technique

To use this technique, soldiers must leave their fighting positions. Selected soldiers move to a company resupply point to the rear of the platoon positions, conduct resupply, and return to their fighting position. This technique is used when contact is not likely and for one or several classes of supplies.

Preposition Technique
In this technique, the company prepositions supplies and equipment along a route to or at a platoon's destination. The company then directs the platoons to the sites. Although this method is often used during defensive operations to position supplies and equipment in subsequent BPs, it can be equally effective in other operations as a cache.

Aerial Resupply
Aerial resupply is not a resupply technique, but it is often used to get supplies and equipment to the platoon. Helicopters are usually more precise than fixed-wing aircraft in delivering supplies, and they are used to deliver supplies and equipment to LZs; fixed-wing aircraft are used for DZs.

Personnel Service Support
The main platoon combat personnel service support functions are strength accounting and casualty reporting. The platoon leader and NCOs are also responsible for handling EPWs and for programs to counter the impact of stress and continuous operations. Platoon leaders coordinate personnel service support provided by the battalion S1, personnel and administration center (PAC), and chaplain through the company headquarters.

Strength Accounting
Leaders use battle rosters to keep up-to-date records of their soldiers and to provide reports to the company at specific intervals. During combat, leaders also provide hasty strength reports upon request or when important strength changes occur.

Casualty Reporting
During lulls in the battle, platoons give by-name (roster line number) casualty information to the company. Forms are completed to report KIAs who were not recovered, as well as missing or captured soldiers. A separate form is used to report KIAs who have been recovered and soldiers who have been wounded.

Handling Enemy Prisoners of War
EPWs are treated in accordance with international law. They are allowed to keep personal protective equipment, are not physically or mentally abused, and are treated humanely. If they cannot be evacuated within a reasonable time, they are given food, water, and, if necessary, first aid.

Other Services
Other personnel service support functions include awards, leaves, mail, financial matters, legal assistance, rest and recreation, and other services related to the morale and welfare of soldiers.

Health Service Support
Health service support consists of the prevention, treatment, and evacuation of casualties.

Prevention
Prevention is emphasized; soldiers can lose their combat effectiveness because of nonhostile injuries or disease. Observing field hygiene and sanitation, preventing weather-related injuries, and considering the soldier's overall condition can cut back on the number of casualties.

Treatment and Evacuation
Casualties are treated where they fall (or under nearby cover and concealment) by the individual himself, a buddy, an aidman, or a combat lifesaver. Casualties are collected at the platoon casualty collection point and separated into treatment and evacuation categories. The casualties' weapons and equipment may be retained and redistributed as necessary or backhauled to the field trains. Machine guns, M203s, and other special weapons are never evacuated but are reassigned to other soldiers. At least one soldier in each squad must be trained as a combat lifesaver to help the aidman treat and evacuate casualties.

ARMORED VEHICLE SUPPORT
Armored units and mechanized infantry units can support infantry units in combat operations. In operations in which dismounted infantry forces predominate, dismounted infantry forces lead the combined arms attack, while all other arms support the infantry. Infantry helps armored forces by finding and breaching or marking antitank obstacles and by providing security for armored vehicles. They detect and destroy or suppress antitank weapons, designate targets for tank main gun fire, and spot the impact of tank rounds for the gunner. Heavy forces help infantry by leading them in open terrain; providing them a protected, fast-moving assault weapons system; suppressing and destroying enemy weapons, bunkers, and tanks by fire and maneuver; and providing transport for the infantry when the situation permits.

Tanks

Tank platoons use the wingman concept: The platoon leader with his wingman and the platoon sergeant with his wingman operate as a four-vehicle platoon. Tank organization tables do not break the organization down further than a platoon. Tanks and infantry must work closely, however. In most operations where they work together, infantrymen must establish direct contact with individual tanks. They will not have time to designate targets or direct fires through the platoon chain of command.

Before an operation, infantry and tank platoon leaders must coordinate communication means and signals. This should include the use of radios, phones, and visual signals such as arm and hand, panel, lights, flags, and pyrotechnics. Most tanks (except the M1) have an external phone on the rear for infantrymen to use. On the M1, the infantryman can run communication wire to the tank commander through the turret. This wire can be hooked into the tank's communication system. Leaders must be confident that tanks and infantry will be able to move and shoot without confusion.

Mechanized Infantry

Mechanized infantry combines the protection, firepower, and mobility of armored forces with the security and close-combat capability of infantry forces. Infantry may work together or in synchronization with mechanized forces to clear a way through obstacles before an armored attack, hold a strongpoint while mechanized infantry maneuvers around it, or conduct military operations in urban terrain (MOUT) missions.

Infantry Riding on Armored Vehicles

Soldiers ride on the outside of armored vehicles routinely. So long as tanks and infantry are moving in the same direction and contact is not likely, soldiers should always ride on tanks. The following must be considered before soldiers mount or ride on an armored vehicle.

- Soldiers must always approach the vehicle from the front to get permission from the vehicle commander to mount. They then mount the side of the vehicle away from the coaxial machine gun and in view of the driver.
- If the vehicle has a stabilization system, squad leaders ensure that it is off before giving the okay for the vehicle to move.
- The infantry must dismount as soon as possible when tanks come under fire or when targets appear that require the tank gunner to traverse the turret quickly to fire.

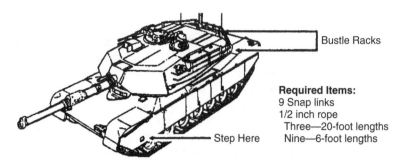

Bustle Racks

Required Items:
9 Snap links
1/2 inch rope
Three—20-foot lengths
Step Here   Nine—6-foot lengths

Soldiers sit facing out. Personal gear is carried in company trains.

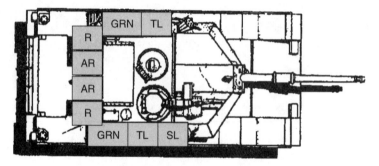

Mounting and Riding on an M1 Tank

- All soldiers must be alert for obstacles that can cause the tank to turn suddenly and for trees that can knock riders off the tank.

The following considerations apply to the M1 tank:

- The M1 tank is not designed to carry riders easily. Riders must not move to the rear deck. Engine operating temperatures make this area unsafe for riders.
- One infantry squad can ride on the turret. The soldiers must mount in such a way that their legs cannot become entangled between the turret and the hull by an unexpected turret movement. Rope may be used as a field-expedient rail to provide secure handholds.
- Everyone must be to the rear of the smoke grenade launchers. This automatically keeps everyone clear of the coaxial machine gun and the laser range finder.
- The infantry must always be prepared for sudden turret movement.
- Leaders should caution soldiers about sitting on the turret blowout panels, because 250 pounds of pressure will prevent the panels from working properly. If there is an explosion in the ammunition rack,

these panels blow outward to lessen the blast effect in the crew compartment.

- If enemy contact is made, the tank should stop in a covered and concealed position and allow the infantry time to dismount and move away from the tank. This action needs to be practiced before movement.
- The infantry should not ride with anything more than their battle gear. Personal gear should be transported elsewhere.

Working in Restricted Terrain
Tanks are more likely to work directly with infantry in highly restrictive terrain. When armored vehicles are buttoned up, crew vision is impaired; dismounted infantry must work near the tanks to provide mutual close protection. At terrain features such as narrow passes or defiles, the dismounted infantry platoon secures the edges using bounding overwatch while the armored vehicles overwatch. The infantry looks for mines, antitank missile systems, and enemy armored vehicles.

Movement and Offensive Operations
Lack of visibility, limited fields of fire, and inability to traverse to targets because of nearby trees are common problems in wooded and jungle terrain. These factors, along with the enemy's antitank capability, determine the lead element in movement.

Armored vehicles lead in open terrain if the antitank threat is light or if fields of fire are too short for wire-guided missiles. Armored vehicles can scan tree lines and other vegetated areas with thermal viewers to provide the infantry with early warning of impending contact and possible bypass routes. Armored vehicles are the first to make contact. They then continue forward to destroy the enemy or to provide a base of fire so that the dismounted infantry can maneuver to destroy or bypass the enemy.

If the antitank threat is medium or heavy, the infantry leads and tanks move from one overwatch position to the next.

Defensive Operations
Armored vehicles provide the infantry with great firepower, but their inability to move quietly may be a disadvantage. Tanks can be positioned at first to provide early warning using thermal viewers. Tanks cover mounted avenues of approach, while infantry covers dismounted avenues of approach. Dismounted infantry support must be placed forward to provide local security for forward tank positions. Tank range finders accurately determine locations of TRPs and other range card data.

PART TWO

Soldier Combat Skills

11

Call for Fire

A call for fire is a concise message prepared by the observer. It contains all information needed by an artillery or mortar fire direction center (FDC) to bring indirect fire on a target. It is a request for fire, not an order. Calls for fire must be sent quickly but clearly enough that they can be understood, recorded, and read back without error, by the FDC.

The normal call for fire is transmitted in three parts consisting of six elements, with a break and read-back after each part. The sequence in which they are transmitted is:
- Observer identification and warning order.
- Target location.
- Description of target, method of engagement, and method of fire and control.

OBSERVER IDENTIFICATION
Despite the availability of attached mortar forward observers (FOs) and artillery fire support teams (FISTs), infantrymen are often in the best location to call for and adjust fire. For the FDC to respond, it needs to know:
- Observer's identity (call sign), which may require authentication to prevent unauthorized use
- Observer's location
- Target identity
- The target's nearness to friendly troops
- Target location in relation to the observer's location or other known locations, such as pre-planned artillery registration or reference points (RPs)
- The direction (azimuth) from the observer to the target, which is referred to as the observer-target line (OTL)

WARNING ORDER

The warning order clears the net for the fire mission and tells the FDC the type of mission and the type of target location that will be used. The basic warning order consists of (1) the type of mission, and (2) the method of target location.

Type of Mission

Adjust Fire

When the observer believes that an adjustment must be made (because of questionable target location or lack of registration corrections), he announces "Adjust fire."

Fire for Effect

The observer should always strive for first-round fire for effect (FFE). When the observer is certain that the target location is accurate and that the first volley should have the desired effect on the target, with little or no adjustment required, he announces "Fire for effect."

Suppression

To quickly bring fire on a target that is not active, the observer announces "Suppress" (followed by the target identification).

Immediate Suppression and Immediate Smoke

When engaging a planned target or target of opportunity that has taken friendly maneuver or aerial elements under fire, the observer announces "Immediate suppression" or "Immediate smoke" (followed by the target location). Though the grid method of target location is the most common, any method can be used in firing an immediate suppression or immediate smoke mission.

Method of Target Location

Polar Plot

If the target is located by the polar plot method of target location, the observer announces, "Polar"; for example, "Adjust fire, polar over."

Shift from a Known Point.
If the target is located by the shift from a known point method of target location, the observer announces "Shift" (followed by the known point); for example, "Adjust fire, shift known point 1, over."

Grid.
If the grid method of target location is being used, the word *grid* is not announced; for example, "Adjust fire, over."

TARGET LOCATION
This element enables the FDC to plot the location of the target to determine firing data.

Polar
In a polar plot mission, the word *polar* in the warning order alerts the FDC that the target will be located with respect to the observer's position, which must be known to the FDC. The observer then sends the direction and distance. A vertical shift tells the FDC how far, in meters, the target is located above or below the observer's location. Vertical shift may also be described by a vertical angle (VA), in mils, relative to the observer's location.

Grid
In a grid mission, six-place grids normally are sent. Eight-place grids should be sent for registration points or other points for which greater accuracy is required. The observer-target (OT) direction normally is sent after the entire initial call for fire, since it is not needed by the FDC to locate the target. Note: Direction is expressed to the nearest 10 mils.

Shift
In a shift from a known point mission, the point or target from which the shift will be made is sent in the warning order. Both the observer and the FDC must know the point. The observer then sends the OT direction. Normally, it is sent in mils, but, the FDC can accept degrees or cardinal directions, whichever is specified by the observer. The corrections are sent next:
- The lateral shift—how far left or right the target is—from the known point
- The range shift—how much farther (add) or closer (drop) the target is in relation to the known point, to the nearest 100 meters

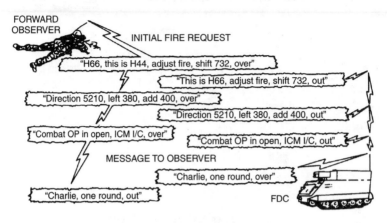

Shift Request

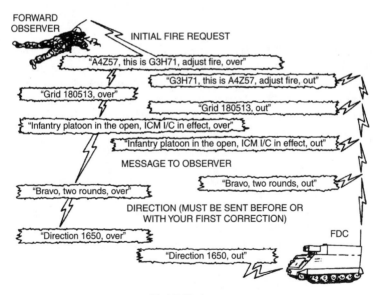

Grid Request

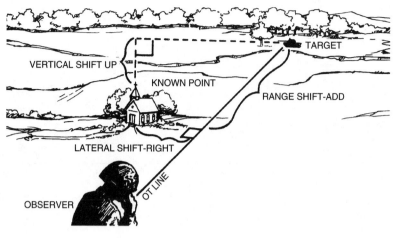

Shift From a Known Point

- The vertical shift—how much the target is above (up) or below (down) the altitude of the known point, to the nearest 5 meters (the vertical shift is ignored unless it exceeds 30 meters)

TARGET DESCRIPTION

The observer must describe the target in enough detail so that the FDC can determine the amount and type of ammunition to use. The observer should be brief but accurate. The description should contain the following:
- What the target is (troops, equipment, supply dump, trucks, and so forth).
- What the target is doing (digging in, in an assembly area, and so forth).
- The number of elements in the target (squad, platoon, three trucks, six tanks, and so forth).
- The degree of protection (in open, in foxholes, in bunkers with overhead protection, and so forth).
- The target size and shape, if these are significant; for example, "rectangular, 400 meters by 200 meters; circular, radius 200 meters." Linear targets may be described by length, width, and attitude.

METHOD OF ENGAGEMENT
The observer may indicate how he wants to attack the target. This element consists of the type of adjustment, trajectory, ammunition, and distribution. "Danger close" and "Mark" are included as appropriate.

Type of Adjustment
Two types of adjustment may be employed—precision and area. Unless precision fire is specified, area fire will be used. Precision fire is conducted with one weapon on a point target. It is used either to obtain registration corrections or to destroy a target. If the target is to be destroyed, the observer announces "Destruction." Area fire is used to attack an area target.

Danger Close
"Danger close" is included in the method of engagement when the target is (rounds will impact) within 600 meters of friendly troops for mortar and artillery, 750 meters for naval guns 5-inch and smaller, and 1,000 meters for naval guns larger than 5-inch. For naval 16-inch ICM, danger close is 2,000 meters.

In the event that fire is required within 600 meters of friendly troops, the following guidelines apply:
- Announce "Danger close" to the FDC.
- The initial target location is reported on the enemy side of the target.
- Creeping procedures are used to adjust danger-close fire. Range corrections should not exceed 100 meters. Do *not* bracket. It could cause friendly casualties.

Mark
"Mark" is included in the method of engagement to indicate that the observer is going to call for rounds to orient himself in his zone of observation or to indicate targets to ground troops, aircraft, or fire support.

Trajectory
Low-angle fire is standard for field artillery. If high-angle fire is desired, it is requested immediately after the type of engagement. If high angle is not specified, low angle will (normally) be used. If the firing unit determines that high angle must be used to attack a target, the unit must inform the observer that high angle will be used. Mortars fire only high angle.

Ammunition

The observer may request any type of ammunition during the adjustment or the FFE phase of his mission. Shell HE with fuse quick is normally used in adjustment. If that is what the observer desires, he need not request it in his call for fire. Examples of requests for other than HE projectiles are "Illumination," "ICM," and "Smoke."

Volume of Fire

The observer may request the number of rounds to be fired by the weapons firing in effect. For example, "3 rounds" indicates that the firing unit will fire three volleys. When a battery has six guns, each gun will fire three rounds.

METHOD OF FIRE AND CONTROL

The method of fire and control element indicates the desired manner of attacking the target, whether the observer wants to control the time of delivery of fire, and whether he can observe the target. "At my command" (AMC) and "Time on target" (TOT) are especially useful methods of control in massing fires.

At My Command

If the observer wishes to control the time of delivery of fire, he includes "At my command" in the method of control. When the pieces are ready to fire, the FDC announces "Platoon [or battery or battalion] is ready, over" (call signs are used). The observer announces "Fire" when he is ready for the pieces to fire. "At my command" remains in effect throughout the mission until the observer announces "Cancel. At my command. Over."

Cannot Observe

"Cannot observe" indicates that the observer cannot see the target (because of vegetation, terrain, weather, or smoke); however, he has reason to believe that a target exists at the given location and that it is important enough to justify firing on it without adjustment.

Time on Target

The observer may tell the FDC when he wants the rounds to impact by requesting "Time on target [so many] minutes from now, over" or "Time on target 0859, over." The FO must conduct a time check to ensure that 0859 on his watch is 0859 on the FDC's watch.

Check Firing
"Check firing" is used to cause an immediate halt in firing.

Repeat
"Repeat" can be given during adjustment or FFE missions. During adjustment, "repeat" means fire another round(s) with the last data and adjust for any change in ammunition, if necessary. During FFE, "Repeat" means fire the same number of rounds using the same method of FFE as last fired.

Corrections of Errors
Errors are sometimes made in transmitting data or by the FDC personnel in reading back the data. If the observer realizes that he has made an error in his transmission or that the FDC has made an error in the readback, he announces "Correction" and transmits the correct data.

ADJUSTING FIRE
Adjust fire onto the target using the bracketing method of adjustment.

Spot each round when it impacts as over or short, right or left of the target. When the first range spotting is observed, make a range correction that would result in a range spotting in the opposite direction. For example, if the first round is short, add enough to get an *over* on the next round.

Use the following guide to establish a bracket:

"BRACKET"

400 METERS
200 METERS
100 METERS
50 METERS

TARGET

Successive Bracketing

Round Impact From Target	Add or Drop + or −
Over 400 meters	800 meters + or −
200–400	400 meters + or −
100–200 meters	200 meters + or −
Less than 100 meters	100 meters

1. *Deviation.* Measure the horizontal angle in mils, using either fingers or the reticle pattern in the binoculars. Estimate the range to the

target and divide by 1,000. This is the OT factor. If the OT distance is 1,000 meters or greater, the OT factor is expressed to the nearest whole number. If the OT distance is less than 1,000 meters, the OT factor is expressed to the nearest tenth. For example, 800 = 0.8. Multiplying the OT factor by the deviation measured in mils produces deviation in meters.

For example, if we measure the round 100 mils right of the target and estimate the range to be 2,200 meters, the OT factor is 2. For adjustment purposes, we express the OT factor to the nearest whole number. Example: 1.1 would be 1; 1.8 would be 2; 2.5 would be 2. Multiplying the angle (100 mils) by the OT factor (2), we get the deviation in meters (200 meters right).

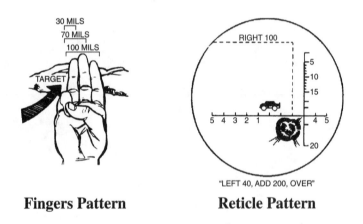

"LEFT 40, ADD 200, OVER"

Fingers Pattern   **Reticle Pattern**

2. *Transmit corrections to the FDC in meters.* The initial correction should bracket the target in range. Deviation correction should be made to keep the rounds on the observer target line. The accompanying figure shows the impact of the initial round. Since the round is beyond the target, you must drop. You estimate that the round is 250 meters beyond the target. Therefore, a 400-meter drop will give you a bracket. The round impacted 50 mils left of the target. With an OT factor of 2, the round impacted 100 meters left. Your correction to the FDC is "Right 100, drop 400, over."

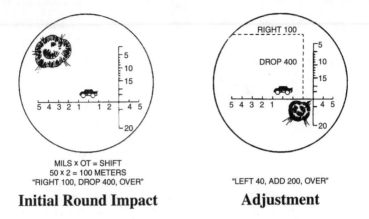

MILS x OT = SHIFT
50 x 2 = 100 METERS
"RIGHT 100, DROP 400, OVER"

Initial Round Impact

"LEFT 40, ADD 200, OVER"

Adjustment

3. *Continue splitting the range bracket until a 100-meter bracket is split or a range correct spotting is observed, maintaining deviation on line.*
4. *Initiate fire for effect.* When a 100-meter bracket is split or a range correct spotting is made, the fire-for-effect phase is entered, and the call is "Fire for effect."
5. *Observe the results of fire for effect and report the results.* When the smoke clears, tell the FDC what the results are. Such things as the number of casualties, damaged equipment, stalled tracks, and so forth are important.

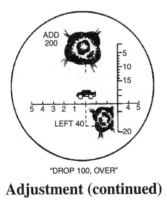

"DROP 100, OVER"

Adjustment (continued)

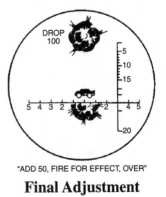

"ADD 50, FIRE FOR EFFECT, OVER"

Final Adjustment

12

Camouflage

Camouflage is anything a soldier uses to keep himself, his equipment, and his position from looking like what they are. Both natural and manmade material can be used for camouflage. Change and improve camouflage often. Natural camouflage often dies or fades, and manmade camouflage may wear off or fade. When this happens, a soldier may no longer blend with the surroundings.

Each soldier is responsible for camouflaging himself, his equipment, and his position. Camouflage reduces the probability of the enemy placing aimed fire on the soldier.

The soldier uses natural and artificial materials for camouflage. Natural camouflage includes defilade, grass, bushes, trees, and shadows. Artificial camouflage includes the battle dress uniform (BDU), lightweight camouflage screening system (LCSS), skin paint, and natural materials removed from their original positions. To be effective, artificial camouflage must blend with the natural background.

Noise, movement, and light discipline all contribute to individual camouflage. Effective noise discipline muffles and eliminates sounds made by soldiers and their equipment. Movement discipline minimizes movement within and between positions and limits movement to routes that cannot be readily observed by the enemy. Light discipline controls the use of lights at night. Examples are not smoking in the open or walking around with a lit flashlight.

Dispersal, the spreading of soldiers and equipment over a wide area, is a key individual survival technique. It creates a smaller target mass for enemy sensors and weapon systems. Dispersal, therefore, not only reduces casualties and losses in the event of an attack but also makes enemy detection efforts more difficult.

Camouflage

CAMOUFLAGE CONSIDERATIONS

Movement
Movement draws attention, whether it involves vehicles on the road or individuals walking around. The naked eye, as well as infrared and radar sensors, can detect movement. Soldiers should minimize movement while they are in the open. They should remember that darkness does not prevent observation by an enemy equipped with modern sensors. When movement is necessary, slow, smooth movement attracts less attention than quick, irregular movement.

Shape
The soldier should use camouflage materials to break up the shapes, outlines, and shadows of positions and equipment, as all three are revealing. As shadows can visually mask objects, soldiers should stay in shadows

whenever possible, especially when moving. When conducting operations close to the enemy, disguise or distort the shape of the helmet and the human body with artificial camouflage materials, as they are easily recognized by the enemy at close range.

Shine and Light

Gloss or shine can also attract attention. Pay particular attention to gloss and shine caused by light reflecting from smooth or polished surfaces, such as mess kits, mirrors, eyeglasses, watch crystals, windshields, and starched uniforms. Plastic map cases, dust goggles worn on top of the helmet, and clear plastic garbage bags also reflect light almost as well as windshields and mirrors. Cover or remove these items from exposed areas. Vehicle headlights, taillights, and safety reflectors reflect not only light but also laser energy used in weapon systems. Cover this equipment when the vehicle is not in operation. Red filters on vehicle dome lights and flashlights, while designed to protect the soldier's night vision, are extremely sensitive to detection by night vision devices. A tank's red dome light, reflecting off the walls and out through the sight and vision blocks, can be seen from as far away as 4 kilometers with a starlight scope. Red-lensed flashlights, as well as cigarettes and pipes, are equally observable. To reduce the chances of detection, soldiers should replace red with blue-green filters and practice strict light discipline. Soldiers should also use measures to prevent shine at night, because moonlight and starlight can be reflected as easily as sunlight.

Color

The contrast of skin, uniforms, and equipment with the background helps the enemy detect opposing forces. Individual camouflage should blend with the surroundings; at a minimum, objects must not contrast with the background. Therefore, the proper camouflage technique is to blend colors with the background or to hide objects with contrasting colors.

HOW TO CAMOUFLAGE

Before camouflaging himself, his equipment, and his position, a soldier should study the nearby terrain and vegetation. His reconnaissance should incorporate an analysis of the camouflage considerations listed above. He then chooses camouflage materials that best blend with the area. When moving from one area to another, change camouflage as required. What works well in one location may draw fire in another.

Soldier Camouflage

Skin

Exposed skin, even very dark skin, reflects light. Camouflage paint sticks cover these oils and provide blending with the background. Avoid using oils or insect repellent to soften the paint stick, because doing so defeats the purpose by making the skin shiny. Soldiers applying camouflage paint should work in pairs and help each other. Self-application may leave gaps, such as behind the ears. Paint high, shiny areas (forehead, cheekbones, nose, ears, and chin) a dark color. Paint low, shadow areas a light color. Paint the exposed skin on the back of the neck, arms, and hands with an irregular pattern. When camouflage paint sticks are not available, use field expedients such as burnt cork, bark, charcoal, lampblack, or mud. Mud contains bacteria, so consider it a last priority for field-expedient paint.

Uniform

BDUs, which have a camouflage pattern, often require additional camouflage, especially when operating very close to the enemy. Soldiers should attach leaves, grass, small branches, or pieces of LCSS to their uniforms and helmets. These items assist in distorting the shape of the soldier and in blending colors with the natural background. The BDU provides visual as well as near infrared (NIR) camouflage. Do not starch BDUs; doing this counters the infrared properties of the dyes. Replace excessively faded and worn BDUs, because they lose their camouflage effectiveness as they wear.

Equipment

Soldiers should inspect their personal equipment to ensure that shiny items are covered or removed. Take corrective action on items that rattle or make other noises when moved or worn. Soldiers assigned equipment such as vehicles or generators should be knowledgeable of the appropriate techniques to camouflage them.

Individual Fighting Position

While building a fighting position, soldiers should camouflage it and carefully dispose of the earth spoil. They must also remember that too much camouflage material applied to a position can actually disclose it. Soldiers should obtain camouflage materials from a dispersed area to avoid drawing attention to the position due to the stripped area around it.

Camouflage the position as it is built. To avoid disclosing a fighting position, soldiers should observe the following guidelines:

- Do not leave shiny or light-colored objects exposed.
- Do not remove shirts while in the open.
- Do not use fires.
- Do not leave tracks and other signs of movement.
- When aircraft fly overhead, refrain from looking up, as one of the most obvious features on aerial photographs is the upturned faces of soldiers.

When camouflage is complete, inspect the position from the enemy's viewpoint. Check camouflage periodically to see that it stays natural looking and conceals the position. When camouflage materials become ineffective, change or improve them.

13

Land Navigation
and Map Reading

COMPASS

Compasses are the primary tools to use when moving in an outdoor world where there is no other way to find directions. The lensatic compass is the most common and simplest instrument for measuring direction. The lensatic compass consists of the following major parts:

- The *cover* protects the floating dial. It contains a sighting wire and two luminous sighting slots or dots used for night navigation.
- The *base* or body of the compass contains a thumb loop and moving parts that include the floating dial, which is mounted on a pivot and rotates freely when the compass is held level. Printed on the dial in luminous figures are an arrow and the letters *E* and *W*. The arrow always points to magnetic north, and the letters rest at east (90 degrees) and west (270 degrees). There are two scales, the outer denoting mils and the inner (normally in red) denoting degrees. Encasing the floating dial is a glass containing a fixed, black index line.
- The *bezel ring* is a ratchet device that clicks when turned. It will make 120 clicks when rotated fully; each click is equal to 3 degrees. A short, luminous line that is used in conjunction with the north-seeking arrow is contained in the glass face of the bezel ring.
- The *lens* is used to read the dial. It contains the rear-sight slot used in conjunction with the front sight for sighting on objects. The rear sight must be opened more than 45 degrees to allow the dial to float freely.

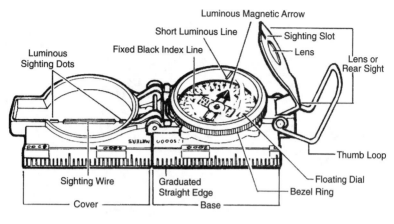

Lensatic Compass

Handling the Compass

The compass is a delicate instrument and should be closed and in its case when not being used. Metal objects and electricity can affect the performance of a compass. Nonmagnetic metals and alloys do not affect the compass. To ensure its proper functioning, observe these suggested safe distances:

High-tension power lines	55 meters
Field gun, truck, or tank	18 meters
Telegraph or telephone wires and barbed wire	10 meters
Machine gun	2 meters
Steel helmet or rifle	$1/2$ meter

Using the Compass

The compass must always be held level and firm when sighting on an object. Some of the techniques are as follows:

Centerhold

Open the compass to its fullest so that the cover forms a straightedge with the base. Place your thumb through the thumb loop, form a steady base with your third and fourth fingers, and extend your index finger along the side of the compass. Place the thumb of the other hand between the lens (rear sight) and the bezel ring; extend the index finger along the other side of the com-

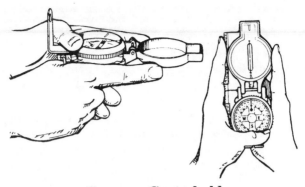

Compass Centerhold

pass and the remaining fingers around the fingers of the other hand. Pull your elbows in firmly to your sides—this places the compass between your chin and belt. To measure an azimuth, simply turn your entire body toward the object, pointing the compass cover directly at the object. Then look down and read the azimuth from beneath the fixed, black index line.

Compass-to-Cheek
Open the cover of the compass containing the sighting wire to a vertical position, and fold the rear sight slightly forward. Look through the rear-sight slot, and align the front-sight hairline with the desired object in the distance. Then glance down at the dial through the eye lens to read the azimuth.

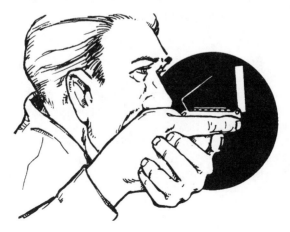

Compass-to-cheek

Presetting a Compass

In Daylight or with a Light Source
Hold the compass level in the palm of the hand. Rotate it until the desired azimuth falls under the fixed, black index line. Turn the bezel ring until the luminous line is aligned with the north-seeking arrow. The compass is now preset.

To follow the azimuth, use the centerhold technique and turn your body until the north-seeking arrow is aligned with the luminous line. Then proceed forward in the direction of the front cover's sighting wire, which is aligned with the fixed, black index line.

In Darkness or Limited Visibility
Set the azimuth by the click method (each click equals a 3-degree interval). Rotate the bezel ring until the luminous line is over the fixed, black index line. Find the desired azimuth and divide it by three. The result is the number of clicks that you have to rotate the bezel ring. If the desired azimuth is smaller than 180 degrees, the number of clicks on the bezel ring should be counted in a counterclockwise direction. If the desired azimuth is larger than 180 degrees, subtract the number of degrees from 360 degrees and divide by three to obtain the number of clicks. Count them in a clockwise direction. For example, if the desired azimuth is 330 degrees, then 360–330 = 30 divided by 3 = 10 clicks clockwise.

With the compass preset, use the centerhold technique and rotate your body until the north-seeking arrow is aligned with the luminous line on the bezel. Then proceed forward in the direction of the front cover's luminous dots, which are aligned with the fixed, black index line.

Offset
A deliberate offset is a planned magnetic deviation to the right or left of an azimuth to an objective. It is used when the objective is located along or in the vicinity of a linear feature such as a road or stream. Because of errors in reading the compass or map, you may reach the linear feature without knowing whether the objective lies to the right or left. A deliberate offset by a known number of degrees in a known direction compensates for possible errors and ensures that upon reaching the linear feature you will know whether to go left or right.

Orienting Compass and Map
Place the compass on the map so that the cover of the compass is pointing toward the top of the map. Align the sighting wire or the straightedge of the

compass over a north-south grid line, and rotate the map and compass together until the north arrow of the compass points in the same direction and number of degrees as shown in the current, updated grid-magnetic angle.

DETERMINING DIRECTIONS WITHOUT A COMPASS

Using the Sun

The sun is a natural source of direction. Weather permitting, you can determine true north by using the sun and an accurate but time-consuming emergency method called *equal shadow*. The *watch method* can be used to determine approximate true north and true south. This method can be in error, however, especially in the lower latitudes. The best improvised method is called *shadow tip*—it is simple and accurate and can also be used to determine the approximate time of day. Another method of finding the approximate time of day is the *shortest shadow.*

Equal Shadow Method

The shadow of a vertical rod at two hours before midday is the same length as the shadow from the same object two hours after midday. Place a stick upright into the ground in direct sunlight. In the morning, draw a circle with the base of the stick as center and the length of the shadow as radius. Mark the point where the tip of the shadow falls. As the sun rises, the shadow will get shorter. In the afternoon, the shadow lengthens. When it again touches the circle, mark again. The halfway point between the two marks is due north of the stick.

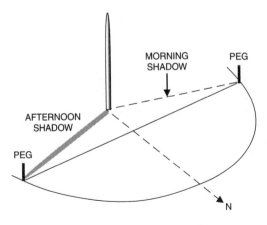

Equal Shadow Method

Watch Method

A watch can be used to determine approximate true north and true south. In the north temperate zone only, the hour hand is pointed toward the sun. A south line can be found midway between the hour hand and 1200 hours, standard time. If daylight saving time is in effect, the north-south line is found between the hour hand and 1300 hours. If there is any doubt as to which end of the line is north, remember that the sun is in the east before noon and in the west after noon.

A watch may also be used to determine direction in the south temperate zone, but the method is different. The 1200-hour dial is pointed toward the sun, and halfway between 1200 hours and

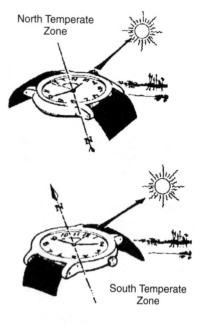

Watch Method

the hour hand is the north line. If on daylight saving time, the north line lies midway between the hour hand and 1300 hours.

The watch method can be in error, especially in the lower latitudes, and may cause circling. To avoid this, make a shadow clock and set your watch to the time indicated. After traveling for an hour, take another shadow-clock reading. Reset your watch if necessary.

Shadow-Tip Method

This method requires only 10 to 15 minutes in sunlight and is much more accurate than the watch method. Mark the tip of the shadow cast from a 3-foot stick. Mark the tip again after about 10 minutes. A straight line through the two marks is an approximate east-west line from which any desired direction of travel can be obtained. Draw a north-south line at right angles to the east-west line at any point to assist in orienting yourself.

If you are ever uncertain which is east and which is west, observe this simple rule: The sun rises in the east and sets in the west. The shadow tip moves just the opposite. Therefore, the first shadow tip mark is always toward the west, and the second mark is always to its east—everywhere on earth.

To find the time of day using the shadow-tip method, move the stick to the intersection of the east-west and north-south lines and set it vertically in the ground. The west part of the east-west line indicates 0600 hours, and the east part is 1800 hours, anywhere on earth. The north-south line is the noon line. The shadow of the stick is the hour hand in the shadow clock, and you can estimate the time using the noon line and the 6 o'clock line as your guides. Depending on your location and the season, the shadow may move either clockwise or counterclockwise, but this does not alter the reading of the shadow clock. The shadow clock is not a timepiece in the ordinary sense. It makes every day 12 unequal hours long and always reads 0600 hours at sunrise and 1800 hours at sunset. The shadow clock time is closest to conventional clock time at midday, but the spacing of the other hours compared with conventional time varies somewhat with the locality and the date. However, it provides a satisfactory means of telling time in the absence of properly set watches. The shadow-tip system is not intended for use in polar regions, which the Department of Defense defines as being above 60 degrees latitude in either hemisphere.

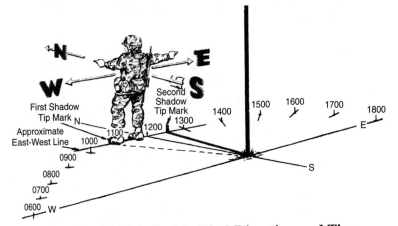

Shadow-Tip Method to Find Direction and Time

Shortest Shadow Method

The sun is at its highest at noon; therefore, shadows are at their shortest then. Put a stick or rod as vertical as possible in a level place. Check its vertical alignment by sighting along the line of a makeshift plumb bob. Sometime before midday, begin marking the position of the end of the stick's shadow. Continue marking until the shadow definitely lengthens. The time of the shortest shadow is when the sun passed the local meridian at solar noon.

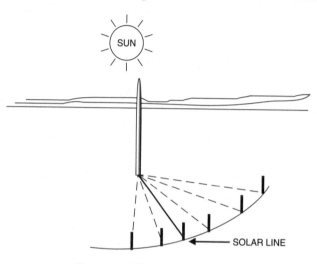

Shortest Shadow Method

Using the Stars

Less than 60 of approximately 5,000 stars visible to the eye are used by navigators. The stars we see when we look up at the night sky are not evenly scattered across the whole sky; they are grouped in constellations. Which constellations we see depends on where we are, the time of the year, and the time of the night. The night sky changes with the seasons because the earth revolves around the sun, and it also changes from hour to hour because the rotation of the earth makes some constellations seem to travel in a circle. But the North Star, also known as the Polar Star or Polaris, is in almost exactly the same place in the sky all night long every night. The North Star is less than 1 degree off true north and does not move because the axis of the earth is pointed toward it. The North Star is the last star in the handle of the Little Dipper. Two stars in the Big Dipper are a help in finding the North Star. They are called the Pointers, and an imaginary line drawn through them five times their distance points to the North Star. There are many stars brighter than the North Star, but none is more important. However, the North Star can be seen only in the Northern Hemisphere, so it cannot serve as a guide south of the equator. The farther north one goes, the higher the North Star is in the sky; above latitude 70 degrees, it is too high in the sky to be useful.

Depending on the star selected for navigation, azimuth checks are necessary. A star near the north horizon serves for about a half hour. When moving south, azimuth checks should be made every 15 minutes. When traveling east or west, the difficulty of staying on azimuth is more likely caused by the star climbing too high in the sky or disappearing below the horizon than by the star changing direction angle. When this happens, it is necessary to choose another guide star.

The Southern Cross is the main constellation used as a guide south of the equator, and the general directions above for using north and south stars are reversed. When navigating using the stars as guides, the user must know the different constellation shapes and their locations throughout the world.

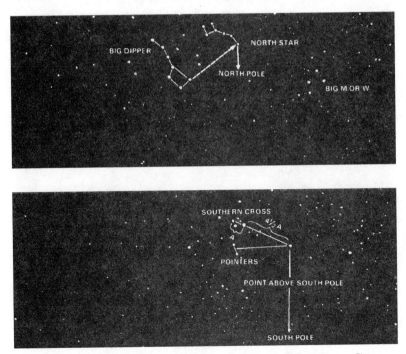

Determining Direction by the North Star and Southern Cross

MAP READING

To be in the right place at the right time is essential on the battlefield, so map-reading and land-navigation skills are important for every soldier.

Military Grid System

A military grid system is a network of squares formed by north-south and east-west grid lines placed on a map. The distance between grid lines represents 1,000 or 10,000 meters, depending on the scale of the map. A grid system enables the map reader to locate a point on a map quickly and accurately.

A grid line is identified by a specific number printed in the margin directly opposite the line it indicates. Any point on a map can be identified by coordinates. Following are rules for reading grid coordinates:

1. Large, bold-faced numbers in the margin label each grid line.
2. Starting at the lower left-hand corner of the map, read right and up.
3. Write the coordinates as a continuous series of numbers. The first half of the total number of the digits represents the "right" reading; the last half represents the "up" reading.

Examples (using a map with 1,000-meter grid squares):

- Location of a point within a 1,000-meter grid square is used to designate an object that is easily identifiable within a large area. Identify the grid square by using the numbers of the two grid lines intersecting at the lower left-hand corner, e.g., 9176.
- Location of a point within 100 meters. Use the appropriate corner of a coordinate scale that breaks the 1,000-meter square into 10 equal parts along each side (100-meter segments are indicated by longer lines on the coordinate scale). Place the coordinate scale along the east-west grid at the lower left-hand corner of the grid square, then slide it eastward to the center of the object. Location is expressed as a six-digit coordinate. The third digit is the longer line nearest grid line 91, and the sixth digit is the longer line nearest the spot elevation (SE), e.g., 915761.
- Location of a point within 10 meters. The short lines divide 100-meter segments into 20-meter segments. To read to the nearest 10 meters, interpolate along the scale. The coordinate will be an eight-digit coordinate, e.g., 91547614.

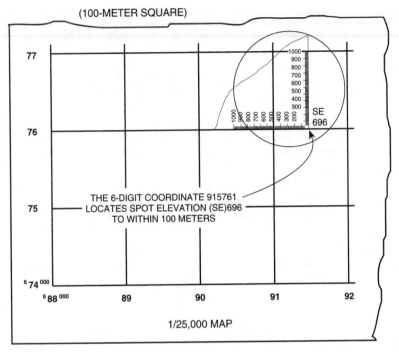

(100-METER SQUARE)

THE 6-DIGIT COORDINATE 915761
LOCATES SPOT ELEVATION (SE)696
TO WITHIN 100 METERS

1/25,000 MAP

The Six-digit Coordinate

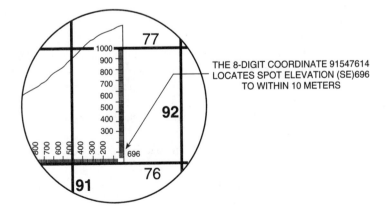

THE 8-DIGIT COORDINATE 91547614
LOCATES SPOT ELEVATION (SE)696
TO WITHIN 10 METERS

The Eight-digit Coordinate

Scale

Scale is defined as the fixed relationship between map distance (MD) and the corresponding ground distance (GD). It is expressed as a representative fraction (RF):

$$RF = \frac{MD}{GD}$$

The RF appears in the margin of the map as 1/25,000 or 1:25,000, each of which means that one unit of measure on the map represents 25,000 similar units of measure on the ground.

The graphic scale is printed in the margin as a special ruler and is used to measure ground distances on a map. Military maps normally have three graphic scales, expressed in miles, meters, and yards.

Direction

Direction is defined as an imaginary straight line on the map or ground and is expressed as an azimuth.

Azimuth

An azimuth is a horizontal angle measured clockwise from a north baseline. All directions originate from the center of an imaginary circle called the azimuth circle. This circle is divided into 360 equal units of measurement, called degrees. The degrees are numbered in a clockwise direction, with east at 90 degrees, south at 180 degrees, west at 270 degrees, and north at 360 or 0 degrees. Distance has no effect on azimuth.

Back Azimuth

The back azimuth of a line differs from its azimuth by exactly 180 degrees. The rules for determining back azimuth are as follows:

- If the azimuth is less than 180 degrees, the back azimuth is the value of the azimuth *plus* 180.
- If the azimuth is more than 180 degrees, the back azimuth is the value of the azimuth *minus* 180.
- If the azimuth is 180 degrees, the back azimuth is 0 degrees or 360 degrees.

Measuring Azimuths on a Map

Map azimuths are measured with a protractor. The issue protractor (MR-1) is graduated in two scales—0 to 180 degrees, and 180 to 360 degrees—to represent the complete azimuth circle.

To read a map azimuth between any two points:

• Draw a line connecting the two points.
• Place the index at the point from which you are measuring, ensuring that the baseline of the protractor is on or parallel to a north-south grid line.
• Read the azimuth at the point where the line intersects the scale.

To plot an azimuth on a map:

• Place the protractor on the map with the index at the initial point and baseline parallel to a north-south grid line.
• Place a dot on the map at the desired azimuth reading.
• Remove the protractor; connect the initial point and the dot with a line.

Base Direction

There are three base directions: true north, grid north, and magnetic north.

1. *True North.* Direction to the north pole. The symbol is a star.
2. *Grid North.* Direction of the north-south grid lines. The symbol is GN.
3. *Magnetic North.* Direction in which the magnetic arrow of a compass points. The symbol is a half arrow.

The angular relationships among these three directions are shown by a declination diagram in the margin of a map.

Grid-Magnetic Angle

To understand the grid-magnetic (G-M) angle, you must know the meaning of azimuth. Map readers are concerned with two base directions: grid north, from which we read grid azimuths (protractor and map), and magnetic north, from which we read magnetic azimuths (compass and ground).

Grid azimuth is a horizontal angle measured clockwise from grid north. *Magnetic azimuth* is a horizontal angle measured clockwise from magnetic north. *G-M angle* is the angular difference between grid north and magnetic north, measured from grid north.

To use a grid azimuth in the field with a compass, you must first change it to a magnetic azimuth. To plot a magnetic azimuth on a map, you must first change it to a grid azimuth. To make either of these changes, you must use a G-M angle diagram as shown in the diagram.

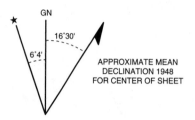

APPROXIMATE MEAN
DECLINATION 1948
FOR CENTER OF SHEET

Draw this current G-M angle.

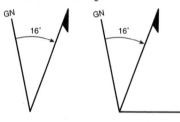

From the base of the G-M angle, draw a line to the right; this line represents any azimuth.

To use the G-M angle diagram in working with a map having an EAST G-M angle:

1. Convert magnetic azimuth to grid azimuth.

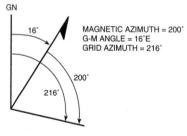

MAGNETIC AZIMUTH = 200°
G-M ANGLE = 16°E
GRID AZIMUTH = 216°

2. Then convert grid azimuth to magnetic azimuth.

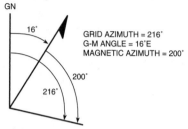

GRID AZIMUTH = 216°
G-M ANGLE = 16°E
MAGNETIC AZIMUTH = 200°

When working with a map having a WEST G-M angle:

1. Convert magnetic azimuth to grid azimuth.

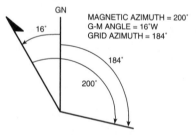

MAGNETIC AZIMUTH = 200°
G-M ANGLE = 16°W
GRID AZIMUTH = 184°

2. Then convert grid azimuth to magnetic azimuth.

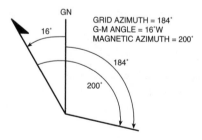

GRID AZIMUTH = 184°
G-M ANGLE = 16°W
MAGNETIC AZIMUTH = 200°

You should construct and use the G-M angle diagram *each time* conversion of azimuths is required. As a time-saving procedure when working frequently with the same map, construct a G-M angle conversion table on the margin. The following is an example, using a map having a G-M angle of 16 degrees east:

For Conversion of:

Magnetic azimuth to grid azimuth: Add 16 degrees
Grid azimuth to magnetic azimuth: Subtract 16 degrees

Intersection

Distant or inaccessible objects can be located on a map by intersecting lines from two known points. For example, a magnetic azimuth from a known OP to a distant point is converted to a grid azimuth and drawn on the map. Another magnetic azimuth from another OP to the same distant point is converted to a grid azimuth and drawn on the same map. The intersection of the two lines on the map is the location of the known point.

Resection

The resection method lets you locate your position on a map. Take magnetic azimuths to two distant points on the ground that can be identified on the map. Change these azimuths to back azimuths, convert to grid azimuths, and draw the *converted* azimuths from the known points on the map. Your location is where these two lines intersect. To verify and make a final determination of your position, compare ground features with those shown on the map.

Modified Resection

Modified resection is a method of locating your position on a map when you are on a road, stream, or other linear feature identified on the map. Take a magnetic azimuth to a distant point that can be identified both on the ground and on the map. Change this to a back azimuth, and convert to a grid azimuth. Draw this *converted* azimuth on the map from the known point. Your position is where the azimuth line on the map crosses or intersects the linear feature.

Elevation and Relief

Elevation is height expressed in feet or meters above or below mean sea level. *Relief* is the variation in the height and shape of the earth's surface. Elevation and relief may be shown on a map by hachures (short, broken lines used to show mountain ranges, peaks, and plateaus), layer tinting, or contour lines. On large-scale maps, contour lines are used.

Contour lines are imaginary lines on the ground connecting points of equal elevation. On a map they are shown in brown or gray. The *contour interval*—the vertical distance between contours—is stated as marginal information. Normally every fifth contour is printed more heavily than the others and is numbered to show the height above or below mean sea level. These lines are known as *index contours.*

Following are some characteristics of contours:

- Contours are smooth curves that always close to form irregular circles.
- When crossing a valley or a stream, contours form Us or Vs, with the base of the U or V pointing toward higher ground (or upstream).
- When crossing ridges, contour lines form Us or Vs with the base of the U or V pointing away from high ground.
- Contours far apart indicate a gentle slope; contours close together indicate a steep slope.
- On uniform slopes, contours are evenly spaced; on irregular slopes, they are unevenly spaced.
- The last (inmost) closed contour indicates a hilltop.
- Movement parallel to contours is relatively level; movement across contours is up- or downslope.

Terrain Features

All ground forms may be classified as one of the following primary terrain features: hilltop, ridge, valley, saddle, or depression. Contour lines are used to indicate these ground forms on a map.

The relationship between contour lines and actual ground forms is illustrated as follows. To determine the elevation of a point that falls between two adjacent contours, estimate the point's relative distance between the two contours, and add the same proportion to the elevation of the lowest-valued contour line. For example, a point located seven-tenths of the distance

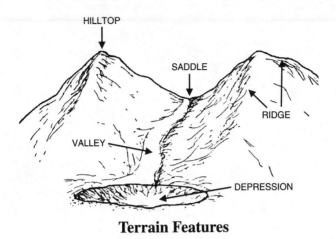

HILLTOP

SADDLE

RIDGE

VALLEY

DEPRESSION

Terrain Features

between the 70-foot contour and the 80-foot contour would have an elevation of 77 feet.

A rule of thumb to determine the elevation of a hilltop is to take the elevation of the last closed contour line and add to it one-half the contour interval. To determine the elevation of a depression, subtract one-half the contour interval from the last depression contour line.

Use of a Map in the Field

To determine your location on the map and on the ground, use the following procedure: Orient the map to the north. Inspect the surrounding area or ground to determine all distinct terrain features. On the map, look for an area having the same types of features in the same relative positions as those observed on the ground. Through comparing the map to the ground and using a process of elimination, isolate the terrain feature on which you are located. Confirm this terrain feature by assuring that the direction to, distance from, and difference in elevation from all adjacent terrain features are identical on the map and on the ground. Determine your exact location on the isolated terrain feature by a detailed analysis of all the immediate terrain features.

Hilltop

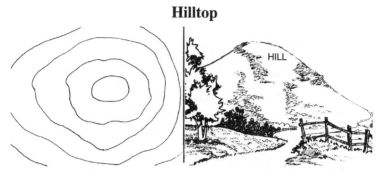

(On Map)
Last closed contour.

(On Ground)
When you are located on a hilltop,
the ground slopes down in all directions.

Ridge

(On Ground)
When you are located on a ridge,
the ground slopes down in three
directions and up in one direction.

(On Map)
U- or V-shaped contours with the base
of the U or V pointing away from
higher ground.

Saddle

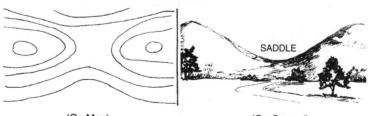

(On Map)
Hourglass or figure eight–
shaped contours.

(On Ground)
When you are located in a saddle,
there is higher ground in two directions
and lower ground in two directions.

Valley

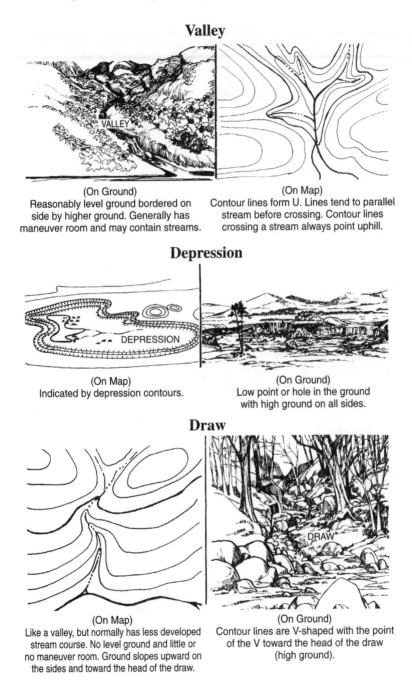

(On Ground)
Reasonably level ground bordered on
side by higher ground. Generally has
maneuver room and may contain streams.

(On Map)
Contour lines form U. Lines tend to parallel
stream before crossing. Contour lines
crossing a stream always point uphill.

Depression

(On Map)
Indicated by depression contours.

(On Ground)
Low point or hole in the ground
with high ground on all sides.

Draw

(On Map)
Like a valley, but normally has less developed
stream course. No level ground and little or
no maneuver room. Ground slopes upward on
the sides and toward the head of the draw.

(On Ground)
Contour lines are V-shaped with the point
of the V toward the head of the draw
(high ground).

Spur

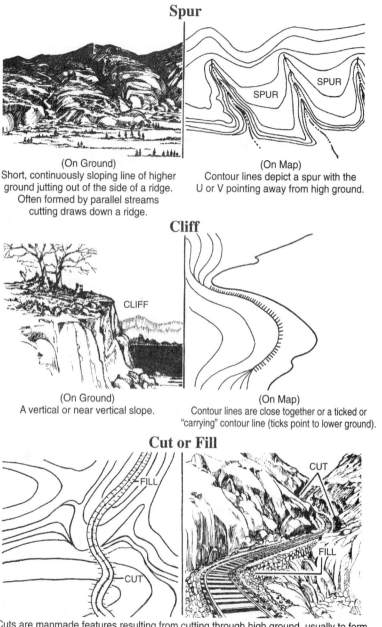

(On Ground)
Short, continuously sloping line of higher ground jutting out of the side of a ridge. Often formed by parallel streams cutting draws down a ridge.

(On Map)
Contour lines depict a spur with the U or V pointing away from high ground.

Cliff

(On Ground)
A vertical or near vertical slope.

(On Map)
Contour lines are close together or a ticked or "carrying" contour line (ticks point to lower ground).

Cut or Fill

Cuts are manmade features resulting from cutting through high ground, usually to form a level bed for a road or railroad track. Fills are manmade features resulting from filling a low area, usually to form a level bed for a road or railroad track.

GROUND NAVIGATION

Ground navigation is movement between two points in which an individual, using terrain features as guides, knows both his map and ground location throughout the movement. Ground navigation demands a thorough knowledge of terrain features as they appear on the map and on the ground. Since terrain features are used as guides during movement, use of the compass is minimal. Two basic rules must always be applied:

1. Begin from a known location on both the map and the ground.
2. Then orient the map to the ground and keep it oriented throughout the movement.

With the basic rules established, the following steps outline the ground (land) navigation procedure:

1. Through a map study of the terrain, determine the most practical route to your destination, and select terrain features along this route to guide your movement.
2. Determine the general direction of movement.
3. Begin movement, considering the horizontal and vertical distances between terrain features along the route.
4. Confirm your location at selected terrain features (checkpoints) along the route.
5. Upon arrival at the final destination, confirm your location by a detailed comparative analysis between the ground position and the plotted map position.

Mounted Navigation

With the addition of more combat vehicles to the Army, your chances of having to navigate while mounted are increasing. The major difference between navigating while mounted and while dismounted is the speed at which you travel. When moving mounted, it is important to designate a navigator who makes sure that the correct distance and direction are followed and recorded, beginning with the leg from the start point to the first prominent feature and then to subsequent easily identifiable features on the ground. The navigator prepares a log to record azimuths and distances for each leg of the movement. During movement, the navigator must face in the direction of travel to keep his map oriented and to identify terrain features.

Mounted navigation with a compass requires determination of the amount of deviation caused by the vehicle. This can be done in the following manner:

1. The navigator dismounts and moves 50 meters in front of the vehicle.
2. The navigator determines an azimuth from his position to a fixed object at least 50 meters to his front.

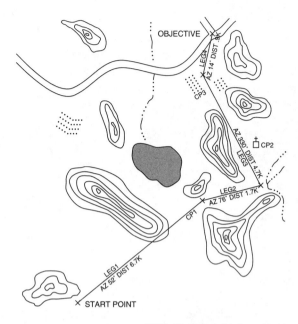

NOTE: All azimuths in this figure are grid.

Mounted Movement

3. The driver moves the vehicle forward, keeping it centered on the navigator, and stops as close to him as safely possible.

4. The navigator then gets back into the vehicle and measures the azimuth to the fixed object from the vehicle. The vehicle's engine must be running. The difference between the two azimuths is the deviation. The deviation is logged and added to or subtracted from the azimuth to be followed. This procedure should be followed for any change of direction of 10 degrees or more.

   Be aware that distance measured on a vehicle's odometer during mounted movement may be greater than that measured on the map, since the map measurements do not take into consideration the rise and fall of the land.

How to Fold a Map
Use the following steps to fold a map:

1. Lay the map flat, faceup, north at the top. Fold it in half, turning the bottom edge up to the top.

2. Crease map into three equal parts parallel to the center fold just made.

3. Open the map completely, faceup. Turn it so east is at the top.
4. Repeat the folding procedures of steps 1 and 2.
5. Open the map again, faceup, placing north at the top. With a sharp blade, neatly cut the map as shown in Sketch 1, along heavy lines.
6. Grasp as in Sketch 2, drawing paper up at the crease. Fold over toward the top edge.
7. Repeat step 6 with the second crease from the bottom, folding to meet the top edge of the map. Fold up the remaining flap. The edge view of the map should look like Sketch 3.
8. From the center V, open the map to center section without unfolding the remainder. Turn the map so east is at the top.
9. Follow the same creasing and folding procedures as in steps 6 and 7.
10. Again open the map at the center V without unfolding the rest, exposing the center section.
11. Without unfolding the map, carefully glue or tape together the eight places where the edges you have cut come together.
12. You now have three sections, each of which may be used like a book map. You can fold the entire map so that only the desired "book" is exposed for use.

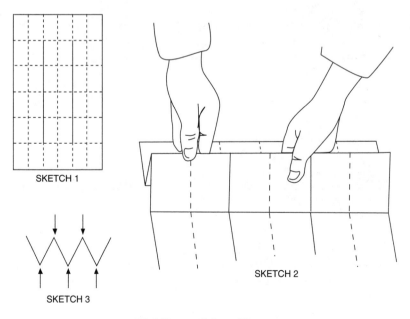

SKETCH 1

SKETCH 2

SKETCH 3

Folding a Map Sheet

14

Fighting Positions

Infantrymen use a variety of fighting positions ranging from the one-man hasty position to the well-prepared three-man position meant for a deliberate defense. Soldiers must construct fighting positions that protect them and allow them to fire into their assigned sectors, remembering that effective weapons use is the primary mission.

Fighting positions protect soldiers by providing *cover* through sturdy construction and by providing *concealment* through positioning and proper camouflage. The enemy must not be able to identify the position until it is too late and it has been effectively engaged. When possible, soldiers should site positions in nonobvious places, behind natural cover, and in an easy-to-camouflage location. The most important step in preparing fighting positions is to make sure that they cannot be seen. In constructing fighting positions, soldiers should always:

- Dig the position armpit deep.
- Fill sandbags about 75 percent full.
- Revet excavations in sandy soil.
- Check stabilization of wall bases.
- Inspect and test the position daily, after heavy rain, and after receiving direct or indirect fires.
- Maintain, repair, and improve positions as required.
- Use proper materiel and use it correctly.

Soldiers must be able to engage the enemy within their assigned sectors of fire. They should be able to fire out to the maximum effective range of their weapons with maximum grazing fire and minimal dead space. Soldiers and leaders must be able to identify the best location for their positions that meet these criteria. Leaders must also ensure that fighting positions provide interlocking fires. This allows them to cover the platoon's sector from multiple positions and provides a basis for final protective fires.

Leaders must ensure that their soldiers understand when and how to prepare fighting positions based on the situation. Soldiers normally prepare hasty fighting positions every time the platoon halts (except for short security halts), and a good percentage of the platoon digs in and conducts other priorities of work while the rest maintain security. Soldiers prepare positions in stages that require a leader to inspect the position before moving on to the next state.

Stage 1. The leader checks the fields of fire from the prone position and has the soldier emplace sector stakes.

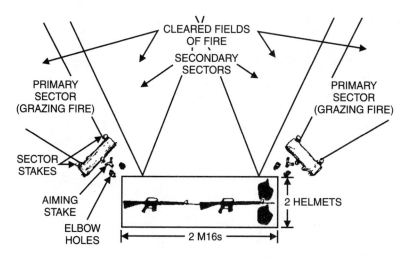

■ Sector stakes emplaced (primary sector).

■ Grazing fire log or sandbag positioned between the sector stakes.

■ The aiming stake, if required, is emplaced to allow limited-visibility engagement of a specific target area.

■ Elbow holes are scooped out.

■ The outline of position is traced on the ground.

■ Fields of fire are cleared (primary and secondary sectors).

■ The leader inspects the position.

Stage 1

Stage 2. The retaining walls for the parapets are prepared at this stage. These ensure that there is at least one helmet distance from the edge of the hole to the beginning of the front, flank, and rear cover.

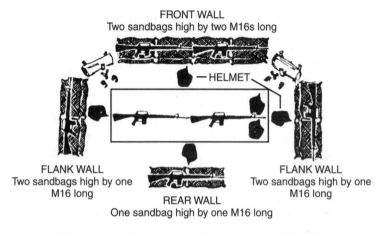

FRONT WALL
Two sandbags high by two M16s long

—HELMET

FLANK WALL
Two sandbags high by one M16 long

FLANK WALL
Two sandbags high by one M16 long

REAR WALL
One sandbag high by one M16 long

- The front wall is two to three sandbags (or logs) high. For a two-soldier position, it is about two M16s long.

- The flank walls are the same height, but only one M16 long.

- The rear wall is one sandbag high by one M16 long.

- If logs are used, they must be held firmly in place with strong stakes about 2 to 3 inches in diameter and 18 inches long.

- The leader inspects the position.

Stage 2

Stage 3. The position is dug and the dirt is thrown forward of the parapet retaining walls and then packed down hard.

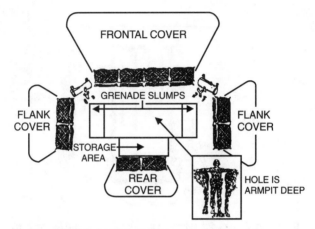

- The position is dug armpit deep.

- The parapets are filled in order of front, flanks, and rear.

- The parapets and the entire position are camouflaged.

- Grenade sumps are dug and the floor sloped toward them.

- Storage areas for the two rucksacks may also be dug into the rear wall.

- The leader inspects the postions.

Stage 3

Stage 4. The overhead cover is prepared . Camouflage should blend with surrounding terrain. At a distance of 35 meters, the position should not be detectable.

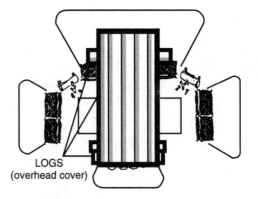

LOGS
(overhead cover)

- Five to six logs 4 to 6 inches in diameter and two M16s long are placed over the center of the position.

- Waterproofing (plastic bags, poncho) are placed on top of these logs.

- Six to 8 inches of dirt or sandbags are put on top of the logs.

- The overhead cover and the bottom of the position are camouflaged.

- The leader inspects the position.

Stage 4

TYPES OF FIGHTING POSITIONS

There are many different types of fighting positions. The number of personnel, types of weapons, time available, and terrain are the main factors that dictate the type of position.

Hasty Fighting Position

Soldiers use this type of position when there is little or no time to prepare. They locate it behind whatever cover is available. It should give frontal protection from direct fire while allowing fire to the front and obliquely. A hasty position may consist simply of a rucksack placed beside a tree or large rock. For protection from indirect fire, a hasty fighting position should be in a small depression or hole at least 18 inches deep. The term *hasty position* does not mean that there is no digging. In only a few minutes, a prone shelter can be scraped out or dug to provide some protection. This type of position is well suited for ambushes or for protection of overwatching elements during raids and attacks. Hasty positions can also be the first step in the construction of more elaborate positions.

Hasty Fighting Position

One-Soldier Fighting Position

This type of position allows choices in the use of cover; the hole needs to be large enough for only one soldier and his gear. It does not have the security of a two-soldier position. The one-soldier fighting position must allow a soldier to fire to the front or obliquely from behind frontal cover.

One-Soldier Fighting Position

Two-Soldier Fighting Position

A two-soldier fighting position can be prepared in close terrain. It can be used where grazing fire and mutual support extend no farther than to an adjacent position. It can be used to cover dead space just in front of the position. One or both ends of the hole are extended around the sides of the frontal cover. Changing a hole this way allows both soldiers to see better and have greater sectors of fire to the front. Also, during rest or eating periods, one soldier can watch the entire sector while the other sleeps or eats. If they receive fire from the front, they can move back to gain the protection of the frontal cover. By moving 1 meter, the soldiers can continue to find and hit targets to the front during lulls in enemy fire. This type of position requires more digging and is harder to camouflage. It is also a better target for enemy hand grenades.

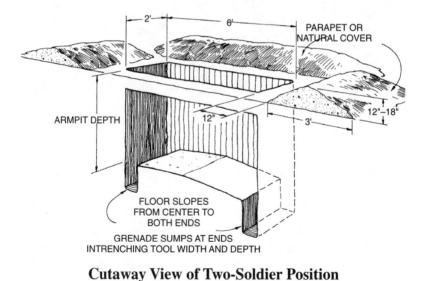

Cutaway View of Two-Soldier Position

Modified Two-Soldier Fighting Position
A modified two-soldier fighting position may be prepared in close terrain, where grazing fire and mutual support extend no farther than to an adjacent position, or it can be prepared to cover dead space just in front of the position. This is done by extending one or both ends of the hole around the sides of the frontal cover.

Positions on Steep Terrain
On a steep slope, a soldier in a hole behind frontal cover cannot shoot attackers without standing up and exposing himself. To overcome this, the hole is dug and firing ports are dug out at each end of the hole. The ground between the firing ports then serves as frontal cover for the position.

Steep Terrain Position

Three-Soldier Fighting Position
A three-soldier position has several advantages over the other positions. There is a leader in each position, which makes command and control easier. It supports continuous, secure operations better than other positions. One soldier can provide security; one can do priority work; and one can rest, eat, or perform maintenance. It allows the platoon to maintain combat power and security without shifting personnel or leaving positions unmanned. It provides 360-degree observation and fire.

The leader must consider the following with three-person positions:
- Either the distance between positions must be increased or the size of the squad's sector reduced. The choice depends mainly on visibility and fields of fire.

- Because the squad leader is in a fighting position that will most likely be engaged during the battle, he cannot exert personal control over the other two positions. The squad leader keeps control over the battle by:
  — Clearly communicating plans and intent to his squad, including control measures and fire plans
  — Using prearranged signals such as flares, whistles, or tracers
  — Positioning key weapons in his fighting position
  — Placing his fighting position so that it covers key or decisive terrain
  — Placing his fighting position where his team might be able to act as a reserve

The three-soldier emplacement is the T-position. This basic design can be changed by adding or deleting berms, changing the orientation of the T, or shifting the position of the third soldier to form an L instead of a T. Berms, camouflage, and overhead cover are similar to other fighting positions.

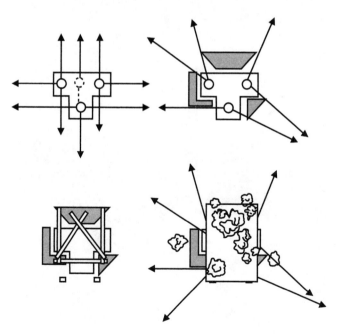

Three-soldier T-position

MACHINE GUN POSITIONS

The primary sector of fire is usually situated obliquely so that the gun can fire across the platoon's front. The tripod is used on the side with the primary sector of fire, and the bipod legs are used on the side with the secondary sector. When changing from primary to secondary sectors, the machine gun is moved, but the tripod is left in place. Dig a trench for the bipod legs in the secondary sector. After the platoon leader positions the gun and assigns sectors of fire, mark the position of the tripod legs and the limits of the sector of fire. Then trace the outline of the hole and the frontal cover.

The gun is lowered by digging down the firing platforms where the gun will be placed. The platforms must not be so low that the gun cannot be traversed across the sector of fire. Lowering the gun reduces the profile of the gunner when he is shooting and reduces the height of the frontal cover needed. Dig the firing platform first, to lessen the gunner's exposure in case firing is required before the position is completed.

After the firing platforms have been dug, dig the hole, placing the dirt first where frontal cover is needed. The hole is dug deep enough to provide protection and still let the gunner shoot, usually about armpit deep. When the frontal cover is high and thick enough, the rest of the dirt is used to build the flank and rear cover. Three trench-shaped grenade sumps are dug at various points so that grenades can be kicked into them.

Machine Gun Position Preparation

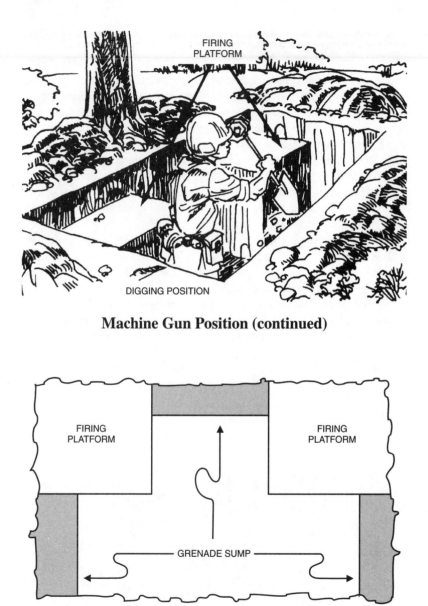

FIRING
PLATFORM

DIGGING POSITION

Machine Gun Position (continued)

FIRING
PLATFORM

FIRING
PLATFORM

GRENADE SUMP

Machine Gun Position (continued)

DRAGON POSITIONS

The Dragon has a primary fighting position and one or more alternate firing positions to cover its primary sector of fire. Additionally, each Dragon may have supplementary firing positions for coverage of other sectors of fire.

The backblast and the muzzle blast must be considered when employing the weapon. When the weapon is fired from an improved position, the muzzle end of the launcher must extend 6 inches beyond the front of the hole. The rear of the launcher must extend out over the rear of the hole. As the missile leaves the launcher, stabilizing fins unfold that require at least 6 inches of clearance above the ground. The position is only waist deep so that the gunner can move while firing. A trench for the bipod is dug 6 inches in front of the hole.

The position should be protected in the front by a parapet or some natural or manmade cover. The ground in front of and behind the position should be free of rocks, sand, and debris to prevent a dust cloud caused by the firing from obscuring the gunner's vision.

When the Dragon is to fire in only one direction, a one-soldier fighting position can be prepared. The Dragon should be positioned to fire obliquely so that its position can be protected from frontal fire while the target is being engaged.

The two-soldier fighting position is triangular. It is best suited for use when more than one sector of fire can be covered from a single position. The design of the position gives the gunner frontal protection and allows targets to be engaged obliquely or from the flank.

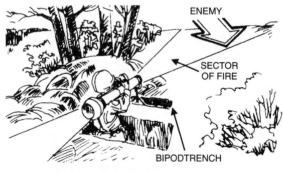

Position Preparation

Dragon Position

Two-Soldier Dragon position

Overhead cover is placed on the flanks of the one- or two-soldier Dragon position.

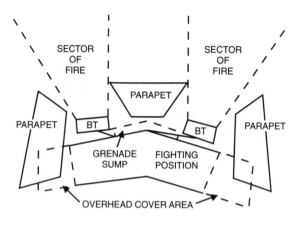

BT = BIPOD TRENCH

Two-Soldier Dragon Position—Overhead Cover

MORTAR POSITIONS
The standard dug-in mortar position has three stages of construction:
1. Mortar pit
2. Personnel shelters
3. Ammunition bunker

A dug-in position for 81-mm or 60-mm mortars is the same as for 4.2-inch mortars, with only slight changes in dimensions. The standard mortar position should be constructed on reasonably flat ground. It can be constructed totally below, partially above, or completely above ground, depending on the time and material available and the composition of the ground.

Stage 1. After the general location is selected, the exact baseplate position is marked, and construction of the mortar pit is begun.

Stage 2. As soon as the mortar pit is completed and as time allows, personnel shelters with overhead cover are constructed. Firing ports should be built into the personnel shelter and positioned as determined by assigned sectors of fire. There should be a blast barrier at least two sandbags thick separating the personnel shelters from the mortar pit.

Stage 3. If time and resources permit, ammunition bunkers are constructed. Each bunker is divided into four sections for each type of ammunition: white phosphorus (WP), illumination, final protective fire (FPF), and high explosive (HE).

Camouflaging the position is done in conjunction with construction through all stages.

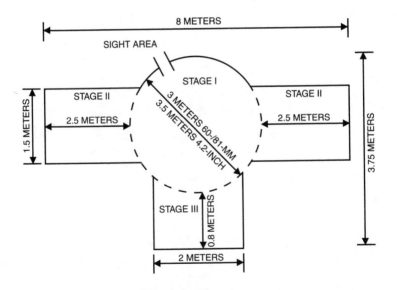

Mortar Position.
Three stages of construction: (1), mortar pit;
(2), personel shelters; (3), ammunition bunker

VEHICLE POSITIONS

The deliberate position is constructed in four parts: hull defilade, concealed access ramp or route, hide location, and turret defilade. The access ramp from the hide location to the hull defilade usually provides turret defilade for a vehicle at some point on the ramp. This location is marked to allow the driver to drive to it during daylight and darkness.

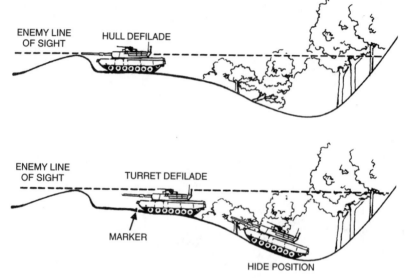

Vehicle Position

15

First Aid

Soldiers may have to depend on their first-aid knowledge and skills to save themselves or other soldiers. They may be able to save a life, prevent permanent disability, or reduce long periods of hospitalization by knowing what to do, what not to do, and when to seek medical assistance. Most injured or ill soldiers are able to return to their units primarily because they are given appropriate and timely first aid followed by the best medical care possible.

EVALUATING A CASUALTY
All casualties should be evaluated in eight steps, checking for:
1. Responsiveness
2. Breathing
3. Pulse
4. Bleeding
5. Shock
6. Fractures
7. Burns
8. Head injury

Seek medical aid as soon as possible, but do not stop treatment. If the situation allows, send another person to find medical aid. If there are any signs of chemical or biological poisoning, immediately mask the casualty. If it is nerve agent poisoning, administer the appropriate antidote, using the casualty's injector.

1. RESPONSIVENESS
Check the casualty for responsiveness by gently shaking or tapping him while calmly asking, "Are you okay?" Watch for a response. If the casualty does not respond, go to step 2. If the casualty responds, you can assume that he is breathing and has a pulse and continue the evaluation at step 4. If the casualty is conscious, ask him where he feels different from usual or where

it hurts. Ask him to identify the location of pain if he can, or to identify the area in which there is no feeling.

2. BREATHING

Check for breathing. If the casualty is breathing, proceed to step 4. If the casualty is not breathing, stop the evaluation and begin treatment. Lack of oxygen intake (because of a blocked airway or inadequate breathing) can lead to brain damage or death in only a few minutes.

Open the Airway

Head-Tilt/Chin-Lift Technique
In most cases, the airway can be cleared by simply using the head-tilt/chin-lift technique. Place one hand on the casualty's forehead and apply firm, backward pressure with the palm to tilt the head back. Place the fingertips of the other hand under the bony part of the lower jaw and lift, bringing the chin forward. The thumb should not be used to lift the chin. If the casualty does not resume breathing, give mouth-to-mouth resuscitation.

Once the rescuer uses one of the techniques to open the airway, he should maintain that head position to keep the airway open. If the casualty does not promptly resume adequate spontaneous breathing after the airway is open, rescue breathing (artificial respiration) must be started.

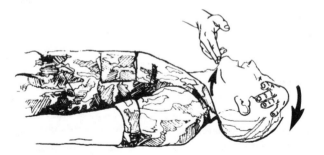

Give Artificial Respiration
Rescue breathing, or artificial respiration, is performed at the rate of about one breath every 5 seconds (12 breaths per minute), with rechecks for pulse and breathing after every 12 breaths. Rechecks can be accomplished in 3

to 5 seconds. Continue rescue breathing until the casualty starts to breathe on his own, until another person relieves you, or until you are too tired to continue.

Mouth-to-Mouth Method

While maintaining an open airway, take a deep breath and place your mouth (in an airtight seal) around the casualty's mouth. Blow two full breaths into the casualty's mouth (1 to 1¹/₂ seconds per breath), taking a breath of fresh air before each blow. Watch out of the corner of your eye for the casualty's chest to rise. If the chest rises, sufficient air is getting into the casualty's lungs. After giving two breaths that cause the chest to rise, attempt to locate a pulse on the casualty. If a pulse is found and the casualty is not breathing, continue rescue breathing.

PRESS CHEEK FIRMLY AGAINST NOSE, OPEN YOUR MOUTH WIDE, AND BLOW UNTIL CHEST RISES, LISTEN AND LOOK FOR SIGNS OF THROAT OBSTRUCTION OR CLOGGED AIR PASSAGE.

Mouth-to-Mouth Resusitation Method

Mouth-to-Nose Method

The mouth-to-nose method is performed in the same way as the mouth-to-mouth method, except that you blow into the nose while you hold the lips closed with one hand at the chin. You then remove your mouth to allow the casualty to exhale passively. It may be necessary to separate the casualty's lips to allow the air to escape during exhalation.

OPEN YOUR MOUTH WIDE AND BLOW INTO NOSE UNTIL CHEST RISES. LISTEN AND LOOK FOR SIGNS OF THROAT OBSTRUCTION OR CLOGGED AIR PASSAGE.

Mouth-to-Nose Method

3. PULSE

If a pulse is present and the casualty is breathing, proceed to step 4. If a pulse is not found, seek medically trained personnel for help.

4. BLEEDING

Look for spurts of blood or blood-soaked clothes. Also check for both entry and exit wounds. If the casualty is bleeding from an open wound, stop the evaluation and begin first-aid treatment.

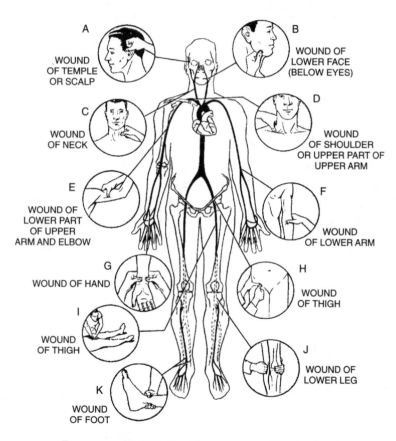

Pressure Points for Temporary Control of Arterial Bleeding

Arm or Leg Wound

Use the casualty's first-aid dressing; remove it from the wrapper and pull the dressing open with the white side down. Place the dressing directly over the wound without touching the sterile white side of the dressing. Wrap both tails of the dressing around the injured limb in opposite directions until the edges of the dressing are sealed. Leave enough tail for a knot. Tie the knot over the outer edge of the dressing but not directly over the wound. The dressing should be tied firmly enough to stop the bleeding, but without causing a tourniquet-like effect.

If the bleeding continues after applying field dressing, apply firm pressure with the hand over the dressing for 5 to 10 minutes, or have the casualty do it if he is conscious. Elevate the wound slightly above the heart to stop the bleeding.

If the bleeding continues, use a pressure dressing (a wad of padding or cloth). Place it directly over the wound and use a cravat or improvised dressing to wrap the padding tightly over the previously placed field dressing. Tie the ends together in a nonslip knot directly over the wound site. Continue to elevate the wound.

Place Dressing Directly Over Wound   Tie Tails Into Nonslip Knot
                                                                (Not Over Wound)

Tourniquet

If the bleeding still continues and all other measures have failed, or if the limb is severed, apply a tourniquet. A tourniquet is a constricting band placed around an arm or leg to control bleeding. A soldier whose arm or leg has been completely amputated may not be bleeding when first discovered, but a tourniquet should be applied anyway. If the pressure dressing under firm hand pressure becomes soaked with blood and the wound continues to bleed, apply a tourniquet. If left in place too long, a tourniquet can cause loss of an arm or leg. Once applied, however, it must stay in place, and the casualty must be taken to the nearest medical treatment facility as soon as possible. Do not loosen or release a tourniquet after it has been applied and the bleeding has stopped.

In the absence of a specially designed tourniquet, one can be made from strong, pliable material such as gauze or muslin bandages, clothing, or kerchiefs. An improvised tourniquet is used with a rigid sticklike object. To minimize skin damage, ensure that the improvised tourniquet is at least 2 inches wide. Place the tourniquet around the limb, between the wound and the body trunk (or between the wound and the heart). Place the tourniquet 2 to 4 inches from the edge of the wound site. Never place it directly over a wound or fracture or directly on a joint (wrist, elbow, or knee). For wounds just below a joint, place the tourniquet just above and as close to the joint as possible. The tourniquet should have padding underneath. If possible, place the tourniquet over the smoothed sleeve or trouser leg to prevent the skin from being pinched or twisted. If the tourniquet is long enough, wrap it around the limb several times, keeping the material as flat as possible. Damaging the skin may deprive the surgeon of skin required to cover an amputation. Protection of the skin also reduces pain.

1. Tourniquet placed 2 to 4 inches above wound

2. Rigid object on top of half knot

3. Full knot over rigid object

4. Twist the stick and align it lengthwise with the limb

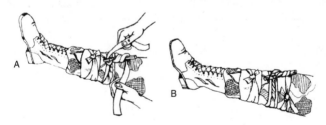

5. Free ends looped and tied off

Applying a Tourniquet

Open Abdominal Wound

Position the Casualty
Place and maintain the casualty on his back with his knees in an upright (flexed) position, unless other wounds prevent such action. The knees-up position helps relieve pain, assists in the treatment of shock, prevents further exposure of the bowel (intestines) or abdominal organs, and helps relieve abdominal pressure by allowing the abdominal muscles to relax.

Expose the Wound
Remove the casualty's loose clothing to expose the wound. However, *do not* attempt to remove clothing that is stuck to the wound; it may cause further injury. Gently pick up any organs that may be on the ground. Do this with a clean, dry dressing or with the cleanest available material. Place the organs on top of the casualty's abdomen.

Apply the Field Dressing
If the field dressing is not large enough to cover the entire wound, the plastic wrapper from the dressing may be used to cover the wound first (placing the field dressing on top). If necessary, other improvised dressings may be made from clothing, blankets, or the cleanest materials available. Field dressings can be covered with improvised reinforcement material (cravats, strips of torn T-shirt, or other cloth), if available, for additional support and protection.

   Do not give casualties with abdominal wounds food or water, although moistening the lips is allowed.

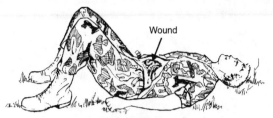

1. Place the casualty on his back with knees flexed

2. Before applying dressings, carefully place protruding organs near the wound to protect them and control contamination

3. Dressing applied and tails tied with nonslip knot (side of wound)

4. Field dressing covered with improvised material and loosely tied (opposite side)

Open Abdominal Wound

Open Chest Wound

Expose the Wound
Follow the same procedure as for an open abdominal wound. Expose the wound. Listen for sucking sounds to determine if the chest wall is punctured. If there is an object extending from (impaled in) the wound, *do not* remove it. Apply a dressing around the object and use additional improvised bulky materials or dressings (use the cleanest materials available) to build up the area around the object. Apply a supporting bandage over the bulky materials to hold them in place.

Dress the Wound
The field dressing plastic wrapper is used with the field dressing to create an airtight seal. If a plastic wrapper is not available or if an additional wound needs to be treated, cellophane, foil, the casualty's poncho, or similar material may be used. The covering should be wide enough to extend 2 inches or more beyond the edges of the wound in all directions.

1. Open chest wound sealed with plastic wrapper

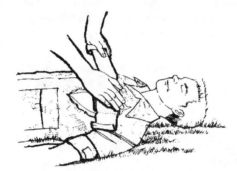

2. Field dressing placed on plastic wrapper

3. Tails of dressing tied into nonslip knot over center of dressing

Open Chest Wound

5. SHOCK

Signs of shock are sweaty but cool (clammy) skin, paleness of skin, rest-lessness or nervousness, thirst, loss of blood, confusion, faster than normal breathing rate, blotchy or bluish skin, especially around the mouth, and nausea and/or vomiting.

In the field, the procedures to treat shock are identical to those used to prevent shock:

* Move the casualty to cover.
* Lay the casualty on his back. If shock occurs after a heart attack, chest wound, or breathing difficulty, the casualty may breathe easier in a sitting position. If this is the case, allow him to sit upright, but monitor him carefully in case his condition worsens.
* Elevate the casualty's feet higher than the level of his heart.
* Loosen clothing at the neck, waist, or wherever it may be binding.
* Prevent chilling or overheating.
* Calm the casualty.

Do not give a shock casualty any food or drink. If you must leave the casualty or if he is unconscious, turn his head to the side to prevent him from choking should he vomit.

6. FRACTURES

Signs of a broken bone include tenderness over the injury with pain on movement, inability to move the injured part, unnatural shape, swelling, and discoloration of the skin. All these signs may or may not be present with a fracture; if you are not sure, give the patient the benefit of the doubt and treat it as a fracture.

Handle with care. Prevent shock and further injury. Broken ends of bone can cut nerves, blood vessels, and so on. Do not move the patient unless necessary. If he must be moved, splint the fracture first.

If there is a wound, apply dressing as for any other wound. If there is bleeding, it must be stopped. If a tourniquet is necessary, do not place it over the site of the fracture. If time permits, improvise splints (sticks, blankets, poncho, and the like); if a weapon is used for a splint, unload it first. Pad splints well with soft material to prevent pressure and rubbing. The splint should extend from above the joint above the fracture to below the joint below the fracture. Bind splints securely at several points, but not so tightly as to interfere with blood flow (check pulse).

One of the quickest ways to splint a broken leg is by tying it to the uninjured leg (do not use narrow materials such as wire). Use padding between the legs, and tie at several points above and below the break. Tie the feet together.

Support a fracture of the arm or shoulder with a sling (do not try to bend an injured elbow if it is straight).

Back and Neck
Check for signs or symptoms of a back or neck injury, such as pain or tenderness, cuts or bruises, numbness, and inability to move (paralysis). Look for unusual body or limb position. Unless there is immediate life-threatening danger, *do not* move a casualty who has a suspected back or neck injury. Movement may cause permanent paralysis or death.

Spinal Column Fractures
If a casualty does not have any feeling in his legs and cannot move them, he has a severe back injury that should be treated as a fracture. If the casualty is lying faceup, slip a blanket or other like material under the arch of his back to support the spinal column in a swayback position. If he is lying facedown, *do not* put anything under any part of his body.

If the casualty must be transported to a safe location and is in a faceup position, transport him by litter or use a firm substitute. Loosely tie the casualty's wrists together over his waistline and his feet together to avoid accidental shifting of the body. Lay a folded blanket or substitute across the litter

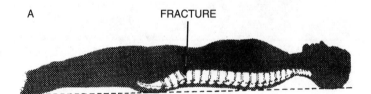

A   FRACTURE

In this position, bone fragments may bruise or cut the spinal cord

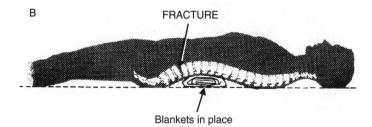

B   FRACTURE

Blankets in place

Broken Back

where the arch in the back is to be placed. Use a four-man team and place the casualty on the litter without bending his spinal column or his neck. If the casualty is in a facedown position, he must be transported in this same position. Keep the spinal column in a swayback position, and use a blanket or substitute placed on the litter where the chest will be placed to maintain this position.

Neck Fractures

A fractured neck is extremely dangerous. Moving the casualty may cause death. *Leave him in the position in which he is found.* If his neck or head is in an abnormal position, immediately immobilize the neck and head. If he is lying faceup, raise his shoulders slightly, and slip a roll of cloth that has the bulk of a bath towel under his neck. The roll should be thick enough to arch his neck only slightly, leaving the back of his head on the ground. Place heavy objects such as rocks or the casualty's boots on each side of his head to immobilize it. If it is necessary to use boots, fill them with stones, gravel, sand, or dirt and tie them tightly at the top. *Do not* move the casualty in any way or place any objects under his neck if he is lying facedown.

Casualty with roll of cloth (bulk) under neck
and boots used to immobilize head

Broken Neck

7. BURNS

Look carefully for reddened, blistered, or charred skin; also check for singed clothing. If burns are found, stop the evaluation and begin treatment.

Minor burns (no charring or blistering) of small skin areas should be covered with a first-aid packet or other dry, sterile dressing. Otherwise, leave them uncovered.

If a burn is severe (blistered or charred or covers a large area of body), infection and shock must be prevented. Cover the burned area with a dry, sterile dressing. Do not touch the burn with anything but sterile dressings, except in the case of mass casualties. Then cover their burns with clean sheets, T-shirts, and the like. Leave a severe burn uncovered only as a last resort. Do not place the dressing over the face or genital area. Do not pull clothes over the burned area, try to remove pieces of cloth sticking to skin, try to clean the burned area, break a burn blister, or put grease, Vaseline, or ointment on a burn.

Prevent shock by placing the casualty's head and shoulders lower than the rest of the body and by replacing body fluids. If the casualty is conscious, is not vomiting, and has no belly wound, give small amounts of cool or cold water. Give a few sips every few minutes; increase amounts until one-third of a canteen cupful is drunk every hour. If the casualty vomits or acts as if he might, do not give him anymore water. Do not use warm water, which can cause vomiting.

8. HEAD INJURY

A head injury may be opened or closed. In open injuries, there is a visible wound and the brain may be seen. In closed injuries, no visible injury is seen, but the casualty may experience the same signs and symptoms. If you suspect a severe head injury, evaluate the casualty for loss of consciousness, nausea or vomiting, convulsions, slurred speech and confusion, sleepiness, dizziness, clear or bloody fluid leaking from the ear or nose, headache, paralysis, black eyes, or other obvious signs.

The casualty should be continuously monitored for the development of conditions that might require basic lifesaving measures. Treat the injury as a suspected neck or spinal injury until proved otherwise. Place a dressing over the wounded area, and keep the casualty warm. Place the casualty in a position with the head slightly elevated if there is no accumulation of fluid or blood in the casualty's throat. When there is bleeding from the mouth and throat, place the casualty on his side or face so the blood can run out of the mouth. Remove all foreign objects and false teeth from unconscious casualties.

Jaw Wounds

Before applying a bandage to a casualty's jaw, remove all foreign material from the mouth. If the casualty is unconscious, check for obstructions in the airway. When applying the bandage, allow the jaw enough freedom to permit passage of air and drainage from the mouth. If the casualty is unconscious, place him on his belly or side with the head lower than the body and turned slightly to one side.

MISCELLANEOUS INJURIES

FOREIGN BODIES

In the Eye
Do not rub eye. Tears frequently flush out the particle. If not, pull the eyelid up or down and attempt to remove the particle with the corner of a moist, clean handkerchief. If unsuccessful, or if the foreign body is glass or metal, blindfold both eyes and evacuate to medical facilities.

In the Ear, Nose, or Throat
Never probe for a foreign object in the ear or nose. A live insect in the ear may be removed by attracting it with a flashlight or by pouring water into the ear to drown it and flush it out. Do not attempt to flush a foreign object out of the ear with water if the object will swell when wet.

Remove foreign objects from the nose by blowing.

Coughing frequently dislodges a foreign object from the throat. If this fails and the object can be reached, try to remove it with the fingers, but be careful not to push it deeper.

HEAT INJURIES
Heat injuries are disabling to varying degrees and can be fatal. They occur when water and salt lost in sweat are not replaced. Heat injuries are especially liable to occur in individuals who are not acclimatized (accustomed) to the heat and in those who are overweight, have fevers (sunburn, infection, reaction to immunizations), or are already dehydrated (have insufficient water in their bodies) because of diarrhea, alcohol consumption, or simply not having drunk enough water.

Sweating
The evaporation of sweat is the only way the body can cool itself when the temperature is above 95° Fahrenheit; evaporation is less efficient and more water intake is required, in the humid jungle than in the dry desert. More than 3 gallons of water and salt may be lost and need to be replaced by soldiers working hard in the heat.

Water
It's best to replace water as it is lost—soldiers should drink when thirsty. There is no benefit in withholding water until later. It is impossible to train soldiers to get by on less water than the amount required to replace that lost in sweat. Water requirements can be reduced only if sweating is reduced by working during the cooler hours of evening, night, and early morning.

Salt
Extra salt is required when soldiers are sweating heavily. Salt tablets should *not* be used to prevent heat injury, however. Usually, eating field rations or liberal salting of the garrison diet provides enough salt to replace what is lost.

Heat Cramps
Heat cramps are cramps of the muscles of the belly, arms, or legs. They occur when a person sweats a lot and has not consumed extra water.

Heat Exhaustion
The victim of heat exhaustion may have a headache and be dizzy, faint, and weak. He has cool, pale (gray), moist (sweaty) skin and loss of appetite. Move him to a shady area or improvise shade and have him lie down. Loosen or remove clothing and boots, pour water on him, and fan him if it is hot. Elevate his legs, and have him slowly drink at least one canteen of water. The patient should not participate in further strenuous activity and should be evacuated if symptoms persist.

Heatstroke
Heatstroke is a medical emergency and can be fatal if not treated promptly and correctly. It is caused by failure of the body's cooling mechanisms. Inadequate sweating is a factor. The casualty's skin is flushed, hot, and dry. He may experience dizziness, confusion, headaches, seizures, and nausea, and his respiration and pulse may be weak. Cool the casualty immediately by moving him to a shaded area; remove outer clothing, pour water on him or immerse him in water, and fan him to permit the cooling effect of evaporation. Massage his skin, elevate his legs, and have him slowly drink water. Get him to a medical facility as soon as possible.

COLD INJURIES
Cold injuries are caused when the body loses heat. They can cause the loss of toes, fingers, feet, ears, and so on.

Frostbite

If body heat is lost quickly and the tissues actually freeze, the injury is called frostbite. Frostbite usually affects the face, hands, or feet. There may be no pain. Frostbitten parts of the body become grayish or white and lose feeling. Use a buddy system to keep watch on one another for signs of frostbite.

Treat frostbite by removing the casualty's clothing (boots, gloves, socks) and thawing the area by placing it next to a warm part of his or somebody else's body. Warm (not hot) water may be used. Remove constrictive clothing that interferes with circulation. Do not rewarm by walking, massage, exposure to open fire, cold water, or rubbing with snow. After the part has been warmed, protect it from further injury by covering it lightly with a blanket or dry clothing. Do not use ointments or other medications.

Trenchfoot (Immersion Foot)

Trenchfoot or immersion foot resembles frostbite but occurs when the feet are exposed to cold and wet conditions. (See the section on Foot Care.)

Prevention of Cold Injuries

Cold injuries can be prevented by proper leadership and by training in conserving body heat.

Leadership—command interest—is essential. Personnel must be taught how to prevent cold injuries. Reduce their exposure to cold, wet, and wind when possible. Rotate individuals and units to warming tents. Provide changes of dry clothing, hot food, and drinks.

Individuals can take the following steps:

- Do not stand in wet positions—build them up with branches and the like.
- Carry extra dry socks, and change after marching or standing.
- Remove cold and wet boots and socks before going to sleep.
- Sleep back to back with a buddy to prevent loss of body heat.
- Massage the feet several times daily, especially when changing socks.
- Do not touch bare metal with bare skin.

To dress properly, remember C-O-L-D:

C: Keep *clean*. Dirty clothing has less insulating quality.

O: Avoid *overheating*. Overheating causes sweating, and clothing wet from sweat causes cold injury.

L: Wear *loose* and in *layers*. Warm air is trapped between layers and acts as insulation. Tight clothing, boots, and gloves leave no room for a warm air layer or for the exercise of fingers and toes and may act as a tourniquet to shut off circulation.

D: Keep *dry.* Dry clothing retains heat; wet clothing conducts heat away from the body.

SNAKEBITES

Keep the bitten person quiet, and do not let him walk or run. Kill the snake, if possible, and keep it for identification. If the bite is on an extremity, do not elevate the limb; keep it level with the body. If the bite is on an arm or leg, place a constricting band (narrow gauze bandage) one to two finger widths above and below the bite. If the bite is on a hand or foot, place the band above the wrist or ankle.

The band should be tight enough to stop the flow of blood near the skin, but not so tight as to interfere with circulation. It should not have a tourniquet-like effect. Get the casualty to medical treatment as soon as possible.

FOOT CARE

Socks

Wash and dry socks daily. Start each day with a fresh pair. After crossing a wet area, dry your feet, put on foot powder, and change socks if the situation permits. Avoid worn or tight-fitting socks. Carry an extra pair in a pack or inside the shirt.

Blisters

Wash the area, open the blister, drain, and cover with adhesive tape.

Athlete's Foot

Keep feet clean and dry. Use foot powder.

16

Reporting Enemy Information

Commanders get information about the enemy from many sources, but the individual soldier is their best source. You can collect information from the following other sources:

- Prisoners of war (PWs)
- Captured documents
- Enemy activity
- Local civilians

WHAT TO REPORT

Report all information about the enemy to your leader quickly, *accurately,* and *completely.* Such reports should answer the questions who, what, where, and when. It is best to use the SALUTE format (size, activity, location, unit, time, and equipment) when reporting. Use notes and draw sketches as aids in remembering details.

Size

Report the number of soldiers and vehicles you saw. For example, report: "ten enemy infantrymen" (not "a rifle squad") or "three enemy tanks" (not "an enemy tank platoon").

Activity

Report what you saw the enemy doing—for example, "emplacing mines in the road."

Location

Report where you saw the enemy. If you have a map, try to give a six-digit coordinate, such as "GL567345." If you do not have a map, related the location to some key terrain feature, such as "on the Hann Road, about 300 meters south of the Kelly River bridge."

Unit

If the enemy's unit is not known, report any distinctive features, such as bumper markings on trucks or type of headgear. Some armies have distinctive uniforms and headgear, or colored tabs on their uniforms, to identify types of units. A unit's action may also indicate its type. The kind of equipment observed may me peculiar to a certain type of unit. For example, a BRDM may indicate a reconnaissance unit.

Time

Report the time you saw the enemy activity, not the time you report it. Always report local or Zulu times.

Equipment

Report all of the equipment the enemy is wearing or using. If you do not recognize an item of equipment or a type of vehicle, sketch it and submit the sketch with the report

The following is an example of a SALUTE report:

"Combat OP sighted four enemy tanks moving west along secondary road at grid NB612297 at 241730Z. Tanks traveling at approximately 5 KMH. Hatches are open, and visible enemy personnel are wearing protective masks."

PRISONERS OF WAR (PW) AND CAPTURED DOCUMENTS

Enemy prisoners of war (EPW) are a good source of information. They must be handled without breaking international law and without losing a chance to gain intelligence. Treat EPWs humanely. Do not harm them either physically or mentally. Do not give them candy, cigarettes, or other comfort items. EPWs who receive favors or are mistreated are poor interrogation subjects. In handling PWs, follow the five Ss:

- *Search* EPWs as soon as they are captured. Take their weapons and papers, except identification cards and protective masks. Give them a written receipt for any personal property and documents taken. When searching an EPW, have one may guard him while another searches him. A searcher must not get between the guard and the PW. To search a PW, have him spread-eagle against a tree or wall, or get him into a push-up position with his knees on the ground.
- *Segregate* PWs into groups by sex and into subgroups such as officers, enlisted, civilians, and political figures. This keeps the leaders from organizing escape efforts.

- *Silence* PWs and do not let them talk to each other. This keeps them from planning escapes and cautioning each other on security. Report anything an EPW says or does.
- *Speed* PWs to the rear. Turn them over to your leader. He or she will assemble them and move them to the rear for questioning by the S2.
- *Safeguard* PWs when taking them to the rear. Do not let anyone abuse them. Watch out for escape attempts. Do not let EPWs bunch up, spread out too far, or start diversions.

Identification
Before evacuating an EPW, attach a tag to him showing the date and time of capture, place, capturing unit, and circumstances.

Handling Captured Documents and Equipment
Enemy documents and equipment are good sources of information. Documents may be official (maps, orders, records, photos) or personal (letters, diaries).

If such items are not handled properly, the information in them may become outdated. Give them to your leader quickly. Tag each item with information on when and where it was captured; if it was found on a PW, include the PW's name on the tag.

17

Individual
Movement and Security

Use proper movement techniques and security measures to avoid contact with the enemy when you are not prepared for contact.

MOVEMENT SKILLS
Observe the following practices during movement:
- Camouflage yourself and your equipment.
- Tape your dog tags to each other and to the chain to prevent rattle. Tape or pad loose parts of your weapon and equipment so they do not rattle or get snagged. Jump up and down. Listen for rattles.
- Do not carry unnecessary equipment.
- Stop, look, and listen before moving. Be especially alert when birds or animals are alarmed (the enemy may be nearby). Look for your next position before leaving a position. Look for covered and concealed routes on which to move.
- Change direction from time to time when moving through tall grass.
- Use battlefield noises to conceal your movement noises.
- Cross roads and trails at places that have the most cover and concealment (large culverts, low spots, curves, or bridges).
- Avoid steep slopes and places with loose dirt or stones.
- Avoid cleared, open areas and tops of hills and ridges.

MOVEMENT METHODS

Low Crawl
The low crawl gives you the lowest silhouette. Use it to cross places where the concealment is very low and enemy observation prevents you from getting up. Keep your body flat against the ground. Grasp your weapon at the

upper sling swivel with your firing hand. Let the front handguard rest on your forearm and the weapon butt drag on the ground. Push your arms forward, and pull your firing-side leg forward. Then pull with your arms and push with your leg.

High Crawl
The high crawl lets you move faster and still gives you a low silhouette. Use it when there is good concealment but enemy fire prevents you from getting up. Keep your body off the ground and resting on your forearms and lower legs. Cradle your weapon in your arms, and keep its muzzle off the ground. Alternately advance your right elbow and left knee, then your left elbow and right knee.

Rush
The rush is the fastest way to move from one position to another. Rushes are kept short to keep enemy machine gunners or riflemen from tracking you. Each rush should last from three to five seconds, but don't hit the ground just because five seconds have passed—always have cover picked out before moving for your next rush, and get behind it. If you have been firing from one position, the enemy may have spotted you and may be waiting for you to come up from cover. So before rushing, roll or crawl a short distance from your position.

STEALTH
To move with stealth, use the following procedures:
1. Hold your rifle at port arms (ready position).
2. While stepping, make your footing sure and solid by keeping your body's weight on the leading foot.
3. Raise the moving leg high to clear brush or grass.
4. Gently let the moving foot down toe first, with your body's weight on the rear leg.
5. Lower the heel of the moving foot after the toe is in a solid place.
6. Shift your body's weight and balance to the forward foot before moving the rear foot.
7. Take short steps to help maintain balance.

NIGHT MOVEMENT
When moving through dense vegetation, avoid making noise. Hold your weapon in one hand and keep the other hand forward, feeling for obstructions.

When going into the prone position:
1. Hold your rifle with one hand, and crouch slowly.
2. Feel the ground with your free hand to make sure it is clear of mines, trip wires, or other hazards.
3. Lower your knees one at a time, until your body's weight is on both knees and your free hand.
4. Shift your weight to your free hand and opposite knee.
5. Raise your free leg up and back, and lower it gently to that side.
6. Roll quietly into a prone position.

When crawling at night:
1. Crawl on your hands and knees.
2. Hold your rifle in your firing hand.
3. Use your nonfiring hand to feel for and make clear spots for your hands and knees to move to.
4. Move your hands and knees to those spots, and put them down softly.

FLARES

If you are caught in the light of a ground flare, move quickly out of the lighted area. The enemy knows where the flare is and will be ready to fire into that area. Move well away from the lighted area, and look for other team members. If you hear the firing of an aerial flare while you are moving, hit the ground (behind cover, if possible) while the flare is rising and before it illuminates the area.

The sudden light of a flare may temporarily blind both you and the enemy. To protect your night vision, close one eye while the flare is burning.

If you are caught in the light of an aerial flare and you can easily blend with the background (in a forest), freeze in place until the flare burns out. If caught in the open, immediately crouch low or lie down.

SECURITY MEASURES

The enemy must not get information about your operations. This means that you and your fellow soldiers must do the following:
- Practice camouflage principles and techniques.
- Practice noise and light discipline.
- Practice field sanitation.
- Use proper radiotelephone procedures.
- Use the challenge and password properly.
- Not take personal letters or pictures into combat areas.
- Not keep diaries in combat areas.

- Be careful when discussing military affairs.
- Use only authorized codes.
- Abide by the Code of Conduct.
- Report any soldier or civilian who is believed to be serving or sympathetic with the enemy.
- Report anyone who tries to get information about U.S. operations.
- Destroy all maps or important documents if capture is imminent.

SURVIVAL

Continuous operations and fast-moving battles increase your chances of becoming separated from your unit. Your mission is to rejoin your unit. Survival is the action of staying alive in the field with limited resources. You must survive when you become separated from your unit, are evading the enemy, or are a prisoner.

Evasion

Evasion is the action you take to stay out of the hands of the enemy. There are several courses of action you may take:

- You may stay in your current position and wait for friendly troops to find you. This may be a good course of action if you are sure that friendly troops will continue to operate in the area, and if there are a lot of enemy units in the area.
- You may break out to a friendly area. This may be a good course of action if you know where a friendly area is, and if the enemy is widely dispersed.
- You may move farther into enemy territory to temporarily conduct guerrilla-type operations. This is a short-term course of action to be taken only when other courses of action are not feasible. This may be a good course of action when the enemy area is known to be lightly held or when there is a good chance of linking up with friendly guerrillas.
- You may combine two or more of the above. For example, you may stay in your current area until the enemy moves out of the area and then break out to a friendly area.

Enemy

There may be times when you will have to kill, stun, or capture an enemy soldier without alerting other enemy in the area. At such times, a rifle or pistol makes too much noise, and you will need a silent weapon. Some silent weapons are the bayonet, the garotte (a choke wire or cord with handles), and improvised clubs.

RESISTANCE

The Code of Conduct (at the end of this chapter) is an expression of the ideals and principles that traditionally have guided and strengthened American servicemembers. It prescribes the manner in which every soldier of the United States Armed Forces must conduct himself when captured or faced with the possibility of capture. You should never surrender of your own free will. Likewise, a leader should never surrender the soldiers under his command while they still have the means to resist. If captured, you must continue to resist in every way you can, remembering the following:

- Make every effort to escape and help others to escape.
- Do not accept special favors from the enemy.
- Do not give your word not to escape.
- Do nothing that will harm a fellow prisoner.
- Give no information except name, rank, social security number, and date of birth.
- Do not answer any questions other than those concerning your name, rank, social security number, and date of birth.

ESCAPE

Escape is the action you take to get away from the enemy if you are captured. The best time for you to escape is right after you are captured. You will probably be in your best physical condition at that time. The following are other reasons for making an early escape:

- Friendly fire or air strikes may cause enough confusion and disorder to provide a chance of escape.
- The first guards you have probably will not be as well trained as guards farther back.
- Some of the first guards may be walking wounded who are distracted by their own condition.
- You know something about the area where you are captured and may know the location of nearby friendly units.

The way you escape depends on what you can think of to fit the situation. The only general rules are to escape early and escape when the enemy is distracted.

Once you escape, it may not be easy to contact friendly troops, even when you know where they are. You should contact a friendly unit as you would if you were a member of a lost patrol. Time your movement so that you pass through enemy units at night and arrive at a friendly unit at dawn. A good way to make contact is to find a ditch or shallow hole to hide in where you have cover from both friendly and enemy fire. At dawn, attract the attention of the friendly unit by an action such as waving a white cloth, shouting, or showing a panel. When the friendly unit has been alerted, shout who you are and what your situation is, and ask for permission to move toward the unit.

NIGHT VISION EQUIPMENT

Poor visibility adds to command and control problems. Modern technology has produced devices that soldiers can use to reduce the effects of limited visibility. Reconnaissance, surveillance, and target acquisition (RSTA) devices available in a Bradley-equipped platoon include the following:

AN/PVS-4 Individual Weapon Night Vision Device. A small, lightweight, image-intensification device used on the M16A1 rifle. It can also be handheld. It is a 3.8X telescopic device and has a range of 400 meters in starlight and 600 meters in moonlight.

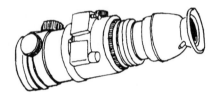

AN/PVS-4

AN/PVS-5 Night Vision Goggles. This is both an active and a passive night vision device worn on the head. It has a built-in infrared light source for close-up viewing within 2 meters. This mode can be used to read maps, orders, and overlays or for vehicle maintenance. The goggles have a range of 150 meters in the passive mode.

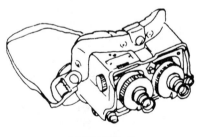

AN/PVS-5

AN/PVS-7A and AN/ PVS-7B Night Vision Systems. The AN/PVS-7A and AN/ PVS-7B are self-contained night vision systems worn on the head or handheld. They provide improved night vision capabilities using available light from the sky and moonlight. The goggles enable the user to perform normal tasks such as reading, walking, driving, or surveillance during times of darkness. The goggles may be used with or without the standard battle helmet and provide capabilities for all infantry tasks. The head harnesses differ slightly. The 7B version has some improvements over the 7A version. The 7A version has an effective range of 100 meters, and the 7B version has an effective range of 300 meters under optimal conditions.

AN/PVS-7

AN/TAS-5 Dragon Thermal Night Vision Sight. This is a passive thermal imagery system with a range of 1,200 meters.

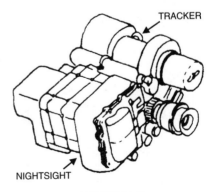

TRACKER

NIGHTSIGHT

AN/TAS-5

AN/VVS-2 Night Vision Driver's Viewer. This image-intensification device is mounted in the Bradley driver's station and has a range in excess of 150 meters. It can observe rounds fired from the 25-mm gun and the 7.62-mm coaxial machine gun out to greater ranges.

AN/VVS-2

Integrated Sight Unit (ISU). The ISU is a thermal imagery sight on the Bradley with 4X and 12X magnification.

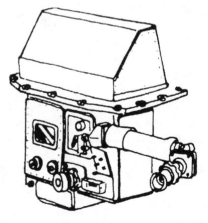

ISU Periscope

CODE OF CONDUCT
For Members of the Armed Forces of the United States

1. I am an American, fighting in the forces which guard my country and our way of life. I am prepared to give my life in their defense.
2. I will never surrender of my own free will. If in command, I will never surrender the members of my command while they still have means to resist.
3. If I am captured I will continue to resist by all means available. I will make every effort to escape and aid others to escape. I will accept neither parole nor special favors from the enemy.
4. If I become a prisoner of war, I will keep faith with my fellow prisoners. I will give no information or take part in any action which might be harmful to my comrades. If I am senior, I will take command. If not, I will obey the lawful order of those appointed over me and will back them up in every way.
5. When questioned, should I become a prisoner of war, I am required to give name, rank, service number, and date of birth. I will evade answering further questions to the utmost of my ability. I will make no oral or written statements disloyal to my country and its allies or harmful to their cause.
6. I will never forget that I am an American, fighting for freedom, responsible for my actions, and dedicated to the principles which made my country free. I will trust in my God and in the United States of America.

18

NBC (Nuclear, Biological, Chemical) Warfare

Avoidance is the most important fundamental of NBC defense, because the best way to survive is to avoid being the object of a chemical or nuclear attack. Avoiding contaminated areas minimizes the risk of additional casualties; it also prevents the degradation of combat power that results when a unit must operate in mission-oriented protective posture (MOPP) level 3 or 4 for extended periods. In addition, the unit is not required to spend the time and resources needed for decontamination. Contamination avoidance measures include using passive avoidance techniques, locating contaminated areas, identifying NBC agents, warning other members of the company team as well as other units, and reporting NBC threats to higher headquarters.

MARKING CONTAMINATION
When contamination is found, it must be marked to prevent other soldiers from being exposed, and then reported. The only exception to marking an area is if the marking would help the enemy avoid contamination. If this exception is approved by the commander, the contaminated area must still be reported. When marking an area, place the markers facing away from the contamination. Markers are placed at roads, trails, and other likely points of entry.

PASSING ALARMS AND SIGNALS
The vocal alarm for any chemical or biological hazard or attack is the word "gas." The person giving the alarm stops breathing, masks, and shouts "Gas" as loudly as possible. Everyone hearing this immediately masks and passes the alarm.

NBC MARKERS

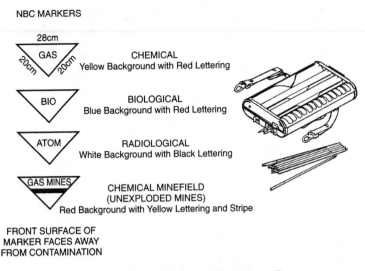

GAS   CHEMICAL
Yellow Background with Red Lettering

BIO   BIOLOGICAL
Blue Background with Red Lettering

ATOM   RADIOLOGICAL
White Background with Black Lettering

GAS MINES   CHEMICAL MINEFIELD
(UNEXPLODED MINES)
Red Background with Yellow Lettering and Stripe

FRONT SURFACE OF
MARKER FACES AWAY
FROM CONTAMINATION

NBC Contamination Marking Set

The first person to hear or see the M8 automatic chemical alarm sound or flash also stops breathing, masks, and yells "Gas."

The all-clear signal is given by word of mouth through the chain of command. The signal is given by leaders after testing for contamination proves negative.

PROTECTING AGAINST NBC ATTACKS

Hardening includes all the things you can do to make yourself more resistant to enemy strikes. Foxholes and bunkers, tanks, and other armored vehicles provide protection. Existing natural and man-made terrain features, such as caves, ditches, ravines, culverts, overpasses, and tunnels, can be used as expedient shelters.

MISSION-ORIENTED PROTECTIVE POSTURE (MOPP)

MOPP is the use of protective clothing and equipment. Wearing MOPP gear can cause heat and mental stress and reduce your efficiency. The leader weighs the needs of individual protection against unit efficiency. Leaders use standard MOPP levels to increase or decrease protection.

MOPP Zero

The protective mask, skin decontamination kit, and detector papers are carried. The overgarment, overboots, chemical protective helmet cover, and gloves are stowed nearby.

MOPP 1

The overgarment is worn. M9 paper is affixed to the overgarment, and the chemical protective helmet cover is worn.

MOPP 2

Add the overboots to MOPP 1.

MOPP 3

The protective mask and hood are added.

MOPP 4

A pair of rubber gloves and cotton liners are put on. The overgarment is closed, and the hood is pulled down and adjusted.

Mask Only

This is not a MOPP level. Only the mask with hood is worn. All exposed skin must be covered with ordinary clothing.

NUCLEAR ATTACK

An enemy nuclear attack rarely is preceded by a warning. The first indication will be a flash of intense light and heat. Initial radiation comes with the light. Blast and hurricane-like winds follow within seconds. There will be a short time to take action, as follows:

- Drop down immediately in a prone, head-on position.
- Protect your exposed skin areas, especially your eyes, face, neck, and hands, which are vulnerable to injury from the dust, sand, and debris blown by the blast wave. Stay down until the blast wave passes in both directions.
- If you are in a tank or other armored vehicle, brace yourself. Stay buttoned up.
- If you are in a building or other shelter, drop to the floor. Get under a desk or table, and keep out of the way of doors and windows. Broken glass fragments flying through the air are dangerous.
- Get out of a wheeled vehicle. You will be safer lying prone than inside a wheeled vehicle.

- If flying in an aircraft, land. If a suitable landing area is not available or dazzle effects prevent landing, turn the aircraft away from the blast and initiate a full-power climb.

Characteristics of Nuclear Explosions

The following are characteristics of nuclear explosions.

Blast

Blast produces an intense shock wave and high winds that create flying debris. It may collapse shelters and some fighting positions.

Thermal Radiation

Thermal radiation (heat and light) causes burns and starts fires. The bright flash at the time of the explosion can cause a temporary loss of vision or permanent eye damage if you look at the explosion, especially at night.

Nuclear Radiation

Nuclear radiation can cause casualties and delay movements. It may last for days and cover large areas of terrain. It occurs in two stages, initial and residual:

1. *Initial radiation* is emitted directly from the fireball in the first minute after the explosion. It travels at the speed of light along straight lines and has high penetrating power.
2. *Residual radiation* lingers after the first minute. It comes from the radioactive material originally in a nuclear weapon or from material, such as soil and equipment, made radioactive by the explosion.

Electromagnetic pulse (EMP)

EMP is a massive surge of electrical power. It is created the instant a nuclear detonation occurs and is transmitted at the speed of light in all directions. It can damage solid-state components of electrical equipment (radios, radars, and so forth). Equipment can be protected by disconnecting it from its power source and placing it in or behind some type of shielding material (armored vehicle or dirt wall) out of the line of sight to the explosion. If no warning is received prior to a burst, there is no effective means of protecting operating equipment.

Effects on Soldiers

Exposure of the human body to nuclear radiation causes damage to the cells in all parts of the body. The damage is the cause of "radiation sickness." The early symptoms of radiation sickness usually appear one to six hours after exposure. These symptoms may include headache, nausea, vomiting, and diarrhea. There is no first aid once someone has been exposed to nuclear radiation. The only help is to get as comfortable as possible while experiencing the early symptoms. If the radiation dose was small, the symptoms will probably go away and not recur. If the symptoms recur, go to an aid station.

Effects on Equipment and Supplies

Blast can crush sealed or partly sealed objects such as food cans, barrels, fuel tanks, and helicopters. Rubble from crumbling buildings can bury supplies and equipment. Heat can ignite dry wood, fuel, tarps, and other flammable material. Nuclear radiation can contaminate food and water.

Post-strike Actions

Take the following actions after a nuclear explosion:
- Assess the situation—how to repair and reinforce your position, assist casualties, improve protection against fallout.
- Put out fires before they can spread.
- Check weapons systems—they may be unserviceable because of sand or dirt blown into them. Field stripping and cleaning may be required before firing.
- Cover foxholes and shelter openings against fallout (a shelter half will do).
- Use MOPP gear to keep fallout off your skin and out of your body.

CHEMICAL AND BIOLOGICAL WEAPONS

Enemy forces have both chemical and biological weapons. These weapons may be used separately or together, with or without nuclear weapons. Regardless of how they are used, you must be able to survive an attack.

Characteristics

Chemical agents are like poisonous pesticides but are far more powerful. They are meant to kill or injure you and are released to cover large areas. They may be released as gases, liquids, or sprays. The enemy may use a mixture of agents to cause confusion and casualties. Artillery, rockets, mortars, aircraft bombs, and land mines can deliver the agents.

Biological agents are disease-producing germs. They create a disease hazard where none exists naturally. They may be dispersed as sprays by generators or delivered by explosives, bomblets, missiles, or aircraft. They may also be spread by the release of germ-carrying flies, mosquitoes, fleas, and ticks. The U.S. Army does not employ these agents, but other armies may. Toxins are poisonous substances produced by living things (such as snake venom). Toxins are not living things, and in this sense they are chemicals. They would be used in combat in the same way as chemical-warfare agents, and they may disable or kill without warning.

Effects on Equipment
Chemical and biological agents have little direct effect on equipment. Liquid chemical agents can restrict the use of equipment until it is decontaminated.

Effects on Terrain
Liquid agents may restrict the use of buildings. Because it is difficult to decontaminate terrain, it is best to wait for the weather to decontaminate terrain naturally. Bypass contaminated areas if not wearing protective clothing.

Effects on Soldiers
Chemical and biological agents may enter your body through your eyes, nose, mouth, or skin. They can disable or kill.

Liquid agents may be dispersed on you, your equipment, the terrain, and foliage. The agents may linger for days and endanger you when you are unprotected.

Biological agents are hard to detect in the early stages of use. If you find out or suspect that the enemy is using biological agents, report it to your leader.

Decontamination
Immediate decontamination is a basic soldier survival skill carried out as soon as possible after contamination is discovered. Any contact between chemical or toxic agents and bare skin should be treated as an emergency. Some agents can kill if they remain on the skin for longer than a minute. The best technique for removing or neutralizing these agents is to use the M291 skin decontamination kit. Leaders must ensure that their soldiers are trained to execute this technique automatically, without waiting for orders.

Personal decontamination (wipedown) should begin within 15 minutes of contamination. Wipedown removes or neutralizes contamination on the hood, mask, gloves, and personal weapon. For chemical and biological contamination, soldiers use mitts from the M295 individual equipment decontamination kit (IEDK). For radiological contamination, they wipe off the contamination with a cloth or simply brush or shake it away.

Operator's spraydown of equipment should begin immediately after completion of personal wipedown. The spraydown removes or neutralizes contamination on the surfaces that operators must touch to perform their missions. For chemical and biological contamination, operators can use on-board decontamination apparatuses, such as the M11/M13 or the M295 IEDK, to decontaminate surfaces to which decontaminating solution DS2 cannot be applied. Note that the DS2 itself must be washed off surfaces no more than 30 minutes after application. If necessary, use 5-gallon water cans or other water sources to assist in removing DS2. For radiological contamination, brush or scrape away the contamination with whatever is at hand or flush it with water and wipe it away.

19

Radio Sets, Procedures, and Field Antennas

Radios, a common means of communication, are particularly suited for use when you are on the move. Small handheld or backpack radios that communicate for only short distances are found at squad and platoon levels. As the need grows to talk over greater distances and to more units, the size and complexity of radios increase.

ENVIRONMENT
Factors that affect the range of radios are weather, terrain, power, antenna, and the location of the radio. Manmade objects such as bridges and buildings may affect radio transmission. Interference may also come from power lines, electrical generators, bad weather, other radio stations, and enemy jamming. You can correct many of the causes of poor radio communications by using common sense. For example, make sure you are not trying to communicate from under a steel bridge.

RULES FOR RADIO USE
Observe the following rules for radio use:
- Listen before transmitting.
- Avoid excessive radio checks.
- Make messages clear and concise. If possible, write them out before transmitting.
- Speak clearly, slowly, and in natural phrases, and enunciate each word. If the receiving operator must write, allow time for writing.
- Always assume the enemy is listening.
- If jammed, notify higher headquarters by established procedures.
- Maintain whip antennas in a vertical position.
- Make sure the radio is turned off before starting a vehicle.

PROWORDS

The following are frequently used prowords:

All After—Part of the message to which I refer is all of that which follows.

All Before—Part of the message to which I refer is all of that which precedes.

Authenticate—Station called is to reply to the challenge that follows.

Authentication Is—Transmission authentication of this message is.

Break—Indicates the separation of text from other parts of the message.

Correct—What you have transmitted is correct.

Correction—Error has been made in this transmission. Transmission will continue with the last word correctly transmitted.

I Read Back—The following is my response to your instructions to read back.

I Say Again—I am repeating transmission or part indicated.

I Spell—I shall spell the next word phonetically.

Out—This is the end of my transmission to you and no answer is required.

Over—This is the end of my transmission to you and a response is necessary. Go ahead: transmit.

Read Back—Repeat this entire transmission back to me exactly as received.

Roger—Have received your last message satisfactorily.

Say Again—Say again all of your last transmission.

Silence—Cease transmission on this net immediately. (If repeated three or more times, silence will be maintained until lifted.)

Silence Lifted—Silence is lifted (when an authentication system is in force, the transmission imposing and lifting silence is to be authenticated).

Speak Slower—You are transmitting too fast—slow down.

Wait—I must pause for a few seconds.

Wait, Out—I must pause longer than a few seconds.

Wilco—Have received your last message, understand it, and will comply.

SECURITY

Radio is one of the least secure means of communicating. Each time you talk, your voice travels in all directions. The enemy can listen to your transmissions to get information about you and your unit, or to locate your position to destroy you with artillery fire. Communications security keeps unauthorized persons from gaining information of value from radio and telephone transmissions. It includes the following:

- Using authentication to make sure that the other communicating station is a friendly one.
- Using only approved codes.
- Designating periods when all radios are turned off.
- Restricting the use of radio transmitters and monitoring radio receivers.
- Operating radios on low power.
- Enforcing net discipline and radiotelephone procedure (all stations must use authorized prosigns and prowords and must transmit official traffic only).
- Using radio sites with hills or other shields between them and the enemy.
- Using directional antennas when feasible.

RADIO SETS AND RECEIVER-TRANSMITTERS
The Army currently has fielded two series of radio sets, the single-channel ground and airborne radio (SINCGARS) and the older AN/VRC-12 series. Most, but not all, active-duty forces have SINCGARS, as do some reserve component units. The bulk of the reserve component forces, however, still uses the AN/VRC-12 family of radios.

AN/VRC-12 Series
These radio sets provide short-range, two-way, frequency-modulated (FM), radiotelephone communication between vehicles or crew-served weapons. They provide the fast and flexible means of communication necessary in combat operations. Installation kits, provided for specific vehicles, include control boxes, cables, and audio accessories necessary for extending the use of the particular set to various crew members and for furnishing intercommunication facilities.

Receiver-Transmitter, Radio RT-246/VRC, and Receiver-Transmitter, Radio RT-524/VRC
These receiver-transmitters are frequency-modulated. They are identical, except that the RT-246 has 10 preset channels and the RT-524 has none, and the RT-524 has a built-in speaker.

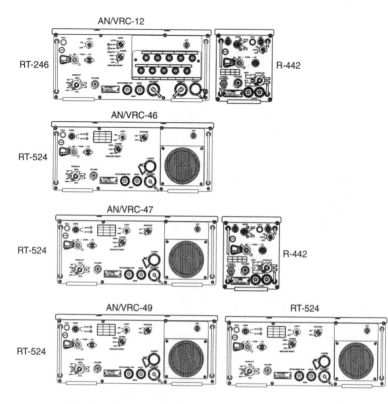

Radio Sets AN/VRC-12, -46, -47, and -49

Characteristics and Capabilities
- Frequency range: 30.00–75.95 MHz
- Type of signals: voice
- Preset frequencies: 10 (RT-246 only)
- Transmission planning range: moving, 15 miles (24 kilometers); stationary, 20 miles (32 kilometers)
- Type of operation: push-to-talk
- Type of control: local or remote
- Antenna: center-fed whip
- Number of channels: 920
- Types of squelch: noise and tone operated
- Pertinent publication: TM 11-5820-401-10, as changed

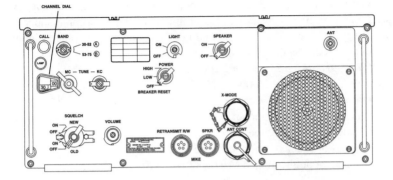

Receiver-Transmitter RT-524/VRC Control Panel

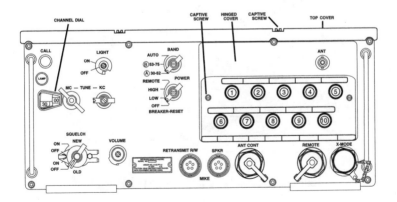

Receiver-Transmitter, Radio RT-246/VRC

Receiver, Radio R-442/VRC

The frequency-modulated receiver, radio R-442/VRC, is used in conjunction with the receiver-transmitter RT-246 or RT-524. This receiver gives the operator a facility for monitoring a frequency in addition to a frequency tuned on the receiver-transmitter. It is common practice for a commander to tune the RT-246 to his own command net and to monitor the next higher headquarters command net on the R-442.

Characteristics and Capabilities

- Frequency range: 30.00–75.95 MHz
- Type of signals: voice
- Preset frequencies: none
- Antenna: multisection whip
- Types of squelch: noise and tone operated
- Pertinent publication: TM 11-5820-401-10, as changed

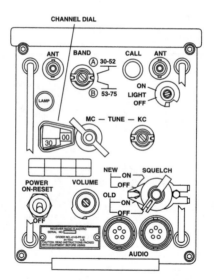

Receiver R-442/VRC Control Panel

Radio Set AN/VRC-12

A receiver-transmitter RT-246, a receiver R-442, and an antenna AS-1729 or AT-912 are components of radio set AN/VRC-12.

Operating Instructions

• Connect audio accessories to control, intercommunication set C-2298/VRC.

• Place the monitor switch in the ALL position.

• Adjust the VOLUME on the control, intercommunication set C-2298/VRC (final adjustment is made at the discretion of the operator).

• Turn the MAIN PWR switch on the amplifier AM-1780/VRC to the NORM position.

• Set the POWER CKT BKR switch to ON.

• If all crew members are to operate the receiver-transmitter, turn the RADIO TRANS switch to CDR & CREW.

• Turn the POWER switch on the receiver-transmitter RT-246 to the LOW position.

• Adjust the VOLUME control on the RT-246 to MAXIMUM.

• If manual tuning is to be used: Turn the BAND switch to A or B, depending on the frequency desired; turn the MC-TUNE and KC-TUNE knobs until the desired frequency appears on the channel dial.

• If pushbutton tuning is to be used: Turn the BAND switch to AUTO; push in the pushbutton for the desired frequency. *Note:* Presetting frequencies is a maintenance function.

• Squelch. Do not move the locking bar that separates the two sectors of the switch. This is a maintenance function.

• Set the POWER switch to REMOTE if you desire to control power and frequency selection from control, frequency selector C-2742/VRC.

• Turn the POWER switch on the receiver R-442/VRC to ON-RESET.

• Adjust the VOLUME control on the R-442/VRC to MAXIMUM.

• Turn the BAND switch to A or B, depending on the frequency desired.

• Turn the MC-TUNE and KC-TUNE knobs until the desired frequency appears on the channel dial.

• Turn the SQUELCH switch to ON.

AN/PRC-126 VHF FM Radio Set

This radio was fielded in 1989–90 as the squad radio (small-unit radio), replacing the PRT-4/PRR-9 and the PRC 68. It operates in the same range as the PRC-119, with a short-range transmission of 500 meters (short antenna) and 3 kilometers (long antenna). The PRC 126 weighs 2.8 pounds with battery.

**AN/PRC-126 VHF FM
Radio**

SINCGARS Ground Combat Net Radio

SINCGARS is a solid-state receiver that operates in the 30- to 87.975 MHz band in a single-channel or frequency-hopping (FH) mode. It is compatible with all current U.S. and allied VHF radios in the single-channel mode on 50-kHz channels. Currently, in the FH mode, SINCGARS is compatible with other Air Force, Marine, or Navy SINCGARS radios. SINCGARS stores eight single-channel frequencies and six separate hopsets. The cue and manual frequencies are included in the eight single-channel frequencies. It is designed for secure voice and data communication and is an antijam radio that is part of a total system. The individual components are interchangeable from one radio set to the next. SINCGARS is compatible with the AN/VRC-12 series tactical radio sets in the single-channel mode and the current VINSON COMSEC. It can provide electronic warfare (EW) protection and reduced electromagnetic signature.

The primary component of SINCGARS is the receiver-transmitter (RT). The most common ground unit version is the RT-1523 integrated COMSEC (ICOM). This RT has almost completely replaced the SINCGARS RT-1439 Non-ICOM, which requires the external COMSEC device known as the VINSON.

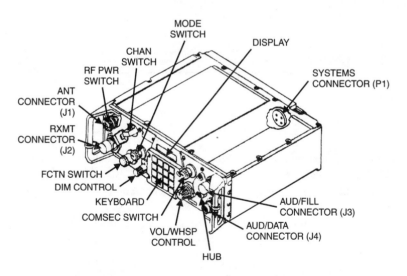

Receiver-Transmitter (RT-1523 Series)

CHARACTERISTICS AND CAPABILITIES

Operating Voltage:	Manpack: 13.5 volts from primary battery.
	Vehicular: 27.5 volts from vehicular battery.
Frequency Range:	30 MHz to 87.975 MHz.
Number of Operating Frequencies:	2320.
Channel Spacing:	25 kHz.
Frequency Stability:	Plus or minus 5 parts per million.
Frequency Offset Ability (SC):	Plus or minus 5 and 10 kHz.
Type of Modulation:	FM.
Audio Response Capability:	300-3000 Hz.
Types of Operation:	Push-to-talk (PTT) and release to receive.
	Retransmit: automatic.
	Remote: push-to-talk, release to receive.
	Data: automatic via data device.
Modes of Operation:	Voice: SC and FH.
	Retransmit: SC to SC, SC to FH, FH to FH.
	Digital data: SC, FH.
	Remote: with AN/GRA-39, CM, or RCU.
	Plain-text or cipher text.
Tuning:	Electronic SC frequency entered manually by using keyboard. Up to eight SC channels and six FH channels can be loaded and later selected using CHAN (channel) switch.

Components

A few components make up the basic radio sets. This simplifies the radio's installation, its tailoring for specific missions, and the maintenance support system. The RT-1523 discussed above is the main component of all radio sets.

- Vehicular mount MT-6352 is common to all vehicular sets. The mount fits into the same drilled hole footprint as the previous AN/VRC-12 series radios.
- Mounting adapter AM-7239 converts the vehicle power supply to the various operating voltages for radio and amplifier operation. The

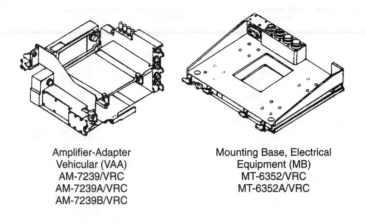

Amplifier-Adapter
Vehicular (VAA)
AM-7239/VRC
AM-7239A/VRC
AM-7239B/VRC

Mounting Base, Electrical
Equipment (MB)
MT-6352/VRC
MT-6352A/VRC

adapter provides surge protection for the radio if the vehicle is started when the radio is on. The adapter interfaces the vehicle intercom system and provides amplified output to power an external speaker. The adapter can house two RTs and one power amplifier in the same space that a single AN/VRC-12 radio previously occupied.

- Power amplifier AM-7238 provides up to 50 watts output power from the radio in vehicle mounts. A single amplifier mounts in the mounting adapter to the side of the radio.
- SINCGARS uses broad-band antennas that do not have to be changed when changing frequency (for example OE-254 ground-plane or AS-3900 vehicular whip antennas). The output frequency can change over a wide range between hops due to the FH nature of SINCGARS. Therefore, conventional antennas with narrow bands of operation (for example, the RC-292 ground-plane antenna) cannot be used.
- Voice input must be through the H-250 handset. Output is obtained through either the handset or the LS-671 auxiliary speaker. The LS-454 speaker can be used with the AN/VRC-12 and the SINCGARS family of radios.

Common components are the key to tailoring radio sets for specific missions. The components included in the radio set determine its capabilities. The number of RTs and amplifiers, an installation kit, and a backpack component determine the model. The RT is the basic building block for all radio configurations.

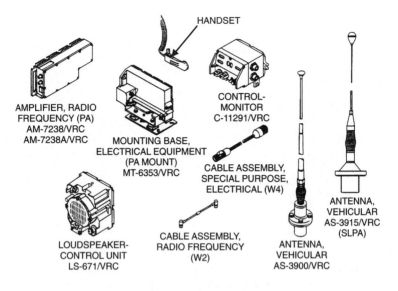

HANDSET

AMPLIFIER, RADIO
FREQUENCY (PA)
AM-7238/VRC
AM-7238A/VRC

MOUNTING BASE,
ELECTRICAL EQUIPMENT
(PA MOUNT)
MT-6353/VRC

CONTROL-
MONITOR
C-11291/VRC

CABLE ASSEMBLY,
SPECIAL PURPOSE,
ELECTRICAL (W4)

LOUDSPEAKER-
CONTROL UNIT
LS-671/VRC

CABLE ASSEMBLY,
RADIO FREQUENCY
(W2)

ANTENNA,
VEHICULAR
AS-3900/VRC

ANTENNA,
VEHICULAR
AS-3915/VRC
(SLPA)

Radio Set Components

VERSIONS
The versions consist of manpack (AN/PRC-119A), six ground versions (AN/VRC-87A through AN/VRC-92A), and three airborne versions (RT-1476, -1477, and -1478). The "A" at the end of the nomenclature means that the radio is ICOM.

Manpack Radio AN/PRC-119A
The manpack radio replaces the AN/PRC-77 and AN/PRC-25. It consists of one RT, a battery box, a handset, a manpack antenna, and an all-purpose lightweight individual carrying equipment (ALICE) pack.

MANPACK RADIO

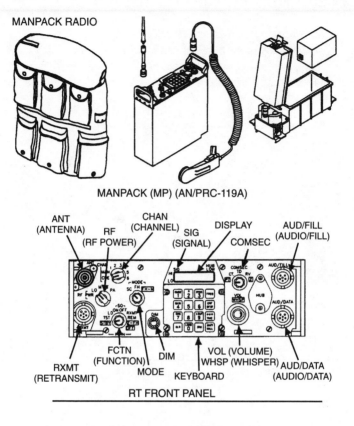

MANPACK (MP) (AN/PRC-119A)

RT FRONT PANEL

RT KEYBOARD

Ground Versions

Vehicular Short-Range Radio AN/VRC-87A

The AN/VRC-87A is the base vehicular radio set. It consists of one RT, a radio mount, a mounting adapter, a vehicular antenna, and associated handsets and cabling. The AN/VRC-87A replaces the AN/GRC-53 and AN/GRC-64.

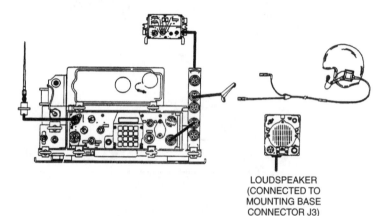

LOUDSPEAKER
(CONNECTED TO
MOUNTING BASE
CONNECTOR J3)

Short Range (SR)
Mounted in Mounting Adapter
(AN/VRC-87A or AN/VRC-88A)

Dismounted Short-Range Radio AN/VRC-88A

The AN/VRC-88A adds the components needed to operate as a manpack radio (battery box, manpack antenna, and ALICE pack); otherwise, it is identical to the AN/VRC-87A. The AN/VRC-88A replaces the AN/GRC-125 and AN/GRC-160.

Vehicular Long-Range/Short-Range Radio AN/VRC-89A

The AN/VRC-89A is built from the AN/VRC-87A by adding another RT and a power amplifier. The AN/VRC-89 replaces the AN/VRC-12 and AN/VRC-47, which have a single RT and an auxiliary receiver. The additional RT replaces the auxiliary receiver in the previous versions. The RT provides increased capabilities over a receiver alone.

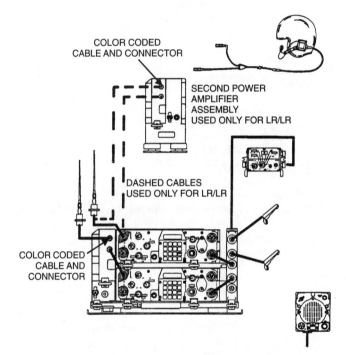

COLOR CODED CABLE AND CONNECTOR

SECOND POWER AMPLIFIER ASSEMBLY USED ONLY FOR LR/LR

DASHED CABLES USED ONLY FOR LR/LR

COLOR CODED CABLE AND CONNECTOR

**Long Range/Short Range (LR/SR)
(AN/VRC-89A or AN/VRC-91A)
Long Range/Long Range (LR/LR)
(AN/VRC-92A)**

Vehicular Long-Range Radio AN/VRC-90A
The AN/VRC-90A is an AN/VRC-87A with a power amplifier added for
long-range capability. It replaces the AN/VRC-43 and AN/VRC-46.

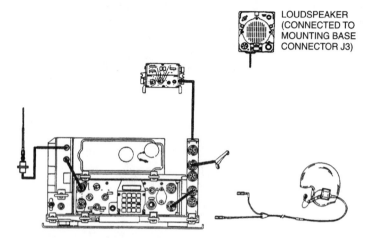

LOUDSPEAKER
(CONNECTED TO
MOUNTING BASE
CONNECTOR J3)

Long Range (LR)
Mounted in Mounting Adapter (AN/VRC-90A)

Vehicular Short-Range/Long-Range Dismountable Radio AN/VRC-91A
The AN/VRC-91A adds the components needed to operate as a manpack
radio; otherwise, it is identical to the AN/VRC-89A. It does not replace any
similar single radio set. The closest configuration would be a combination
of manpack (AN/PRC-77) radio and a vehicular radio (AN/VRC-43 or
AN/VRC-46) kept in the same vehicle.

Vehicular Dual Long-Range/Retransmission Radio AN/VRC-92A
The AN/VRC-92A adds a second power amplifier to the AN/VRC-89 to
provide high-power capability for both radios in the mount. The second
amplifier has its own mount (MT-6353/VRC) and obtains its power from a
cable connected to one of the auxiliary power outputs from the radio mount.
In the mounting adapter, the co-mounted amplifier can be used only with the
lower radio, and the separate amplifier can be used only with the upper
radio. The AN/VRC-92A replaces the AN/VRC-45 and AN/VRC-49.

Airborne Versions
The airborne and ground versions are interoperable. They appear physically different from the ground models and from each other. The only change in the airborne models is the faceplate that is attached to the different configurations. The RT is identical to all three models, but the add-on modules change the capabilities of the base RT.

Planning Ranges
The ranges shown in the accompanying chart are based on line of sight and are average for normal conditions. Range depends on location, sighting, weather, and surrounding noise level, among other factors. Use of OE-254 antenna increases range for both voice and data transmissions. Enemy jamming and mutual interference conditions degrade these ranges. In data transmissions, use of a lower baud rate will increase range.

VOICE TRANSMISSION MAXIMUM PLANNING RANGES:

TYPE RADIO	RF SWITCH POSITION	PLANNING RANGES
Manpack/Vehicular	LO (low) M (medium) HI (high)	200 M – 400 M 400 M – 5 KM 5 KM – 10 KM
Vehicular Only	PA (power amplifier)	10 KM – 40 KM

DATA TRANSMISSION MAXIMUM PLANNING RANGES:

TYPE RADIO	BAUD RATE USED	RF SWITCH POSITION	PLANNING RANGES
Manpack/Vehicular (Short Range)	600 – 4800 BPS 16,000 BPS (16 KBPS)	HI (high) HI (high)	3 KM – 5 KM 1 KM – 3 KM
Vehicular (Long Range)	600 – 2400 BPS 4800 BPS 16,000 BPS (16 KBPS)	PA (power amp) PA (power amp) PA (power amp)	5 KM – 25 KM 5 KM – 22 KM 3 KM – 10 KM

Loading Frequencies
The procedure for loading single-channel (SC) frequencies requires setting the proper switches, pressing the correct number keys for the frequency you wish to load, and storing the load in RT permanent memory by pressing the STO (storage) button. Loading secure frequencies requires special

COMSEC devices that transmit the proper "FILL" data to the radio, including frequencies, FH data, secure transmission data, and other necessary information. The current component or device is called an ANCD (automated net control device), AN/CYZ-10. Correct operating instructions may be obtained from various technical manuals and the unit signal officer.

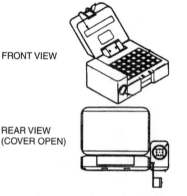

FRONT VIEW

REAR VIEW
(COVER OPEN)

AUTOMATED NET CONTROL DEVICE (ANCD), AN/CYZ-10

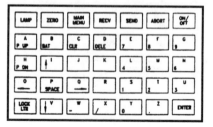

ANCD KEYPAD

FIELD EXPEDIENT ANTENNAS

Expedient antennas are temporary antennas designed and constructed by the user to increase the range of tactical radio sets. Antennas that are components of tactical radio sets are, for the most part, vertical antennas, resulting in the signal being radiated equally in all directions. Expedient antennas increase the operating range of a given radio set, providing increased efficiency through the use of an antenna specifically designed for the operating frequency in use, elevation of the antenna above the ground, or concentration of the radiated signal along a given direction. Field expedient antennas are easily constructed from field wire using poles on trees for support. Whatever antenna is used, remember that the most important considerations are site location and location of the radio set. Before deciding to construct a field expedient antenna, other considerations or operating hints that may improve communications are as follows:

- Use a headset to receive weak signals.
- Speak slowly and distinctly directly into the microphone or handset.
- Use an RC-292 antenna, if available.
- Use continuous wave (CW) in place of voice for increased range on AM radios.

Steel wires should be clipped off, leaving only the copper wires. The copper wires are twisted together and placed into the center hole of the auxiliary antenna connector or the antenna connector, making sure the wires do not touch any other part of the radio set.

If the whip antenna of your radio becomes damaged, try a piece of communication wire tied to a broomstick or a tree limb. Insert the end of the wire in the antenna connector. If you hold the stick or limb in a vertical position, you should be able to communicate. It will not be as effective as with the whip antenna, but it is better than no antenna at all.

Vertical Antennas

Vertical field expedient antennas improve radio set performance by virtue of height above the ground. The most effective height above the ground is equal to one-half the wavelength of the operating frequency in meters. Elevation above this height requires ground plane elements.

Improvised Whip Antenna

Whip antennas may become broken during use, with no replacement antenna readily available. If this should happen, it is possible to improvise a satisfactory replacement by using telephone cable WD-1/TT or by lashing the broken antenna pieces together.

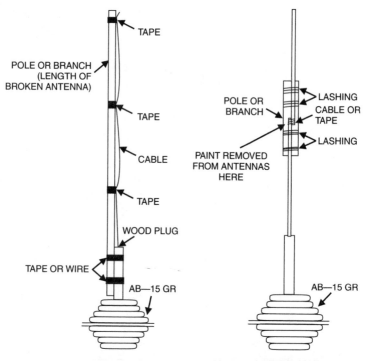

Emergency Repair of Whip Antenna Using Field Wire WD-1/TT

Emergency Repair of Whip Antenna Using Broken Antenna Sections

Patrol Antenna

The patrol antenna is used primarily with FM radios. It is used extensively in heavily wooded areas with the portable radio set AN/PRC-77 to increase line-of-sight communications. Antenna performance increases with height above the ground up to 13 meters.

Length in meters $^1/_2$ wavelength of operating frequency
Height   Variable (lead-in not over 13 meters)
Radiation   360 degrees

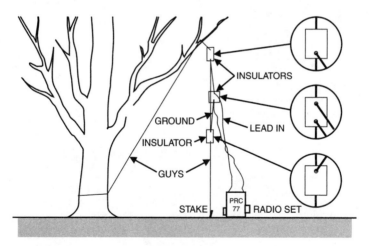

Patrol Antenna

To determine length of antenna in meters, divide 142.5 by your operating frequency.
Example: constant = 142.5 divided by op. freq. 45.0 = 3.17 meters.
Or, constant = 468 divided by op. freq. 45.0 = 10.4 feet.

Bent Bamboo Antenna
The bent bamboo antenna is a variation of the patrol antenna using different
construction materials.

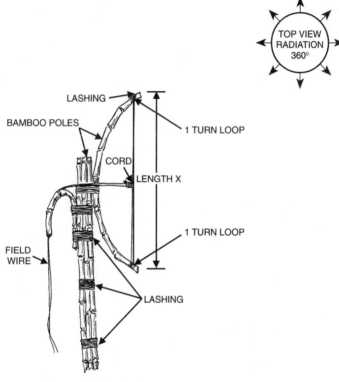

Bent Bamboo Antenna

Ground Plane Antenna

The ground plane antenna is used with FM radios. It is used in place of the RC-292 when such an antenna is not available. The length of the antenna elements listed below may be used for all frequencies of the VRC-12 family radios.

Length	Antenna element–2 meters
	Ground plane elements—$2^1/_2$ meters
Range	Under most conditions will increase the range of the set
Radiation	360 degrees

Note: Portions of the RC-292 may be used to construct a modified version of this field expedient antenna. Only the vertical element, antenna base, ground plane elements, and lead-in cord are needed. The antenna may be erected by fastening insulator material to the top of the vertical elements, attaching a guy rope, and pulling the assembled elements up in a tree.

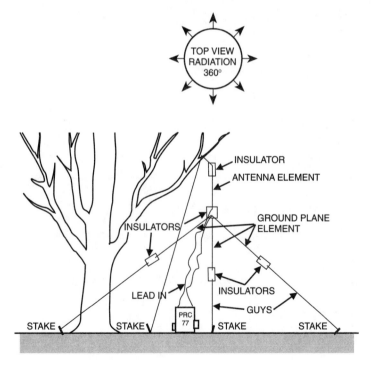

Ground Plane Antenna

Horizontal Antennas

When the situation does not require mobility and the antenna group RC-292 is not available, you can get greater distance by using the long-wire horizontal antenna. The physical length in meters of one wavelength for a given operating frequency can be computed as follows:

$$\text{length (meters)} = \frac{285}{\text{operating frequency (MHz)}}$$

All horizontal antennas described here are fed by connecting the receiver-transmitter to one end of the antenna.

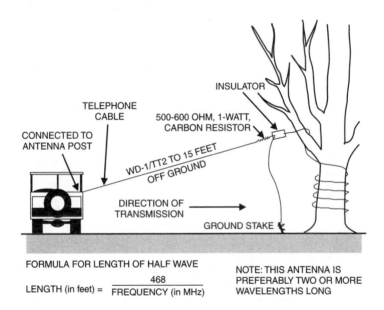

FORMULA FOR LENGTH OF HALF WAVE

$$\text{LENGTH (in feet)} = \frac{468}{\text{FREQUENCY (in MHz)}}$$

NOTE: THIS ANTENNA IS PREFERABLY TWO OR MORE WAVELENGTHS LONG

Horizontal Antenna For Use With AM and FM Radios

Antenna Efficiency
When using WD-1 field wire and the VRC-12 family of radios, antenna efficiency can be estimated by use of the following table:

Antenna Length (wavelengths)	Power Gan Factor
1	1.2
2	1.4
4	2.1
6	3.1
8	4.3

Note: Due to technical characteristics, antenna efficiency begins to decrease when antenna length exceeds eight wavelengths.

Radiation Patterns
In a half-wavelength antenna, maximum radiation occurs in the two directions that are at right angles to the antenna itself, with no radiation off the ends. The direction of maximum radiation moves closer to the direction of the antenna itself as the length of the antenna increases.

The radiation patterns can be modified to make them more directional through the use of a resistor connected to one end of the antenna. The

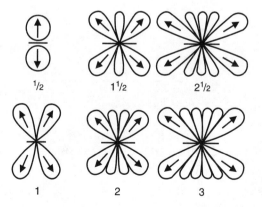

Radiation Patterns for ½- to 3-Wavelength Antennas

antenna may be made of WD-1/TT wire and the resistor fashioned from the carbon pole in a flashlight battery. The radio should be connected to one end of the antenna with the resistor connected between the opposite end and the ground. The antenna must be a minimum of two wavelengths of the transmitting frequency. Maximum signal is radiated off the end of the antenna toward the resistor, and it tends to reject or reduce signals from other directions. The directivity is of value for antijamming and other communications security considerations.

A suspended antenna causes considerable pull on the radio set at the connection. Difficulty may be experienced in keeping the antenna connected to the binding post. One method of overcoming the difficulty is as follows: Remove the regular whip antenna from the mounting base. Place in the mounting base a broken stub. Drill a hole through the broken stub, push the

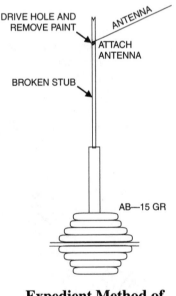

**Expedient Method of
Connecting a Horizontal
Antenna**

end of the antenna through the hole, and tie the antenna to the stub. The connection to the radio set is already on the stub. This expedient will keep the weight of the wire from pulling the wire away from the binding post. Be sure to remove the paint from the area on the stub where the antenna is connected.

Long-Wire Antenna

The long-wire antenna is used with both AM and FM radios to increase the range. It is normally used in open terrain where installation can be accomplished with ease.

Length	5 or 7 wavelengths of operating frequency
Height	3 meters
Range	Up to 2 to 3 times the operating range of set
Resistor	400–700 ohms
Radiation	Without resistor—from both ends
	With resistor—off resistor end only

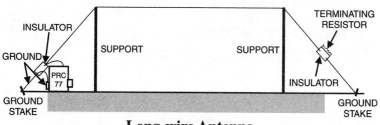

Long-wire Antenna

Vertical Half-Rhombic Antenna

The vertical half-rhombic antenna has the advantage of being smaller in physical size than the horizontal antenna and requires only one pole for construction. It can be made directional with the use of a resistor. The principal disadvantage is that if the angle between the antenna wire and surface of the earth is too small, the signal will be radiated at an upward angle that may be above the intended receiver. A typical vertical half-rhombic antenna consists of 100 feet of field wire WD-1/TT, erected over a single 30-foot support base. One leg of the antenna terminates at the resistor; the other end is connected from the insulator to the radio by a 5-foot lead-in wire.

Length	2 wavelengths of operating frequency, with a 5-foot lead-in
Height	20 meters
Range	Up to 2 to 3 times operating range of set
Resistor	400–700 ohms
Radiation	Without resistor—equally off both ends
	With resistor—off resistor end only

Note: A counterpoise is used as an additional ground in everyday climates. When the counterpoise is used, it is placed on top of the ground and is installed from one ground stake to the other, and then to the battery case clip. If the counterpoise is not used, the ground lead-in is connected from the ground stake to the battery case clip. The insulators and the resistor are installed approximately knee high.

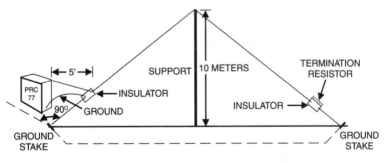

Vertical Half-rhombic Antenna

20

Field Expedient Antiarmor Devices

There are many weapons you can use to destroy a tank or an armored personnel carrier. The weapons most frequently used are the LAW, Dragon, TOW, mines, and high-explosive, dual-purpose rounds of the M203 grenade launcher. There may be times, however, when you will not have these weapons available. In such cases, you may have to use field expedient devices. In order to construct some of these devices, you must know how to prime charges, electrically and nonelectrically.

FLAME DEVICES
Flame devices are used to obscure the vision of a vehicle's crew and to set the vehicle afire.

Molotov Cocktail
A Molotov cocktail is made with a breakable container (usually a bottle), a gas and oil mixture, and a cloth wick. To construct it, fill the container with the mixture, and then insert the cloth wick into the container. The wick must extend both into the mixture and out of the bottle. Light the wick before throwing the container. When the container hits the vehicle and breaks, the mixture will ignite, burning both the vehicle and the personnel around it.

Eagle Fireball
An eagle fireball is made with an ammunition can, a gas and oil mixture, a white phosphorus

WICK

GASOLINE AND OIL MIXTURE

Molotov Cocktail

grenade wrapped with detonating cord, tape, a nonelectric blasting cap, a fuse igniter, and a grapnel (or rope with bent nails).

To construct an eagle fireball, fill the ammunition can with the mixture. Wrap the grenade with detonating cord, and attach a nonelectric firing system to the end of the detonating cord. Place the grenade inside the can with the time fuse extending out. Make a slot in the can's lid for the fuse to pass through when the lid is closed. If available, attach a rope with bent nails or a grapnel to the can. When you throw the can onto a vehicle, the bent nails or the grapnel will help hold the can there. Before throwing the can, fire the fuse igniter.

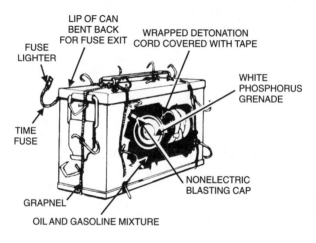

Eagle Fireball

Eagle Cocktail

An eagle cocktail is made of a plastic or rubberized bag (a waterproof bag or a sandbag lined with a poncho), a gas and oil mixture, a smoke grenade, a thermite grenade, tape, string, and communications wire or cord.

To construct an eagle cocktail, fill the bag with the mixture. Seal the bag by twisting its end and then taping or tying it. Attach the thermite and smoke grenades

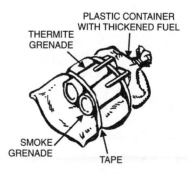

Eagle Cocktail

to the bag using tape, string, or communications wire. When attaching the grenades, do not bind the safety levers on the grenades. Tie a piece of string or cord to the safety pins of the grenades. Before throwing the eagle cocktail, pull the safety pins in both grenades.

EXPLOSIVE DEVICES

Towed Charge
A towed charge is made of rope or communications wire, mines or blocks of explosives, electrical blasting caps, tape, and electrical firing wire.

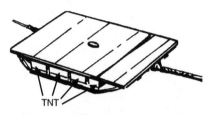

To construct a towed charge, link a series of armed antitank mines together with a rope or communications wire. If mines are not available, use about 25 to 50

Towed Charge

pounds of explosives attached on a board (sled charge). Anchor one end of the rope on one side of the road, and run its other end to a safe position from which the charge may be pulled onto the road. Attach an electric firing system to each mine (or to the explosive), and connect those systems to the firing wire. Tape the firing wire to the rope running to the position from which the charge is pulled onto the road. At that position, conduct a circuit check, and then connect the firing wire to a blasting machine.

Just before a vehicle reaches the site of the towed charge, pull the charge onto the road so that it will be run over by the vehicle. When the vehicle is over it, fire the charge.

Pole Charge
A pole charge is made of explosives (TNT or C4), nonelectric blasting caps, time fuse, detonating cord, tape, string or wire, fuse igniters, and a pole long enough for the mission. Prime the desired amount of explosives with two nonelectric firing systems, and attach the explosives to a board or some other flat material. The amount of explosives you use depends on the target to be destroyed. Tie or tape the board with the explosives to the pole. The time fuse should be only about 6 inches long. Before putting a pole charge on a target, fire the fuse igniters.

Some good places to put a pole charge on a vehicle are under the turret, over the engine compartment, in the suspension system, and in the main gun tube (if the charge is small enough to fit in the tube).

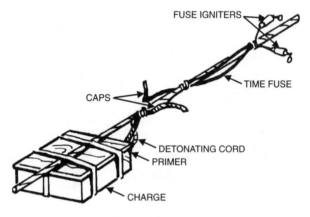

Pole Charge

Satchel Charge

A satchel charge is made of explosives (TNT or C4), nonelectric blasting caps, time fuse, detonating cord, tape, fuse igniters, and some type of satchel. The satchel can be an empty sandbag, a demolitions bag, or other material. To construct the device, fill the satchel with the amount of explosives needed for the mission. Prime the explosives with two nonelectric firing systems. Use only about 6 inches of time fuse. Seal the satchel with string, rope, or tape, and leave the time fuse and igniters hanging out of the satchel. Before throwing a satchel charge onto a target, fire the fuse igniters.

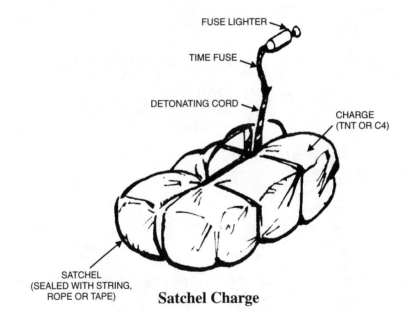

FUSE LIGHTER

TIME FUSE

DETONATING CORD

CHARGE (TNT OR C4)

SATCHEL (SEALED WITH STRING, ROPE OR TAPE)

Satchel Charge

WEAK POINTS OF ARMORED VEHICLES

To use expedient devices, you must know the weak points of armored vehicles. The following are some of the common weak points:

- Suspension system
- Fuel tanks
- Ammunition storage compartments
- Engine compartment
- Turret ring
- Armor on the sides, top, and rear (normally not as thick as that on the front)

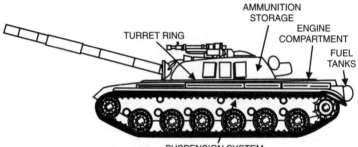

Weak Points of Armored Vehicles

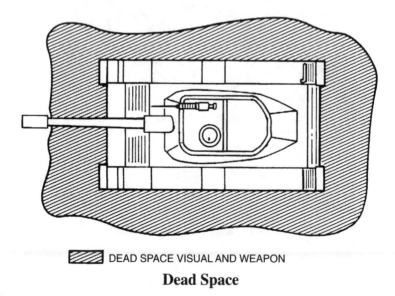

DEAD SPACE VISUAL AND WEAPON

Dead Space

BUTTONED-UP ARMORED VEHICLES

If an armored vehicle is "buttoned-up" and you have no antiarmor weapons, fire your rifle at the vision blocks, at any optical equipment mounted outside the vehicle, into the engine compartment, at any external fuel tanks, or at the hatches. That will not destroy the vehicle but may hinder its ability to fight.

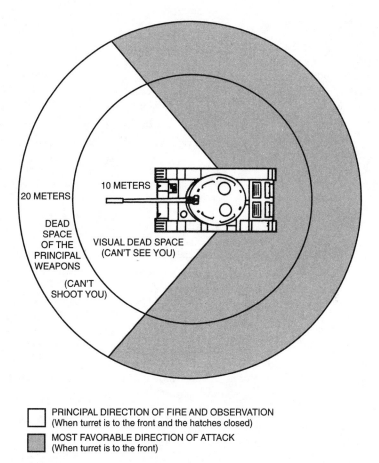

□ PRINCIPAL DIRECTION OF FIRE AND OBSERVATION
(When turret is to the front and the hatches closed)

■ MOST FAVORABLE DIRECTION OF ATTACK
(When turret is to the front)

Dead Space, 10 meters and 20 meters

21

Directed-Energy Weapons

This chapter introduces directed-energy weapons (DEWs) and gives an overview of how to defend against them. These new weapons are radically different in operation and effect from any other weapon in use. They include lasers, microwave radiation emitters, and particle beam generators. Weapon prototypes have been developed using laser and microwave radiation emitter technology.

CHARACTERISTICS
The following are characteristics of DEWs:
- DE (directed energy) is another line-of-sight, direct-fire device. DEWs rely on subatomic particles or electromagnetic waves that impact at or near the speed of light. The time of flight to the target is essentially zero.
- Laser weapons produce intense heat and light on a target; these can burn out optics and blind their operators.
- High-power microwave weapons can burn out electrical systems and components or create an electrical upset.
- A DEW gunner is not required to lead a target, and traditional resupply problems are nonexistent.
- DEWs attack armored vehicles at their most vulnerable points: their "eyes" (optics) and soft electronics.

LASER WEAPONS
The most vulnerable targets of laser weapons are optics, specifically vehicle sights and sighting systems. The two general categories of optical devices on the battlefield today are *direct-view devices* and *electro-optical devices*.

In addition to eyeglasses, contact lenses, and sun-wind-dust goggles, direct-view devices include the following magnifying devices: binoculars; Dragon daysight (X6); daysight (ISU, X4, and X12); backup sight (X4);

M60 series tank sights; and M1 series tank sights (105 series telescopes and .50-caliber sights).

Electro-optical devices include image intensifiers—AN/PVS 4, AN/PVS 5, and AN/VVS 2 (driver's night viewer); thermal devices—thermal night sight, Dragon night sight, and tank thermal sight (TTS); and infrared devices—infrared TOW tracker and infrared Dragon tracker.

Direct-View Optics
A laser weapon targeted on see-through optics will cause damage to the eyes of the operator. The beam passes through the optical device to the eye and burns it, causing either temporary loss of vision (dazzle) or permanent blindness. When the optical device has a magnifying capability, the beam strength is magnified and causes even greater injury.

Electro-Optics
A laser weapon attacks optics that are not see-through by burning the sensor or reticle inside the device. Some of the electrical circuits inside the device may also be damaged by the heat surge, which does not have any effect on the operator.

Personal Injury
Even when not using optical devices, soldiers are susceptible to laser weapons. Laser energy from friendly or enemy systems can cause temporary or permanent damage to the naked, unprotected eye. Laser weapons have a greater effect in darkness than in daylight because the eye is more sensitive to light at night.

Protective Equipment
Protective spectacles, filters, and lenses are being fielded to protect soldiers and optics against lasers.

MICROWAVE WEAPONS
High-powered microwave weapons cause electronic "kills" or electrical upset in electronic equipment. These weapons are effective against command posts, sensors, radar, computers, optical devices, fusing, engines, and a whole variety of electronic communications that use transistors or integrated circuits.

TACTICAL CONSIDERATIONS
With DEWs, an additional direct-fire system now exists that can injure soldiers or damage equipment, but this does not change the nature of tactics.

Standard defensive techniques employed against any direct-fire weapon will provide equal or better protection against personal injury from DEWs because such weapons have no bursting radius. You should observe the following defensive techniques:

- Use terrain for cover and concealment.
- Use weather (fog and rain).
- Use smoke to conceal movement.
- Use artillery, mortars, and direct-fire weapons to suppress known or suspected locations of DEWs.
- Use shoot-and-move tactics to prevent friendly positions from being pinpointed.

Equipment Preparation
Observe the following tactics for preparing equipment:

- Position vehicles and weapons in covered and concealed locations to minimize exposure of glass surfaces to the enemy.
- Cover or shield external glass surfaces until needed. Tape, canvas, empty sandbags, or other materials can be used as covers.
- Open optical protective doors only during required observation or when engaging targets.
- Use a minimum number of optical or electro-optical devices to search for the enemy; protect the rest until they are required for firing weapons.
- Tubular extensions may be fabricated for objective lenses. These decrease detection except from almost head-on.

Soldier Preparation
Prepare soldiers by doing the following:

- Train soldiers to know when they have been engaged by DEWs and what action they can take, such as switching from damaged electro-optical devices to direct-view devices while using laser-protective spectacles.
- Conduct first-aid classes to prepare soldiers to aid injured buddies.
- Teach soldiers that wounds caused by a laser or other DEWs occur in the absence of noise and that the device will probably leave no detectable signature. Although laser burns on the retina do not produce pain, they do cause dark spots in the soldier's vision.
- Train soldiers to wear their protective spectacles whenever they are outside their vehicles, outside their foxholes, or looking out from their foxholes.

Appendix A

NATO Armored Vehicles

Currently, three former Warsaw Pact countries have joined forces with the North Atlantic Treaty Organization (NATO). Leaders and soldiers need to take caution as NATO membership continues to expand, because U.S. forces are likely to come into contact with forces that use weapons and equipment we once identified as foe. The equipment used by some former Warsaw Pact NATO countries is at Appendix B.

CHIEFTAIN—BRITISH
   Large shallow turret with long, sloping front
   Long gun tube with bore evacuator in center
   High, flat engine decks
   6 road wheels with skirting plates covering support rollers

CENTURION—BRITISH
Large square turret
Bore evacuator ²/₃ down from muzzle
6 road wheels with skirting plates covering support rollers

CHALLENGER—BRITISH
Center-mounted turret and fighting compartment
6 road wheels (space between third and fourth); 4 return rollers
5 smoke dischargers each side of main gun
Steel skirting covering upper track

MCV 80—BRITISH
High rear deck
Small, shallow turret
Flat engine decks
6 road wheels

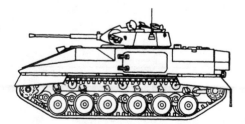

AMX30—FRENCH
Large squat turret
Long gun tube, no bore evacuator
Flat engine decks
5 road wheels with support rollers

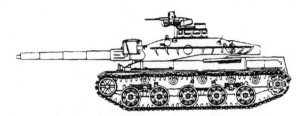

AMX10—FRENCH
Large cupola set to the left
Long thin gun (20 mm)
Flat hull with long, sloping front plate
5 road wheels with support rollers

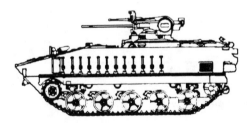

LEOPARD—GERMAN
Large rounded flat turret
Bore evacuator $2/3$ from muzzle
Long sloping-sided hull with horizontal exhaust louvres at rear
7 road wheels with support rollers

LEOPARD II—GERMAN

Large squared turret
7 evenly spaced road wheels
Bore evacuator $^2/_3$ from muzzle
Grenade launchers on rear side of turret
Jagged track skirting

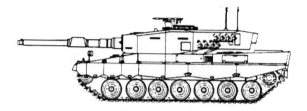

MARDER—GERMAN

Small turret placed centrally on hull
Gun mounted on turret
Long hull with inward-sloping sides, domed cupola at rear
6 road wheels with support rollers

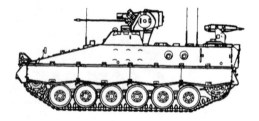

M60—UNITED STATES

High rear deck; prominent cupola
Tortoiseshell-shaped turret
6 road wheels with 3 support rollers

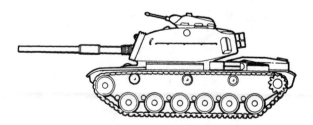

M60A1—UNITED STATES[1]
Wedge-shaped turret
Bore evacuator 2/3 down from muzzle, no blast deflector
6 road wheels with support rollers

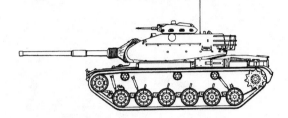

M60A3—UNITED STATES
Wedge-shaped turret
Large thermal sleeve 2/3 down from muzzle
Thermal sight and lazer range finder mounted at body end of gun
(not shown)
6 road wheels with 3 support rollers

M113—UNITED STATES
.50-cal mg, pintle mounted
Rectangular, box-shaped hull
Track—5 road wheels, no support rollers

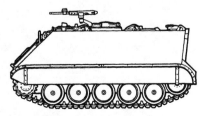

[1] Drawing from Alan K. Russell, *Modern Battle Tanks and Support Vehicles:* Greenhill Books, London and Stackpole Books, Mechanicsburg, PA.

M109A61—UNITED STATES
Self-propelled howitzer with long gun tube
7 evenly spaced road wheels
Large, boxy turret mounted rear of center

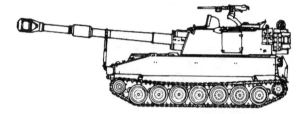

M1 ABRAMS—UNITED STATES
Low, boxy
Low turret—no cupola
7 road wheels covered with skirt

M2 BRADLEY—UNITED STATES
High profile
Distinctive turret in center with tow launcher on left side
6 road wheels, space between third and fourth road wheel
Skirt over road wheels

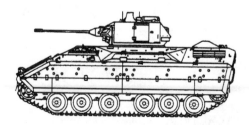

Appendix B

Former Soviet Union Vehicles

PT 76

    Cone-shaped turret set well forward
    Short gun with evacuator at center, muzzle brake at end
    Wide, long, square hull
    Narrow back, 6 road wheels, no support rollers

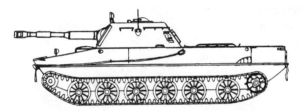

T54/55

    Dome-shaped turret mounted over third road wheel
    Long gun with bore evacuator at muzzle
    Sloped, low-silhouetted hull
    5 road wheels with gap between first and second
    No support rollers
    Infrared searchlight for gun

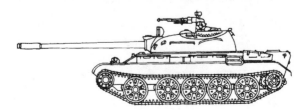

T62

Smooth, round (pear-shaped) turret
Long gun with evacuator $1/3$ down from muzzle
Flat engine deck
5 road wheels, with large gaps between third, fourth, and fifth, no
    support rollers

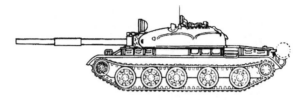

T72

Turret centrally mounted on chassis
Support rollers and 6 road wheels
V-shaped mud deflector on front slope
Infrared searchlight mounted to left of gun tube

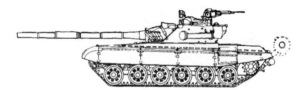

T80

Rounded turret mounted midway on tank
Single snorkel mounted on left side of turret
Long gun with bore evacuator $1/3$ distance from muzzle
6 evenly spaced road wheels with 3 support rollers
Sharply sloped upper glacis with V-shaped splash guard

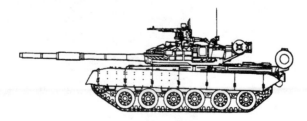

T-10

Turret round, well forward, well sloped
Long gun tube, bore evacuator near end of muzzle break
Hull, narrow; splash guard, wide
7 road wheels, 3 support rollers

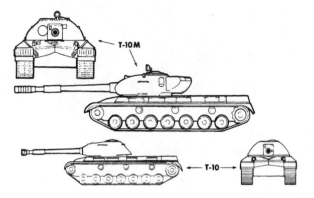

ZSU 23-4

Shallow and square-sided turret
4 antiaircraft guns
Square-sided hull
6 road wheels, no support rollers

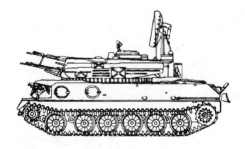

BMD

Same turret and armament as BMP
Driver's hatch centered below main gun
5 road wheels, 4 support rollers
Found with airborne units

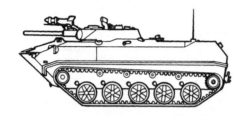

BMP

Circular and cone-shaped turret
Short gun with missile mounted above
Low, wide hull
6 road wheels with support rollers

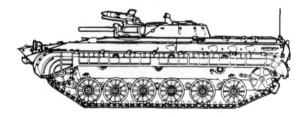

BTR 60P

May have small turret
Machine gun toward front
Large, boatlike hull with sharp square nose
Wheeled—4 large wheels each side

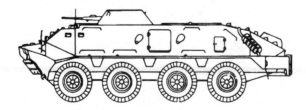

BRDM

No turret

Armament may vary from pintle-mounted machine gun to antitank
   missiles

Long, sloping hood and raised troop compartment

4 wheels

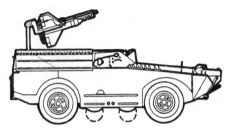

BRDM-2

Small, cone-shaped turret, centered on hull

Machine gun mounted in turret

Square-shaped hull with distinct undercut at nose

Wheeled—2 each side

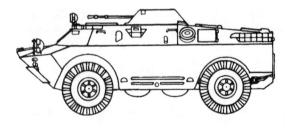

SAU 122

PT-76–type chassis with 7 road wheels

Turret location is rear of center

Infrared searchlight top left of turret

Double-baffle muzzle brake and bore evacuator

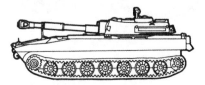

Appendix C

Operational Graphics

Operational graphics (map symbols) depict control measures and friendly and enemy units and equipment. These symbols are normally written on graphical overlays that fit to the individual map scale, to help leaders better identify the battle plan and the placement of units and equipment applicable to the battle.

RULES
Operational graphics depict both the operational and support roles of the battle and have certain rules.

Control Measures
All control measures (obstacles, locations, routes, and lines)—friendly, enemy, neutral, or factional—are drawn using the color green.

Affiliation	Hand-Drawn	Computer-Generated
Friend, Assumed Friend	Blue	Cyan
Unknown, Pending	Yellow	Yellow
Neutral	Green	Green
Enemy, Suspect, Joker, Faker	Red	Red

Unit Symbol Color Defaults

All other friendly graphic control measures are shown in black. All other enemy graphic control measures are shown in red. If red is not available, they are drawn in black with a double line or the abbreviation saying "ENY" placed in at least two locations to avoid confusion. If colors are used to show friendly or enemy (hostile factions), they must be shown in a legend on the overlay describing what the color means.

Unit and Equipment Symbols

Unit and equipment symbols are composed of three components: a frame (geometric border), fill, and icon. Frames are geometric shapes used to display affiliation. The basic affiliation categories are friendly, unknown, neutral, and enemy. The unknown unit frame shape is normally used only for aircraft and ships. The frame shape for suspected friendly, enemy, or neutral is used for ground units not positively identified. The basic frame shapes for units, installations, activities, and logistics sites are shown in the following figure (Unit Installation and Site Symbol Frames).

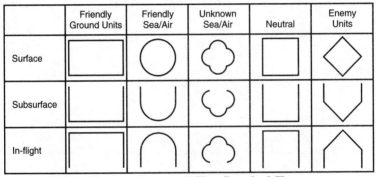

Unit Installation and Site Symbol Frames

Fill refers to the area within the frame. If color is used in a symbol, it indicates affiliation. Generally, black is used for the frame, icon, and modifiers when symbols are displayed on a light background. White is used for these elements when they are displayed on a dark background. A color fill can be used if an icon is displayed within the area of the frame. The figure (Unit Symbol Color Defaults) shows the color defaults for affiliation used for hand-drawn and computer-generated symbols.

The icon is a "role indicator" that shows the warfighting function the unit performs either on the ground, in the air, or at sea. An example is the crossed rifles, which represent an infantry unit.

UNIT SIZE

Squad/crew	Smallest unit/UK section	
Section or unit larger than a squad but smaller than a platoon	Unit larger than a US squad/UK section but smaller than a platoon equivalent	
Platoon or detachment	Platoon/troop equivalent	
Company, battery, or troop	Company/battery/squadron equivalent	
Battalion or squadron	Battalion equivalent	
Group or regiment	Regiment/group equivalent	
Brigade	Brigade equivalent	
Division	Division	
Corps	Corps	
Army	Army	
Army group or front	Army group/front	
Special size indicator for a nonorganic or temporary grouping	Battalion task force	
	Company team	

UNIT TYPE

Adjutant General (personnel services and administration)	AG
Aerial observation	Air Force (surveillance) / Army
Airborne (normally associated with another branch symbol)	
Air cavalry	
Air defense	
Amphibious	
Amphibious engineer	
Antiarmor	
Armor	
Armored cavalry	
Army aviation Rotary wing	
Fixed wing	
Attack helicopter	
Bridging	

UNIT TYPE *(Continued)*

Cavalry or reconnaissance	
Chemical (NBC)	
Chemical (NBC decontamination)	DECON
Chemical (NBC reconnaissance)	
Chemical (smoke generator)	SMOKE
Civil affairs (US only)	CA
Data processing unit	DPU
Dental	D
Engineer	
Electronic warfare	EW
Field artillery	●
Finance/pay	
Infantry	
Light	LT

UNIT TYPE *(Continued)*

	Mechanized APC	
	BIFV (mounted)	
	BIFV (dismounted)	
	Motorized	
Maintenance		
Medical		
Military intelligence (at corps and below, insert is CEWI)		MI
Military police		MP
Motorized		
Mountain		
Ordnance		
Petroleum supply		
Psychological operations		
Quartermaster		

UNIT TYPE *(Continued)*

Ranger	RGR
Rocket artillery	
Service	SVC
Signal/communications	
Sound ranging	
Special forces	SF
Supply	
Supply and maintenance	
Supply and transportation	
Support	SPT
Surface-to-air missile	
Surface-to-surface missile	
Transportation	
Unmanned air reconnaissance (RPV, etc)	

WEAPONS AND EQUIPMENT

Select the appropriate weapon symbol.

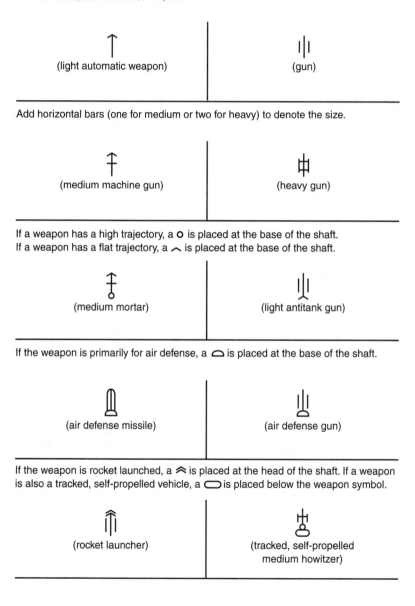

(light automatic weapon)

(gun)

Add horizontal bars (one for medium or two for heavy) to denote the size.

(medium machine gun)

(heavy gun)

If a weapon has a high trajectory, a **o** is placed at the base of the shaft.
If a weapon has a flat trajectory, a **∧** is placed at the base of the shaft.

(medium mortar)

(light antitank gun)

If the weapon is primarily for air defense, a **⌒** is placed at the base of the shaft.

(air defense missile)

(air defense gun)

If the weapon is rocket launched, a **≈** is placed at the head of the shaft. If a weapon is also a tracked, self-propelled vehicle, a **⊂⊃** is placed below the weapon symbol.

(rocket launcher)

(tracked, self-propelled
medium howitzer)

WEAPONS AND EQUIPMENT *(Continued)*

	LIGHT	MEDIUM	HEAVY
Air defense gun			
Antitank gun			
Antitank missile, self-propelled			
Antitank rocket launcher			
Flamethrower	portable	vehicular	
Gun in air defense role, self-propelled			
Gun in antitank role			
Howitzer			
Machine gun/automatic weapon			
Mortar			
Multibarrel rocket launcher			
Surface-to-air missile			
Surface-to-surface missile			

VEHICLES

Armored personnel carrier (APC)	
Armored engineer vehicle	
Armored vehicle launch bridge (AVLB)	
Bradley infantry fighting vehicle (BIFV)	
Cavalry fighting vehicle (CFV)	
Tank	LIGHT MEDIUM HEAVY

LOCATIONS

A solid line symbol represents a present or actual location.	
A broken line symbol indicates a future or projected location.	
Basic symbols other than the headquarters symbol may be placed on a staff that is extended or bent as required. The end of the staff indicated the precise location.	

POINTS

	OWN	ENEMY
General or unspecified point (Exact location is the tip at the bottom of the symbol)		
Coordinating point (Exact location is the center of the symbol)	⊗	⊗
Contact point		
Start point	SP	SP
Release point	RP	RP
Strongpoint (May be combined with unit size symbol)	SP 6 SP 5	SP 2
Checkpoint	8	
Linkup point	• 8	
Passage point	PP 8	
Point of departure	PD	
Pop-up point	▷◁ PUP	
Rally point	RALLY	
Rendezvous point (Letter in circle appears in alphabetical sequence for number of points required)	A RDVU	

LINES

Front lines	Own present	⌒⌒⌒⌒⌒
	Own planned	⌒⌒⌒⌒⌒
	Enemy present	⌒⌒⌒⌒⌒
	Enemy anticipated or suspect	⌒⌒⌒⌒⌒
General tactical boundary	Own present	—— X X ——————
	Own planned	— — — —X X— — — —
	Enemy present	— EN —— III —— EN ——
	Enemy anticipated or suspect	~ EN — —III— — EN ~
Obstacle line (Tips point toward the enemy)		∧‾∧‾∧‾∧‾∧
Fortified line		⊓_⊓_⊓_⊓_⊓

ROUTES

Attack General symbol for main attack—double arrowhead	
General symbol for other than main attack—single arrowhead	
Double arrowhead for direction of main attack and axis of advance for the main attack	
Single arrowhead for supporting direction of attack and supporting axis of advance	
Axis of advance Actual	ALPHA
Proposed with date and time effective	RED EFF 040530Z NOV
Axis of advance for unit designated to conduct main attack	TF 2-7
Bypass Bypass easy	
Bypass difficult	
Bypass impossible	
Direction of attack Direction of attack is shown graphically as an arrow extending from the line of departure. The arrow is not normally labeled.	LD ... X OBJ RED LD ... X
Follow and support mission	

OBSTACLES

Abatis	
Booby trap	
Nonexplosive antitank	
Trip wire	
Wire	
Point Planned abatis reinforced with antipersonnel mines	
Executed or fired demolition reinforced with antitank mines	
Booby-trapped nonexplosive anititank obstacle with target serial number	

Linear Antitank ditch (A rectangle need not be used when the obstacle is drawn to scale on the obverlay. Teeth point toward the enemy.)	 Under preparation	 Completed
Unspecified		
Wire (enemy under preparation)		

Minefields
  Indicators
  Antipersonnel mine		

Antitank mine		

OBSTACLES *(Continued)*

Antitank mine with antihandling device	
Mine cluster	
Mine, type unspecified	O
Conventional A planned minefield consisting of unspecified mines	
A completed minefield consisting of unspecified mines	
Scatterable minefield (DTGs used for self-destruct mines)	
Conventional row mining (outline drawn to scale)	
Nuisance Nuisance minefield	
Phony Phony minefield	
Protective Protective minefield	
Antitank ditch reinforced with antitank mines	
Tactical Tactical minefield of scatterable antitank mines, effective till 101200Z	
Completed antitank minefield (drawn away from the location and connected by a vector)	

FIRE PLANNING

Basic Concentration/point	
Linear concentration/line	
Rectangular target	
Target reference point (TRP)	X1300Z
Concentrations and barrages Linear concentration	AG 1201
Targets and final protective fires Friendly targets (not enemy) are represented by one of the following symbols, as appropriate. Targets for friendly fires are normally designated using two letters followed by four numbers. A linear concentration, target number 1201, on a friendly target effected at 100700Z.	1201 AT100700Z
Final protective fire (identified by unit designation)	A/1-3

NBC

(Height of burst
in meters)

(Target number)

(Delivery unit and
time on target)

(Weapon type and yield)
(For chemical weapons,
type of agent is written
here)

Appendix D

Minefields and
Minefield Recording

Mines are one of the most effective tank and personnel killers on the battle-field. Minefields that an infantry platoon or squad most commonly emplace are the hasty protective, point, and phony.

HASTY PROTECTIVE MINEFIELD

In the defense, platoons and squads lay hasty protective minefields to sup-plement weapons, prevent surprise, and give early warning of enemy advance. A platoon can install hasty protective minefields, but only with permission from the company commander. Hasty protective minefields are reported to the company commander and recorded on DA Form 1355-1-R. The leader puts the minefield across likely avenues of approach, within range of and covered by his organic weapons. If time permits, the mines should be buried to increase effectiveness, but they may be laid on top of the ground in a random pattern. The minefield should be recorded before the mines are armed. The leader installing the minefield should warn adjacent platoons and tell the company commander of the minefield's location. When the platoon leaves the area (except when forced to withdraw by the enemy), it must remove the minefield or transfer responsibility for the minefield to the relieving platoon leader. Only metallic mines are used in hasty protec-tive minefields. Booby traps are not used; they delay removal of the mines. The employing platoon must make sure that the minefield can be kept under observation and covered by fire at all times. The following example describes how to lay a hasty protective minefield.

After requesting and receiving permission to lay the minefield, the pla-toon leader and squad leaders reconnoiter to determine exactly where to place the mines. The leaders determine a need to use antitank mines to block enemy vehicles at the bridge and the ford. The leaders decide that antipersonnel mines are needed to protect the antitank mines and to cover the likely avenues of approach of enemy infantry.

While the soldiers are placing the mines, the platoon leader finds an easily identifiable reference point in front of the platoon's position. The platoon leader records the minefield using a reference point. The row of mines closest to the enemy is designated A and the succeeding rows are B, C, and so on. The ends of a row are shown by two markers. They are labeled with the letter of the row and number 1 for the right end of the row and number 2 for the left end of the row. The rows are numbered from right to left, facing the enemy. The marker can be a steel picket or a wooden stake with a nail or can attached so that it can be found with a metallic mine detector.

From the base reference point (concrete post), the platoon leader measures the magnetic azimuth in degrees and paces the distance to a point between 15 and 25 paces to the right of the first mine on the friendly side of the minefield. This point, B-1, marks the beginning of the second row. The platoon leader places a marker at B-1 and records the azimuth and distance from the concrete post to B-1 on DA Form 1355-1-R.

Next, from B-1 the platoon leader measures the azimuth and distance to a point 15 to 25 paces from the first mine in row A. He places a marker at this point and records it as A-1. The platoon leader then measures the distance and azimuth from A-1 to the first mine in row A and records the location of the mine. He then measures the distance and azimuth from the first mine to the second, and so on until all mine locations have been recorded as

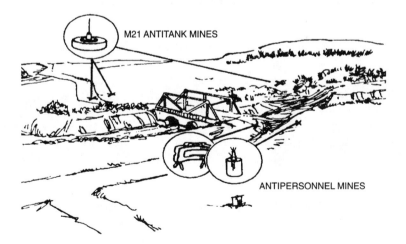

M21 ANTITANK MINES

ANTIPERSONNEL MINES

Antipersonnel and Antitank Mines in a Hasty Minefield

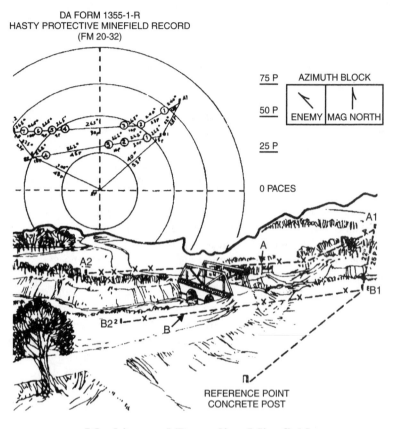

DA FORM 1355-1-R
HASTY PROTECTIVE MINEFIELD RECORD
(FM 20-32)

75 P

50 P

25 P

0 PACES

AZIMUTH BLOCK

ENEMY | MAG NORTH

A1

A

A2

B1

B2

B

REFERENCE POINT
CONCRETE POST

Marking and Recording Minefield

shown. The platoon leader gives each mine a number to identify it in the tabular block of DA Form 1355-1-R. When the last mine location in row A is recorded, the platoon leader measures an azimuth and distance from the last mine to another arbitrary point between 15 and 25 paces beyond the last mine. He places a marker here and calls it A-2. The platoon leader follows the same procedure with row B.

When the platoon leader finishes recording and marking the rows, he measures the distance and azimuth from the reference point to B-2 to A-2, and records them. If antitank mines are being used, it is recommended that they be used at the A-2/B-2 markers, because their large size facilitates retrieval.

The platoon leader now ties in the reference point with a permanent landmark that he found on the map. He measures the distance and azimuth from this landmark to the reference point. The landmark might be used to help others locate the minefield should it be abandoned. Finally, he completes the form by filling in the tabular and identification blocks.

While the platoon leader is tying in the landmark, the soldiers arm the mines nearest the enemy first (row A). The platoon leader reports that the minefield is completed and keeps DA Form 1355-1-R. If the minefield is transferred to another platoon, the gaining platoon leader signs and dates the mines transferred block and accepts the form from the previous leader.

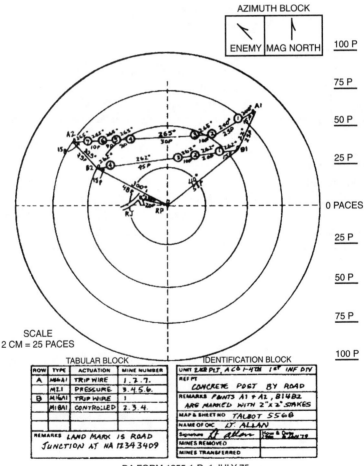

DA FORM 1355-1-R, 1 JULY 75,
REPLACES DA FORM 1335-7, 1 MAR 68, WHICH IS OBSOLETE

Hasty Protective Minefield Record

When the minefield is removed, the form is destroyed. If the minefield is left unattended or abandoned unexpectedly, the form must be forwarded to the company commander. The company commander forwards it to battalion to be transferred to more permanent records.

When retrieving the mines, the soldiers start at the reference point and move to B-1, using the azimuth and distances as recorded. They then move from B-1 to the first mine in row B. However, if B-1 is destroyed, they move from the reference point to B-2 using that azimuth and distance. They will have to shoot the back azimuth from B-2 to the last mine. The stakes at A-1, B-1, A-2, and B-2 are necessary because it is safer to find a stake when traversing long distances than to find a live mine.

POINT MINEFIELDS
Point minefields disorganize enemy forces and hinder their use of key areas. Point minefields are of irregular size and shape and include all types of anti-tank and antipersonnel mines and antihandling devices. They should be used to add to the effect of existing and reinforcing obstacles, or to rapidly block an enemy counterattack along a flank avenue of approach.

PHONY MINEFIELDS
Phony minefields, used to degrade enemy mobility and preserve friendly mobility, simulate live minefields and deceive the enemy. They are used when lack of time, personnel, or material prevents the use of actual mines. Phony minefields may be used as gaps in live minefields. To be effective, a phony minefield must look like a live minefield, which is accomplished by either burying metallic objects or making the ground look as though objects are buried.

Appendix E

Platoon and Squad Organization

All infantry leaders use the same basic doctrinal principles during training and combat, but some differences exist between organizations. Most rifle platoons operate from a modified table of organization and equipment (MTOE) based on their organization, mission, and location. Rifle platoons are organized as light infantry, straight infantry, air assault infantry, airborne infantry, or ranger infantry.

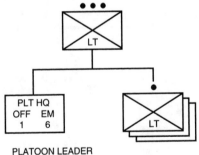

PLATOON LEADER
PLATOON SERGEANT
PLATOON RATELO
2 MACHINE GUNNERS
2 ASSISTANT MACHINE GUNNERS

**Light Infantry Platoon
Organization**

345

The most common organization is that of the light infantry platoon, and it is the easiest to duplicate with soldiers who are not used to being infantry. It consists of three rifle squads and a platoon headquarters with two machine gun teams (if available). Each machine gun team has a gunner and an assistant gunner. The antiarmor weapons are distributed evenly throughout the squads and are usually assigned to more seasoned soldiers.

The most common rifle squad has nine soldiers. It fights as two rifle teams. The squad has one squad leader, two rifle team leaders, and (if weapons are available), two automatic riflemen (M249 SAW), two riflemen (M16), and two grenadiers (M203).

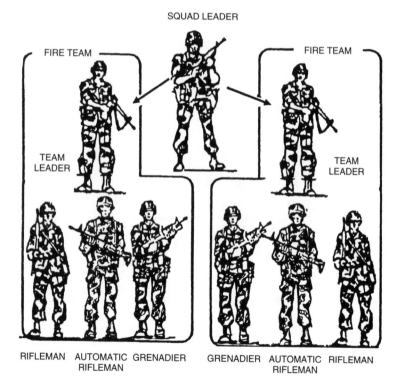

Light Infantry Squad Organization

Appendix F

Organic and Supporting Weapons

	M9 Pistol	M16A2	M249 MG	M203	M60
WEIGHT (lbs)	2.6	8.7	15.5	11	23
LENGTH (in)	8.5	39	41.1	39	43
MAX RANGE (m)	1,800	3,600	3,600	400	3,750
ARMING RANGE (m)	N/A	N/A	N/A	14	N/A
MIN SAFE RANGE (m)	N/A	N/A	N/A	31	N/A
RATE OF FIRE					
CYCLIC (rpm)	N/A	700-800	800	N/A	550
RAPID (m)	N/A	N/A	200*	35	200
SUSTAINED	60	16	85	35	100
EFFECTIVE RANGE					
AREA (m)	N/A	800	800	350	1,100
POINT	50	580	600	160	600
MOVING (m)	N/A	200	N/A	N/A	N/A
AMMUNITION					
TYPE	BALL	BALL, TRACER, DUMMY, PRACTICE, and BLANK	BALL, TRACER, DUMMY, PRACTICE, and BLANK	HE,WP, CS, ILLUM, TP, and BUCK-SHOT	BALL, TRACER, and BLANK
EXAMPLE LOAD (rds)	30	210	600		

* With barrel change.

Organic Weapons

	M72 LAW	M136 AT4	M47 DRAGON
WEIGHT (lbs)	4.7	14.8	68.5
LENGTH (in)	22/35	40	44
MAX RANGE (m)	1,000	2,100	1,000
ARMING RANGE (m)	10	30	65
MIN SAFE RANGE (m)	30	30	65
EFFECTIVE RANGE			
STATIONARY(m)	200	300	1,000
MOVING (m)	125	300	100
BACKBLAST(m)	50	60	50

Antitank Weapons

	FRAG	WP	THERMITE	CONCUSS
WEIGHT (lbs)	1	2	2	1
RANGE (m)	40	30	25	40
(Thrown by average soldier)				
PACKING (box)	30	N/A	16	20
BURST RADIUS (m)	15	17		2
		60-sec burn	40-sec burn	

	M21 ANTITANK MINE	M14 APERS MINE (Toe Popper)	M16A1 APERS MINE (Bouncing Betty)	M18A1 APERS MINE (Claymore)
WEIGHT (lbs)	18	3.6	8.3	3.5
PACKING (box)	4 mines	90 ea mines	4 fuses	6 mines w/accy
	4 fuses	and deton	trip wire	50 meters (eff)
BURST RADIUS (m)	1 tank	1 indiv	30 meters	250 meters (max)

Grenades and Mines

	M2 (.50 CAL)	MK 19	M202 FLASH	M3 RAAWS
WEIGHT (lbs)	84	76	26.7	22
LENGTH (in)	66	43	34.7	42.6
MAX RANGE (m)	6,765	2,212	N/A	
ARMING RANGE (m)	N/A	18	N/A	
MIN SAFE RANGE (m)	N/A	28	20	50 (HEAT)
				500 (illum)
				250 (HE)
				50 (SMOKE)
				50 (TNG)
RATE OF FIRE				
CYCLIC (rpm)	500	375	N/A	
RAPID (rpm)	40*	60	N/A	
SUSTAINED (rpm)	40*	40	N/A	6
EFFECTIVE RANGE				
AREA (m)	1,830	2,212	750	
POINT (m)	1,200	1,500	200	
STATIONARY (m)	N/A	N/A	N/A	700 (HEAT)
MOVING (m)	N/A	N/A	N/A	250
BACKBLAST (m)			50	60
BURST RADIUS (m)			20	
AMMUNITION				
TYPE	BALL, AP,	HEDP, HE,		HEAT, ILLUM,
	TRACER, API,	TP, and		HE, SMOKE,
	API-T, INCEN,	BUCKSHOT		TP, and
	and BLANK			TNG

* With barrel change.

Supporting Weapons

WEAPON	AMMUNITION MODEL	TYPE	METERS MIN RANGE	MAX RANGE***	RATE OF FIRE
M224	M720/M888	HE	70	3,500*	30 rounds per minute
60-mm	M722	WP	70	3,500	for 4 minutes**, then
	M72	ILLUM	200	3,200	20 rounds per minute,
	M302A1	WP	33	1,625	sustained
	M83A3	ILLUM	725	950	
	M49A4	HE	45	1,925	
M29AI	M374A2	HE	70	4,600	12 rounds per minute
81-mm	M374A3	HE	73	4,725	for 2 minutes, then
	M375A2	WP	73	4,775	5 rounds per minute,
	M301A3	ILLUM	100	2,950	sustained
M252	M821/M889	HE	83	5,600	30 rounds per minute
81-mm	M374A3	HE	73	4,775	for 2 minutes, then
	M819	RED P	300	4,875	15 rounds per minute,
	M375A3	WP	73	4,775	sustained
	M853A1	ILLUM	300	5,050	
	M301A1	ILLUM	100	2,950	
M30	M329A2	HE	770	6,850	18 rounds per minute
107-mm	M328A1	WP	720	5,650	for 1 minute, then
	M335A2	ILLUM	400	5,500	9 rounds per minute
					for 5 minutes, then
					3 rounds per minute,
					sustained
M120	M57	HE	200	7,200	15 rounds per minute
120-mm	M68	SMOKE	200	7,200	for 1 minute, then
	M91	ILLUM	200	7,100	4 rounds per minute,
					sustained

*Bipod mounted, charge 4 maximum range handheld is 1,300 meters.
**Charge 2 and above, 30 rounds per minute can be sustained with charge 0 or 1.
***Rounded to nearest 25 meters.

Mortars

	M102	M119	M198
CALIBER	105-mm	105-mm	155-mm
MAX RANGE (For HE) (m)	11,500	14,000	18,100
PLANNING RANGE (m)	11,500	11,500	14,600
MIN RANGE (m)	DIRECT FIRE	DIRECT FIRE	DIRECT FIRE
DANGER CLOSE RANGE	600	600	600

RATE OF FIRE

MAXIMUM (rpm)	10	10	4
SUSTAINED (rpm)	3	3	2

PROJECTILE

TYPE	HE, WP, ILLUM, HEP-T, APICM, CHEM, APERS, RAP	HE, M760, ILLUM, HEP-T, APICM, CHEM, RAP	HE, WP, ILLUM, SMOKE, CHEM, NUC, RAP, FASCAM, CPHD, AP/DPICM

FUSES

TYPE	PD, VT, MT, MTSQ, CP, DELAY	PD, VT, MT, MTSQ, CP, DELAY	PD, VT, CP, MT, MTSQ, DELAY

LEGEND:

AP — Armor-piercing
APERS — Antipersonnel
APICM — Antipersonnel Improved
  Conventional Munitions
CHEM — Chemical
CP — Concrete Piercing
CPHD — Copperhead
DPICM — Dual-Purpose Improved
  Conventional Munitions
FASCAM — Family of Scatterable Mines

HEP-T — High-Explosive Plastic Tracer
ILLUM — Illumination
MT — Mechanical Time
MTSQ — Mechanical Time Super Quick
NUC — Nuclear
PD — Point Detonating
RAP — Rocket-Assisted Projectile
VT — Variable Time
WP — White Phosphorus

Artillery

Appendix G

Acronyms and Abbreviations

AA	assembly area; avenue of approach
ACL	allowable cargo load
ADA	air defense artillery
AG	Adjutant General
AH	attack helicopter
ALICE	all-purpose lightweight individual carrying equipment
AMC	at my command
ANCD	automated net control device
APC	armored personnel carrier
AR	automatic rifle
ASL	assistant squad leader
AT	antitank
ATGM	antitank guided missile
AVLB	armored vehicle launch bridge
BCS	battery computer system
BDU	battle dress uniform
BFV	Bradley fighting vehicle
BIFV	Bradley infantry fighting vehicle
BMP	a Soviet infantry fighting vehicle
BP	battle position
BRDM	a Soviet vehicle used by reconnaissance units
BTR	a Soviet wheeled vehicle
CAS	close air support
CEWI	combat electronics warfare and intelligence
CFV	cavalry fighting vehicle
CH	cargo helicopter
COA	course of action
CP	command post

CS	combat support
CSS	combat service support
CW	continuous wave
DEW	directed-energy weapon
DLIC	detachment left in contact
DTG	data time group
DZ	drop zone
EA	engagement area
EMP	electromagnetic pulse
EPW	enemy prisoner of war
ERP	enroute rally point
EW	electronic warfare
EZ	extraction zone
FA	field artillery
FAC	forward air controller
FDC	fire direction center
FDO	fire direction officer
FEBA	forward edge of battle area
FFE	fire for effect
FFU	friendly forward unit
FH	frequency hopping
FIST	fire support team
FLOT	forward line of own troops
FM	frequency modulation; field manual
FO	forward observer
FPF	final protective fire
FPL	final protective line
FRAGO	fragmentary order
FSO	fire support officer
GD	ground distance
GL	grenade launcher
G-M	grid-magnetic
HALO	high-altitude, low-opening
HE	high explosive
HHC	headquarters and headquarters company
HQ	headquarters
ICM	improved conventional munition
IEDK	individual equipment decontamination kit
IRP	initial rally point
ISU	integrated sight unit (periscope)
ITV	improved TOW vehicle

IVIS	intervehicular information system
KIA	killed in action
LAPES	low-altitude parachute extraction system
LAW	light antitank weapon
LBE	load-bearing equipment
LCSS	lightweight camouflage screening system
LD	line of departure
LMG/COAX	light machine gun/coaxial
LOGPAC	logistical package
LZ	landing zone
MAW	medium antitank weapon
MD	map distance
MEDEVAC	medical evacuation
METT-T	mission, enemy, terrain and weather, troops and equipment, time available
METT-TC	mission, enemy, terrain and weather, troops, time available, and civilian considerations
MG	machine gun
MOPP	mission-oriented protective posture
MOUT	military operations in urban terrain
MRE	meal ready to eat
MTOE	modified table of organization and equipment
NATO	North Atlantic Treaty Organization
NBC	nuclear, biological, chemical
NCO	noncommissioned officer
NVD	night vision devices
OCOKA	observation, cover and concealment, obstacles, key terrain, avenues of approach
OH	observation helicopter
OP	observation post
OPCON	operational control
OPORD	operation order
OPSEC	operations security
ORP	objective rally point
OT	observer target
PAC	personnel and administration center
PCC	precombat check
PCI	precombat inspection
PDF	principal direction of fire
PIR	priority of intelligence requirement
PL	phase line; platoon leader

POSNAV	position navigation
PSG	platoon sergeant
PUP	pop-up point
PW	prisoner of war
PZ	pickup zone
R&S	reconnaissance and security
RATELO	radiotelephone operator
RDVU	rendezvous point
REDCON	readiness condition
RF	representative fraction
ROE	rules of engagement
ROI	rules of interaction
RP	release point
RPV	remotely piloted vehicle
RRP	reentry rally point
RS	road space
RSTA	reconnaissance, surveillance, and target acquisition
RT	receiver-transmitter
SALUTE	size, activity, location, unit, time, equipment
SAW	squad automatic weapon
SC	single-channel
SE	spot elevation
SF	special forces
SINCGARS	single-channel ground and airborne radio system
SL	squad leader
SOI	signal operation instructions
SOP	standing operating procedure
SP	start point
TF	task force
TL	team leader; time length
TLP	troop-leading procedure
TOT	time on target
TOW	tube-launched, optically tracked, wire-guided
TRP	target reference point
UH	utility helicopter
VA	vertical angle
VT	variable time (fuse)
WIA	wounded in action
WP	white phosphorus
XO	executive officer

References

For further information about the subjects discussed in this guide, you should refer to the following publications:

FM 3-7	*NBC Field Handbook,* September 1994
FM 3-100	*NBC Operations,* May 1996
FM 6-30	*Observed Fire Procedures,* July 1991
FM 7-8	*The Infantry Rifle Platoon and Squad,* April 1992
FM 7-10	*The Infantry Rifle Company,* December 1990
FM 20-3	*Camouflage,* November 1990
FM 20-32	*Mine/Countermine Operations,* May 1998
FM 21-11	*First Aid for Soldiers,* October 1988 Change (2)
FM 21-18	*Foot Marches,* June 1990
FC 21-26	*Map Reading and Land Navigation,* May 1993
FM 21-75	*Combat Skills of the Soldier,* August 1984
FM 22-100	*Military Leadership,* August 1998 (Final Draft)
FM 71-1	*Tank & Mechanized Infantry Company Team,* January 1998
FM 90-4	*Air Assault Operations,* March 1987
FM 90-8	*Counterguerrilla Operations,* August 1986
FM 90-10-1	*Infantryman's Guide to Combat in Built-up Areas,* May 1993
FM 90-26	*Airborne Operations,* December 1990
FM 100-5	*Operations,* June 1993
FM 101-5-1	*Operational Terms and Graphics,* September 1997
TM 11-5820-890-10-8	*(SINCGARS) Ground Combat Net Radio (ICOM),* February 1995

Index